INTRODUCTION TO PHILOSOPHY

Themes for Classroom and Reflection

Second Edition

By Brian D. Skelly
University of Hartford

cognella® | ACADEMIC PUBLISHING

Bassim Hamadeh, CEO and Publisher

Kassie Graves, Director of Acquisitions

Jamie Giganti, Senior Managing Editor

Miguel Macias, Senior Graphic Designer

Carrie Montoya, Manager, Revisions and Author Care

Kaela Martin and Christian Berk, Associate Editors

ISBN: 978-1-5165-1006-1 (pb) / 978-1-5165-1007-8 (br)

"Wisdom achieves without competing."
—Laozi

CONTENTS

PART I: Metaphysics

PART II: Epistemology

PART III: Metaethics

PART IV: Normative Ethics

PART V: Social Morality

PART VI: Political Morality

INTRODUCTION

This collection of essays is a bit out of the ordinary in today's college textbook market, so a few words of explanation are in order. To begin, it was not intentionally conceived as a set, but is merely a group of essays I have written over the past years for the purpose of being read and discussed in some incarnation or other of the University of Hartford Philosophy Club. Each essay was written for the purpose of being presented at a club meeting, each topic having been chosen either on account of a student or colleague suggestion or triggered by current events or contemporary cultural dialog. Thus, although the set represents a broad range of philosophical concerns, there has been no attempt at achieving an orderly or systematic representation of philosophical topics. Moreover, there is considerable—though accidental—interaction between some of the essays: some of them overlap one another, while some essays complement one another. For the readers' convenience, the essays have loosely been ordered into thematic areas, which order by no means represents the only way they could have been arranged.

The reader will also note that not all essays are of the same genre. This is explained by the fact that the nature of our Philosophy Club has been evolving since launched on September 13, 2001.

On that first day, the attendants in addition to myself were a Russian student from the Caucasus Mountains, a Saudi, and a medical doctor from the local area who was not a student. Initially, I was not writing essays at all, but just doing short write-ups with bullet points. Then gradually, as professors began attending and the club began to acquire more *gravitas*, I felt the urge to provide more content. Along the way, we temporarily divided our club meetings into a monthly Faculty Seminar, also open to students, to supplement our less formal weekly meetings. As a result of these Faculty seminars, some of the essays appearing in this book are longer and are more formal in nature.

We finally understood that our mission had to be a united one, and as such we should cultivate a Club culture in which students, professors and people from the community could meet as peers. The fact that we have done this on a weekly basis for all these years is a remarkable demonstration of academic collegiality of which all club members are proud. This pride has motivated me to share these essays with a wider audience.

Although this is not reflected in the collection of essays presented here, not all the weekly presentations at the Philosophy Club are done by me. As often as I can, I invite others to present. This includes not only other professors, but students and members of the community at large as well. Still, as it is quite difficult to fill 28 slots per Academic Year with guest speakers, it is not rare that I am called upon to present.

This book may serve as a sourcebook for reflection and classroom discussion on a wide variety of topics, some rarely addressed in print, while others deal with classical themes. I hope you will find the approach to them innovative and refreshing. Each of the essays deals with controversy—and, in each case, my intent is reconciliatory rather than polemic. I am convinced that philosophy cannot meet its purpose unless its intention is ultimately reconciliatory. This does not mean there will be no disagreement or passion, but that underlying these is always a friendly and cooperative intent.

WHAT PHILOSOPHY IS AND HOW IT RELATES TO SCIENCE

Over the years I have heard it said on a number of occasions that Philosophy as an academic discipline cannot be defined, and that it is something that can only be understood by doing it. The implication of this line of thinking is that Philosophy's indefinability is a unique, enigmatic trait. I disagree with this way of thinking, and after explaining why, I will present and discuss what I take to be a suitable definition of Philosophy.

The indefinability claim is based on the exploitation of a fallacious ambiguity between definition and perfect definition. We say Philosophy is undefinable because we recognize that any definition we offer, even if not erroneous, would be found lacking by philosophical scrutiny. At the very least, philosophical scrutiny would reveal at any stage in the defining process that the terms by which philosophy is defined are themselves in need of definition. Recognizing that this sets the stage for an infinite process, we take the shortcut of saying philosophy can't be defined.

It would be more accurate to express this point by saying there is no perfect, finite definition of Philosophy. While this is true, it is not unique to Philosophy. In fact, there is no perfect, finite definition of anything. In other words, there is no finite definition of anything that gives a complete, fully detailed idea of what it is. For example, although we accept that Biology is the empirical study of life, we know that this definition leaves us with work to do. Namely, we have to further clarify Biology's empirical method as well as its subject matter: living things. Both of these tasks are infinite.

Although perfect definitions are always what we seek, we never quite attain them. But we can get closer and closer. It is a remarkable fact about rational awareness that we somehow have a vague sense of the real definitions of things, even though these are infinite, and this vague sense guides us along the way to finding appropriate or suitable finite definitions.

Now there may be more than one suitable definition for the same thing. The suitability of a definition may be at least in part a function of argumentative context. The definition of something is supposed to give the key features of it, from which all other important features might be inferred. But which features of a thing are key may be at least partly a matter of argumentative context.

In the case of defining Philosophy, our argumentative context is as an academic discipline. As such, our task will be analogous to defining any other academic discipline, such as Biology: the definition will have to indicate a method and a subject matter. Of course, as in the case of Biology, this will eventually leave us with two infinite tasks: to capture the complete ideas of the method and the subject matter of Philosophy. But that's okay. It is not the job of a suitable definition to give the complete, infinite idea of thing, but to be a guidepost that correctly points toward it.

Thus, I consider Philosophy to be the dialectic pursuit of answers to general, open questions of controversy. In this definition, 'dialectic' refers to the method of Philosophy, while 'general open questions' refers to the subject matter. Let me elaborate on the latter first.

In §13 of his *Principia Ethica* (1903), G.E. Moore employed the concept of an "open question" to argue against ethical naturalism. According to him, ethical terms are not defined by empirical terms because even if we define goodness as pleasure, it remains an open question whether pleasure in general, or this or that pleasure, is good; this should not be the case if goodness is truly defined as pleasure. The impact of this brilliant distinction on the history of thought was somewhat stymied by an initial narrow interpretation of the concept by Moore's interpreters as signifying nothing more than analytic truth. In fact, the point he was making is that some matters, such as those settled by calculation and observation, are closed to argument, while other matters—namely those which are not settled by observation or calculation, are open to argument. This is the sense in which I use the expression in the definition presented above. I owe much in this regard to Emmett Barcalow, of whose use of the expression in his work *Open Questions* (Wadsworth, 1992, page 5) mine is a variation.[1]

By the definition offered here, then, Philosophy deals only in open questions, namely questions that cannot be answered by observation or calculation. But not all open questions are philosophical questions. Some of them are too particular to be addressed in the public forum, which is Philosophy's "venue". Philosophy only tackles general open questions: open questions general enough not to require access to privileged information, such as that requiring one to live at a certain place or time, know certain people, or be privy to any particular invented games, notions, or social conventions.

To be sure, there is a gray area to manage regarding how general a question has to be to be a philosophical question. Let's probe the gray area a bit with the following example. Consider the question: Q1. Should John marry Sally. Assuming 'John' and 'Sally' are intended to refer to real people, surely this question is not for philosophy, though clearly enough it is an open question, since it can't be answered by observation or calculation. For it could not be meaningfully pondered in the open forum, since to do so would require living at a certain time and place and knowing certain people. Let's see what happens if we generalize the question in successive stages:

Q2. Should John marry?

Q3. (Under what conditions) should anyone marry?

Q4. What is marriage?

Q5. (Under what conditions) should anyone enter trust relationships?

---

1   I say mine is a variation because, unlike Barcalow, I consider a question like "Who was Jack the Ripper?" a closed question, since it could only be answered, if at all, by observation, and hence is closed to argument.

Q6. What is love?

We can see in the above succession of generations that the more general open questions become, the more appropriate they seem to be for philosophical discussion. We can argue over whether Q3 or Q4 should already count as a philosophical question, but this would be based on different takes on whether marriage is natural or a matter of mere human convention.

Of course, Philosophy by its nature focuses on controversial questions. A controversial question is a general open question about which reasonable people can honestly disagree. The fact that there may be a gray area over what counts as controversial only gives Philosophy more to do; for it may be controversial whether a certain question is controversial or not.

Regarding the Method of Philosophy, I borrow the term "dialectic" from Plato and use it straightforwardly in the platonic manner. Dialectic refers to a rigorous, ongoing, progressive, truth oriented form of argument or "dialog"; a form not competitively aimed at defeating one's opponent or winning at all costs, but geared toward a cooperative process of getting closer and closer to the truth of a matter by a process of presenting and defending for the sake of argument argued positions on controversial matters and subjecting the key premises of those positions to rigorous scrutiny. I thus count five steps to this method: presentation of the argument, defense of the premises, criticism of key premises, rebuttal of criticism, and assessment of whether the rebuttal succeeds or fails. This is a reiterative, ongoing process, infinite in principle, but practicable in finite segments.

To those who would criticize this as an excessively narrow description of the philosophical method, I respond that these steps may be taken explicitly or implicitly; but the steps are there in anything that counts as Philosophy. Moreover, if a certain piece of philosophical dialog appears to lack, say, a rebuttal to some criticism, one should keep in mind that the philosophical process is never complete, and that the only philosophy we can do, witness to, or be a part of is incomplete. It is up to all of us, therefore, to pick up where others or we ourselves have left off and advance the process.

This definition establishes a neat theoretical distinction between the respective subject matters of Philosophy and Empirical Science. According to it, there can be no proper dispute between the two, since the former is solely an open-question endeavor while the latter is a closed-question endeavor. To be sure, there are intimate relationships between closed questions and open questions, but these relationships, far from being the cause of competitive rancor, set the stage for a mutually beneficial cooperative venture, Philosophy inspiring Science while Science enlightens Philosophy.

Philosophy inspires science by asking the open questions that lead to their establishment. Biology is inspired by the open question, "What is life?" Now, even though this question cannot be answered by Biology, surely it is the inspiration behind the doing of Biology. Conversely, Biology's finding that *homo sapiens* is a social species ought in all its detail be taken to enlighten the path of Philosophy not only in Ethics, but in Metaphysics and Epistemology as well.

So intimate is the cooperation between Philosophy and Science that Science cannot be done outside a framework set by Philosophy, while Philosophy which ignores Science cannot be relevant.

PART I
Metaphysics

CHAPTER ONE

The Difference between Us and Other Animals

It is undeniable that human beings are animals. Despite its obviousness, we are uncomfortable accepting this fact. The act of conceding that humans are animals is typically accompanied by some significant distinguishing qualification; e.g., we are animals, but we are cleverer, more intelligent, etc. The tension between accepting that we are animals while struggling to find a way to distinguish ourselves from other animals has led through the years to a very interesting disagreement: that is, whether humans are different from other animals merely by degree (i.e., of intelligence, or the naturalist thesis) or categorically (i.e., by type of intelligence). I argue we are distinct from other animals categorically, on the grounds that while we share a type of awareness with them: animal awareness, we have another type of awareness that they lack: rational awareness. Animal awareness (an alternate term might be organismic awareness) is that perspective of consciousness, which is survival oriented or keyed on survival, whereas rational awareness is that oriented to truth.

Animal awareness is survival oriented in that it responds immediately to survival concerns triggered by environmental cues. This response does not always maximize the animal's survival odds and sometimes does the opposite. Nonetheless, its aim or end is survival, and its domain of response cues the animal's immediate survival context.

Just as an animal's survival awareness does not guarantee survival, the truth orientation of rational awareness does not always lead to truth, and sometimes leads away from truth. Nonetheless, the aim or end of rational awareness is not survival, but truth. As such, this form of awareness can compete against or distract us from our animal awareness, sometimes to our loss. (More on this below.) On the other hand, it seems equally clear that, in the long run, our rational awareness has conferred to us collectively a great survival benefit. But this should not be cause for a reduction of rational to survival awareness, since rational awareness does not respond directly to survival cues, but is aimed at gaining an understanding of how things are.

As a result of having two competing types of awareness at work at the same time, we are the only animal among all known species with the telltale characteristic of being existentially distracted; that is, distracted from the animal survival context, which is the focus of our animal awareness. Moreover, because of this unique characteristic among animals of being existentially distracted, we are also the only animals capable of being prejudiced. Prejudice is—or is the product of—a deficiency in judgment whose enabling mechanism is existential distraction. Prejudice is the acceptance of a judgment based on selective denial of evidence in order to support a desired preselected conclusion. The criterion of preselection is the psychological convenience perceived in and desired by human animal awareness. Although human animal awareness per se is not concerned with truth, it can register responses to certain products and activities of rational awareness: boredom, anger, elation, awkwardness, etc.

Everyone who observes dolphins at length marvels at their intelligence. And rightly so. They can accomplish mental feats that one may think impossible for humans to accomplish. They can memorize the details of their immediate environment almost instantaneously.

In fact, dolphins are so intelligent that one wonders why a bucket of fish must always be on hand to reward their performances. In the case of humans working for others, the reward for the work done does not have to be present in the immediate environment to stimulate the workers to work.

This difference between humans and dolphins is not to be understood unless it is recognized that the intelligence of a dolphin, as masterful and as superior to humans as they may be, is contained within the realm of animal awareness. We make a great mistake if we fail to recognize that humans have two types of awareness—animal and rational—whereas dolphins have one. The simplicity of dolphin awareness might even contribute to the dolphin's superiority to us in animal awareness. Since the dolphin has no existential distraction, it pays full attention to the concerns presented to it in animal awareness, whereas we are considerably distracted from the same.

Having two distinct types of awareness makes for a truly distracted mind. This may be the key distinguishing feature of a rational animal. To appreciate this point best requires further elaboration of the distinction between animal and rational awareness. Otherwise, perhaps there is still room for the view that humans and other animals differ only by degree.

One good place to start is language. Language can refer generically to any system of communication between organisms. In that sense, all animals—and probably plants as well—have language. Language in this sense resides in animal/plant awareness and thus is survival oriented. It is largely spontaneous and uninvented, mostly unlearned, and mostly species universal, with much if not most of its content shared or sharable between species. Of its non-spontaneous content, most is triggered more than learned in the proper sense, dependent on a combination of innate capacities and habitual associations.

In contrast, language in the higher sense of the term—what we typically call human language—is only learned with difficulty; is invented and, in fact, continually reinvented; and resides largely in rational awareness, as evidenced by its by its ready detachability from reference to our immediate survival context. Thus has acquisition of human language become a marker of sorts for rational awareness.

There has been some question among social scientists whether human language, at least in some rudimentary form, can be acquired or learned by other animals. A number of experiments have been conducted over the years, particularly with apes, in an attempt to answer this question. If the answer is *yes*, this might be taken to imply that these other animals are also rational to the degree that they can acquire human language. (The implications of a *no* answer are a bit murkier.) Of course, a *yes* answer would also require us to see rationality as a trait possessed more or less rather than entirely or not at all; if the former, this would open the door to the naturalist thesis.

Whereas admittedly it is a scientific question whether other animals can acquire human language, it is a philosophical question to determine the criterion of rudimentary possession. (The failure to carry out this task properly has been the main defect of these animal studies.) If we set the criterion too low—e.g., to the intentional use of proper labels—then the question becomes quite diluted, such that most if not all animals are in play. That this is too low is evidenced by the absurdity of a human language composed entirely of proper labels; clearly the distinctive feature of human language is not proper labels but common labels.

Proper labels are names that label finite classes containing at least one referent, where the reference is made opaquely. Our surnames are no less proper labels than our given names. In either case, the things referred to are by opaque assignment. Proper names as such have no meaning to guide their reference.

Common labels, on the other hand, are names that label infinite classes, the reference to which is guided by meaning. Although we rarely reflect on the marvel of it, whenever we are using human language we are making routine reference to infinite classes of things. We don't understand what "chair" means unless we understand it to refer to an infinite number of things: all possible chairs.

From these considerations it should be clear that even a rudimentary form of human language has to include the intentional use of common labels. This, in turn, should lead us to the recognition that none of the animals we know of besides ourselves is capable of acquiring human language. For its acquisition is contingent on prelinguistic awareness of the infinite—the infinite backdrop of living experience.

This awareness of the infinite is not generated by language itself through some mysterious bootstrapping process. To the contrary, it must be prelinguistic, since any task of labeling requires prior awareness both of the label and the thing to be labeled. This caveat regards attempts to show our conceptualization of the infinite to be by construction. It is easy to see how we can in fact construct infinite sets by means of finite sets of rules. One example of this process, known as mathematical induction, is the following definition of the set of natural numbers:

1. 0 is a natural number.
2. Any natural number plus 1 is a natural number.

In this case, two rules generate the conception of the infinite set of natural numbers. But we must take care to note that by such processes it is only in a formal sense, and not a teleological sense, that we generate the conception of infinite sets. For in the latter sense, we had to already be intuitively aware of the set of natural numbers before we went looking for a formal definition of them. It would be inane to imagine that we just one day became aware of natural numbers by putting the above two rules together for the first time as if by accident.

In fact, it is this spontaneous, ready awareness of the infinite in our experience that constitutes rational awareness. Its absence leaves only brute animal awareness by default, while its presence is a constant reminder that there is more to life than our immediate animal survival context presents to us. Brute animals are limited to the tools of habitual association and recall, are at the mercy of their deliberations, and are forced to accept the choice favored by the greatest coalition of desires and fears that presents itself to them in their immediate survival context. On the other hand, we, due to our constant, immediate awareness of the infinite backdrop to our experience, stand sovereign over our deliberations, since we can never fail to regard the possibility that some further consideration relevant to our present deliberations may be lurking in that background, giving us the option to extend our deliberations until we have searched that infinite data base to our satisfaction—by means of the free association and free recall derived from awareness of the infinite in our experience.

CHAPTER TWO

Rational Deliberation

n conversations about murderers, rapists, and the like, it is typically not long before someone makes the remark that they are "animals" or "have no conscience." But in consideration of the fact that all murderers and rapists in this world are members of the human species, two facts immediately follow:

1. Yes, murderers and rapists are animals, but only in virtue of being human, not in virtue of being murders and rapists.
2. Murderers and rapists, also solely in virtue of being human, **do** have consciences.

That is to say, human beings are animals endowed with the faculty of rational awareness, which is the ability to engage in free deliberation. This is all that having a conscience amounts to, so it is senseless to say that any human being lacks a conscience just because he or she makes terrible choices. Therefore, since deliberation is free, there may be a great deal of variance from individual to individual in the amount or quality of of exercise of conscience.

Failure to make the distinction between not having a conscience and not exercising one's conscience, or mistaking the former for the latter, leads to serious errors in judgment. This failure stems from not having a clear picture of the process of rational deliberation. Let's begin with a description of the basic animal decision-making process, then move on to consider what humans have in addition to this. It will turn out that free association, as opposed to habitual association, is the mechanism that is the basis of free deliberation, hence of rational awareness, hence of conscience.

Here I am drawing on a distinction between two types of awareness: animal awareness, which humans have in common with other animals, and rational awareness, the possession of which by humans is what distinguishes them categorically from other animals. We can call the processes of animal awareness "animal psychology," while the processes of rational awareness may be called "rational psychology."

The decision-making process in animal psychology is based simply on a sort of "free-market competition" among all the desires and fears made present in one's immediate empirical context. This includes all perceptions of bodily yearnings, pains, one's sensible surroundings, and anything else conjured up in recall by habitual association. The decision emerges as that alternative toward which one's greatest present coalition of desires and fears inclines. Awareness of the alternatives from which the choice is to be made is gained through perception, not judgment. Indeed, it is only the awareness of a plurality of incompatible alternatives for action that activates the deliberation process to begin with. Any alternatives not presented in one's immediate perceptual context are simply unrecognizable.

In a nutshell, this is how decisions are made in the animal world. Many philosophers, in line with David Hume, would say this is how decisions are made, **period**. But I disagree.

If we take a closer look, we see that animal decision making involves taking into account all evidence found in one's survival context that it is plainly taken as relevant to the decision to be made. Something sensible is going on here which is not altogether erratic or blind. But what makes it not count as rational is that the evidence-gathering process is not capable of expansion beyond the immediate survival context. That is to say, there is no possibility of taking into consideration any hypothetical evidence, no matter how relevant. There is no ability to consider unexperienced possibilities.

Rational awareness builds on animal awareness, but with two added features which convert it to universality: free association and free recall. These are universalized extensions of two functions of animal cognition: habitual association and habitual recall. Free association is the ability to bring into reflective awareness for deliberative purposes freely imagined unexperienced possibilities beyond that which habitual association offers spontaneously and which might be relevant to the deliberation at hand. Similarly, free recall is the ability to bring into reflective awareness for deliberative purposes freely recalled memories beyond that which habitual recall offers spontaneously and which might be relevant to the deliberation at hand.

At first look, free association and recall may seem to be faculties too trivial to make such a big difference in the deliberation process. The freeness of it brings to mind its absurd, irrelevant applications, such as making up a nonsensical sentence, or listing a number of unrelated items. But, in fact, its relevant application is the cornerstone of rational thought.

The two chief morally relevant uses of free association and recall are:

1. Imagining or employing them to help determine how an action under consideration might be thought of by others.
2. Imagining or employing them to help determine possible future consequences of choices under consideration.

These two are responsible for the generation of moral or universal perspective. From this perspective, every object of awareness is couched in a universe of infinite possibilities within which it is amenable to comparison with all other objects. Here the immediate animal context is no longer master, no longer the dictator of action. Here the agents are not desires and fears in competition with one another, but individuals who guide the deliberation process by the simple act of applying free association and recall. Desires and fears are still the proximate causes of all decisions, but now it becomes our choice the extent to which we expand the domain of relevant desires and fears to be considered.

In sum, our freedom, our rationality, consists simply in the continual spontaneous choosing of whether and how much to apply free association and recall in our deliberations. The default scenario, whereby we choose not to apply it at all, is a backsliding to what appears to be simple animal awareness, where our choices are made by the greatest resulting coalition between the desires and fears conjured up by our immediate animal context. But we should be careful not to identify this with brute animal awareness, since it is arrived at only by a refusal to apply free association and recall. Therefore, no rational animal, no human being, can be said to be a brute, or to be without a conscience. We do have animal awareness, but not in the absence of the faculty of free association and recall.

At this point, one might wonder how human beings can be said to have animal awareness at all, since the presence in humans of the faculties of free association and recall converts animal awareness to rational awareness. But animal awareness is still present in the sense that, whereas rational awareness is something we must choose to activate by choosing to apply free association and recall, animal awareness simply presents itself to us spontaneously. Our first look at things is always the animal look.

In this manner, animal awareness may even compete with rational awareness, both vying for our attention in such a manner that we are distracted, sometimes from our animal concerns by rational concerns, sometimes from our rational concerns by animal concerns. The rational distraction is by our choice and is under our control; the animal distraction is immediate and not under our control.

This distraction of one type of awareness by another in the same animal is the mark that the animal is a rational animal. It is not difficult to tell when an animal is distracted in this way; there is notable behavioral malfunction that is inexplicable under the assumption that all the animal has is animal awareness. Nonrational animals never ignore their survival concerns unless they are distracted by other survival concerns. For them to be distracted from their survival concerns altogether is unheard of.

In contrast, this type of distraction is typical among humans. We fail to be mindful of our basic animal needs whenever our rational awareness is caught up in any particularly intriguing and captivating issue, no matter how abstract.

In light of these considerations, it must be conceded that murderers and rapists are not brute animals, but are, as the rest of us, rational animals, with consciences. The problem is that they have failed to a horrifying degree to exercise well the faculties of free association and recall in their decision making.

It should be clear that all who are endowed with free association and recall are obliged to use it whenever the soundness of a choice might be revealed by evidence outside one's immediate context. These are tools which, through proper use, increases the accuracy of decision making in most situations.

It might even be said that we are obliged to apply free association and recall even to determine whether further application of free association is called for.

What is popularly termed "open-mindedness" may be characterized as the application of free association and recall as far as is practicable. All the various types of provincial attitudes and prejudices can be considered as various kinds of deficiency in being diligent in the application of free association and recall.

It is tempting to issue the challenge that perhaps free association and recall aren't really free, but rather, more elaborately ornamented versions of habitual association and recall, which we have in common with other animals. In this case, the agency that we appear to have through free association and recall is illusory.

For such a challenge to be plausible would require the support of a theory explaining how the appearance of free association and recall is generated. The theory would need to be either genetic or behavioral: either we perform with punctilious precision the actions that have been established by nature to be carried out, or our actions are the product of some elaborate occult system of behavior training. Both these positions are extreme, in that they are incompatible with all we have discovered about human experience up to now. But there is another consideration that dooms them more definitively to the dustbin of determinist ideology: the phenomenon of absurdism.

The point was made earlier that rational deliberation is grounded in the relevant application of free association and recall in decision making. Despite this, it is equally true that the main grounds for proving the existence of real free association and recall in humans lie in its irrelevant applications.

The fact that any relevant application of free association and recall results in a decision or the ordering of a behavior that can always be seen at least largely as a function of its survival context makes it difficult to persuade skeptics that those decisions involved the application of genuine free association and recall. It is too easy for them to insist that the decisions in question were determined by those animal contextual factors alone. This ploy, in fact, works best with well-thought-out decisions, in which the conceptual connection between the decision made and the animal survival context in which it was made is particularly strong.

But there is another class of applications of free associations that are quite more immune to being given a reductive spin. These are the absurd applications. An absurdist application of free association is one that recalls or produces an object of thought which by design has no relation to one's immediate context, or previous thoughts. In contrast with the much-lampooned psychoanalytic tactic of free association, this exercise is one that calls for deliberate effort. An example of this is, say,

purple spoon on Venus

I don't think anyone can seriously argue that there is a determined reason why I thought of purple instead of blue. Yet it is not purely a random function: I was resolved to think up something unconnected to my immediate context. If it was neither produced by a preset random function nor causally determined, then it was freely produced. Such activity is inconceivable as brute animal behavior, since it is unrelated to any conceivable animal interests (i.e., **survival-context-bound** interests).

I can produce these objects at will at any time. It may not be an utterance; it may be a behavior. Most of the time, of course, I have better things to do. Certainly, I always have something relevant to think about, so I am unlikely to resort to this absurdist exercise. But the crucial fact is that I am able to do so.

The fact that whenever I apply free association in an absurdist manner, I have a reason to, e.g., *to prove a point*, does nothing to change the fact that the product of the exercise is unconnected to my context. The **decision** to exercise free association in an absurdist manner is not being claimed to be absurdist; it is just the **product** of the exercise that is absurd.

In short, all humans have free association and recall. They are collectively the cornerstone of rationality and moral responsibility; we are obligated to exercise them in all our decision making; prejudice and closed-mindedness are our result from our deficiency in doing so; and the best proof of free association is its absurdist application. Murderers and rapists, therefore, are not deficient by nature, but are deficient in the relevant exercise of free association and recall. The nature of this deficiency remains to be discussed.

CHAPTER THREE

The Non-Dualist Conception of Soul

Whether humans, animals, or all living things have souls may seem to be an abstract matter without stark or startling consequences either way. But, in fact, the correct understanding of our identity and individuality are at stake. Do we not really have birthdays? Is our individuality really not more than that of a rainbow, or at best, of an accidental machine of nature? To answer yes to such questions seems absurd. But is it a bullet we have to bite?

Our ability to encounter the absurdities of denying that things have souls comes with a closer examination of the non-dualist conception of soul inherited from Aristotelian philosophy. Unlike its more popular dualist counterparts associated with Plato and Descartes, which are grounded in large part on otherworldly assumptions, the non-dualist conception stems from our mindful notice of, and reflection on, living things in this world.

The Aristotelian reflection begins with thinking about physical organisms as we experience them—as (living) bodies. Aristotle accepted as evident in our experience that bodies have unity at any one time and identity over time and physical change. Both of these can be used as grounds to prove that living things have souls. Aristotle's notion of the soul was as the nonphysical organizing principle of the body, which organization is principally evidenced by the unity and identity of the body.

Regarding the proof from identity, it was evident to Aristotle then just as it is to us now that bodies routinely undergo complete turnover of their matter, such that within a certain time period they can be said to have undergone complete physical change. For something to maintain identity despite such change requires that something substantial about that thing not to have changed. We can call this unchanging aspect a thing's principle of identity. By logic, a principle of identity is either physical or nonphysical. But since it is accepted that living things undergo complete physical change, this rules out their possession of a physical principle of identity. Hence, it follows that if a living thing has identity, it is a nonphysical principle of identity, which is a soul.

An example of a physical principle of identity would be the original and still remaining core of matter making up the building that I occupy now. Living things have no such core of matter analogous to this. For even though many organisms have cores of cells—in particular, brain cells—whose lives are or can be coextensive with the life of the organism, the matter composing each of these cells is constantly being turned over.

The only way to deny Aristotle's identity argument is simply to dismiss the notion that living things have real identity, and that the identity we notice in living things is to be explained away as an appearance. If this is the case, then it is in effect a denial that things have birthdays. If I lack real identity, then in a literal biological sense I am unborn and probably will not die—but, as an amoeba that divides into its two daughter cells, I will simply cease to exist. The "I" of which I speak here is this present time-slice "me" in a long, metamorphosing sequence of things related to "me" linking the present "me" indirectly to a "me" who actually was born and, in the other direction, to a "me" who actually does die. It would have to be characterized as a long relay race of organism stages, each of which ever so slightly differs physically from the previous and following stages.

This all seems, at the very least, to be logically possible. And, in fact, a number of metaphysical thinkers in the past century were dedicated to this way of thinking about organisms. Effectively, they are conceding to Aristotle's reasoning, but have chosen to bite the bullet that Aristotle—had he known bullets—would have expected no one to bite: if the consequence of admitting the real identity of living things is to admit the existence of souls as nonphysical principles, some of us have chosen simply to deny the consequent, yielding the opinion of no souls and no identity.

We might just accept this as a stalemate of views were it not for two nagging problems with the option of denial. First, its sequential logic breaks down upon recognition of the fact that the set of elements—the organism stages—to be ordered into a sequence is uncountably infinite. Since to sequence implies to count, then not being able to count implies not being able to sequence. Therefore, what cannot conceivably be counted cannot conceivably be arranged into a sequence.

A set of organism stages is uncountably infinite because the changing life of an organism does not progress through discrete *stases*, or stable, unchanging states, but is continuous. Therefore, this change cannot be accurately characterized by a set of stable organism states, since there is change occurring within any temporal subdivision of a living thing.

Twentieth-century metaphysicians, recognizing the serious challenge this posed to their approach, responded to this by speculating that an organism in fact lives through a series of stages, each of which has a non-negligible duration. This would solve the problem of uncountability if it works; but it could only work as an explanation on the unquestioned assumption that each of these organism stages possessed physical identity throughout its duration, denying the common acceptance that organismic change is continuous. In sum, this attempt at explanation is question-begging, since it attempts to explain organismic change by arbitrarily positing the existence of physically identical organismic minima, from which organisms are constructed as sequences. At best, we have pushed the envelope to puzzling over the identity of organisms to puzzling over the identity of minimal organism stages, and thus are back to the drawing board. In fact, problems such as these cannot be solved by arbitrary definition.

The second problem with denying the reality of organismic identity in favor of positing organisms as sequences of organism stages is that it lacks any motive in its favor, other than the mere insistence upon denying nonphysical reality at all costs. We all reasonably wonder whether life is merely physical or has a substantial nonphysical aspect to it, so it is reasonable to ponder arguments that go one way or the other on the topic. But it is unreasonable to cope with the mystery by simply choosing sides from the beginning and using that as our unconditional theoretical point of departure. Instead, we should start, as Aristotle did, by due reflection upon the evidence lying in our intuited experience.

Although, to be sure, it may be useful to reverse-engineer possible explanations from hypothetical positions, this should not be mistaken for explanation. Of course, if there happens to be no nonphysical aspect to life, then our best chance at understanding living things might be as sequences of organism stages. But the fact that this approach looks not only to be questionably motivated, but also to be fatally crippled by logical problems, argues for taking Aristotle's approach more seriously. Although physical explanation, where it works, is to be favored over nonphysical explanation, our insistence upon the former even where it doesn't work is irrational.

The same tack can be used to argue for the existence of the soul based on the unity of the body. We notice bodies to be richly endowed with a coordinated intricacy of detail that is infinite, in the sense that we know we can never know a body completely. If such unity of the body is real, then there must be an organizing principle to account for it. Once again, such an organizing principle in this case would have to be nonphysical, since bodies do not have unchanging physical cores, but undergo complete physical change.

Once again, the only way to deny this proof is to deny the evidence: in this case, the real unity of the body. Doing this would give us the onus of explaining away the appearance of bodily unity. Our choices are three: to consider the body akin to how we know the rainbow to be, which is an indefinite aggregate; akin to a statue, which is a definite aggregate; or as an accidental machine of nature, which is an accidentally mechanized aggregate.

Rainbows seem as unities, but in fact they are just manifolds of water droplets diffracting the sunrays to our eyes at varying angles as these move through the sky. Rainbows seem to have shape and to occupy a certain space, but they do neither. In fact, if you and I are looking at the same rainbow at any instant, we are not even looking at the same collection of water droplets. The appearance of unity is therefore not even objective, but at least in a sense, subjective. Hence, rainbows, as we understand them, are not unities at all. They are not even definite aggregates, since even at any one time the "same" rainbow is composed of different water droplets from different points of view. Rainbows, therefore, are simply accidental indefinite physical phenomena.

Statues have more unity than rainbows only in that they are definite aggregates. Their reality consists in a definite chunk of matter, such as anyone beholding it is beholding the same chunk of matter. But the unity of a statue is clearly for that reason due to a physical principle.

The prospects for considering bodies akin to rainbows or statues are nil, since, in the first case, we notice upon closer examination that rainbows lack unity, whereas the study of bodies only yields an ever-greater appreciation of their unity upon deeper investigation. As for statues, their unity is clearly due to an unchanging physical core, whereas bodies are known to lack unchanging physical cores.

As to the consideration of bodies to be accidental machines of nature, we first have to at least concede that machines do exist—in fact, we create them. Moreover, the machines we create are not substantial but only accidental unities. They are aggregates of parts that have been coordinated from without and that by and large do not provide their own principle of organization such that they could be called alive. Furthermore, the machines we create are finite in intricacy, such that we can comprehend them by analysis into and study of their simple parts. This analysis goes from complexity at the highest level to simplicity at the lowest, each successive level of analysis becoming less complex.

Also, some things in nature seem to be mechanical in a similar way as the machines we create are mechanical. Subatomic particles build up very nicely into atoms, which can be understood by analysis into and study of their parts. The same goes for atoms building into molecules. In fact, we have found many cases that we can refer to as mechanical strands of explanation in the study of nature.

So why not just give in and concede that living things must be machines of nature? First, a closer look at the apparently mechanical things in nature reveals they are not exactly like the machines that we know and create. To begin, we cannot ultimately break them down to simple, unchanging, stable parts. Subatomic particles such as nucleons are analyzed down to particles such as quarks and all types of other energy particles.

Also, unlike machines, the understanding of which becomes increasingly simple as we analyze them down to simpler and simpler parts, the smaller "parts" of natural things do not seem to be any less rich in detail and complexity than the things they compose. Nobody really knows what the elementary particles of physics, such as quarks, really are, or electrons, or photons, for that matter. Whatever they are, their richness of detail and intricacy belies their ever being considered as "simple parts."

In short, whereas the machines we ourselves create are finitely and discretely intricate in detail, we notice the intricacy of living things to be infinitely and continuously intricate; continuous in the sense that there is no ultimate reduction to simple parts, and infinite in the sense that their intricacy is not something we can ever get to the bottom of. We recognize there are no prospects of our ever finishing physics or chemistry, let alone biology or psychology. There will always be more intricacy to uncover, no matter how far we progress in its study.

Given that our options appear to have been exhausted in explaining away the unity of living things as non-substantial appearances, it seems irrational not to accede to the Aristotelian position, that living things have real unity accounted for by a nonphysical organizing principle, i.e., the soul.

What makes Aristotle's approach to the soul preferable to the dualism of Plato or Descartes is that the latter ignores the evidence of the body in coming to their conclusions, relying solely on our acceptance that some of our life functions do not pertain to the body and, hence, are evidence of a soul. This counts only for humans, for the most part, who possess rational awareness, something that could readily be considered to be a non-bodily function, since it has an agenda quite distinct from animal awareness, which is straightforwardly linked to the body's survival orientation. But the fact that rational awareness is not exercised separately but in tandem with animal awareness makes it difficult for us to draw a line neatly between the two. Thus, naturalists might go on insisting that, after all, rational awareness is in fact reducible to animal awareness, which, in turn, as a bodily function can be thought to be reducible to the body. In this manner, dualist theories of the soul at best lead to a stalemate, whereas Aristotle's non-dualist conception of the soul has the clear advantage over its opponents when carefully examined, as we have done here.

Whether souls are immortal is another matter. Aristotle's position on the souls of living things generally was that they are not, since the soul's activity of organizing the body is interrupted by death. Unless the soul has an activity that does not get interrupted by death, it cannot be immortal. But Aristotle seemed to have left the door open specifically for human immortality by noting that human rational thought is an activity that does not pertain to the body. At any rate, it is a matter of less philosophical certainty than the existence of the soul *per se*.

CHAPTER FOUR

Confusion Regarding Natural Explanation

To the extent that we have truth-oriented awareness, we seek to know the sufficient reason of things or, as Leibniz put it, the reason why things are just as they are and not otherwise. This is our rational mandate, and per se implies no a priori limitation as to how that knowledge is to be gained. The search for sufficient reason can be considered, most generically, critical dialog, and takes two distinct forms: experimental dialog, or science, and ongoing argumentative dialog, or philosophy. Here, science and philosophy are taken in a wider sense, which includes both more formal and less formal versions of them.

Science is a closed-question enterprise in that it seeks answers to questions whose answers are to be gained by some combination of observation and calculation. These questions are closed in the sense that they are closed to argument: no amount or quality of argument will lead to knowledge of their answers. Questions answered by calculation alone are also therefore closed questions, since their answers will not be gained by an ongoing argumentative process, but only by axiomatic calculation.

Philosophy, on the other hand, handles open questions, that is, questions open to argument, since they cannot be answered directly by observation or calculation. Unlike the mathematical disciplines, the ongoing argumentative process of philosophy is not considered axiomatic on the grounds that although it may appeal to principles, these principles are subject to criticism along the way, whereas axioms as such are accepted without criticism. Calculation, then, is typically considered as ancillary to science, but in certain cases it may also be considered as ancillary to philosophy.

In fact, science, philosophy, and mathematics have all sorts of interactions; but this should not make us any less mindful of the distinctions between them. If we let the notice of one disappear as it were by absorption into another, it will be at the expense of both.

In the history of western thought, the gradually achieved division between science and philosophy was preceded by another distinction, that between natural and supernatural explanation. The latter makes references to divinity and other-worldly spiritual forces, while the former methodologically abstains from reference to such. This division was already evident in the Ionian Pre-Socratic philosophers of Asia Minor, now eastern Turkey.

In contrast to the classical Greeks, the ancient Hebrews, who also had spawned a great tradition of dialog, never made the methodological division between natural and supernatural explanation. As heir to both of these traditions, we now feel conflicted in our notion of how to approach our search for sufficient reason. Is it rational to coordinate natural with supernatural explanation, or not? If not, should one typically natural explanation take precedence, while the other is altogether abandoned? Or should they be compartmentalized as separate, noninteractive endeavors? All of these approaches are exemplified by some notable element of our society, and we have yet to reach consensus as to the proper course.

This confusion regarding the relationship between natural explanation and the rational mandate is compounded by our recent loss of focus regarding the proper role of argument in natural explanation. In Aristotelian thought, for example, even his discussion of the soul as the nonphysical organizing principle of the body—in particular of its unity and identity—was clearly not considered by him to be anything other than natural explanation. His concern in speaking of the souls of living things was not religious or theological, and was not used as leverage to speak of immortality or otherworldly existence. Quite to the contrary, he argued that the souls of living things are not immortal, since a soul would cease to exist when the body which it organized ceased to exist. Nonphysical things, according to him, can exist only by acting, and therefore they cease to exist once their activity ceases. This, in a nutshell, is Aristotle's natural explanation of bodies.

So what ever happened to argument in natural explanation, or natural argument? To be sure, it is not that we no longer engage in such activity, but that we have lost confidence in it after centuries of confusion between it and science proper.

The gradual division between science and philosophy was not a univocal process, but was accepted in some times and in some places more than others. The Muslim philosophers, for example, had a good sense of the importance and distinction of both. Nonetheless, by the Renaissance, seeds of dissension were already being sown in the form of a basic distrust in philosophy. Look at all that science had done in advancing human civilization; yet what had philosophy done in the meantime but heap more confusion upon us! It was time for philosophy, a less substantial enterprise, to yield to science, the more substantial enterprise, and to get out of its way! This led to the birth of positivism.

Positivism is the ideology that knowledge can only come from observation, or what could count as scientific evidence. If so, then argument can be of little value to us, since the evidence upon which it is based—reasons favoring the truth of argued claims—is not evidence in the scientific or closed-question sense. For example, Aristotle's evidence for the soul was the noticed unity and identity of bodies; but this kind of notice is of an intuitive sort which does not meet the quantitative, categorical demands of science.

The positivist movement would eventually advance from the position that observational claims alone were knowable to the position that only they were meaningful. So at its high-water mark of neo-positivism, Aristotle's theory of souls could be summarily dismissed as a meaningless claim, worthy of being ignored.

To be sure, neopositivism is no longer officially in vogue. But some of its effects have remained intact, such as our tendency to ignore less tangible concerns in the professions—regardless of import—in favor of more tangible ones.

In the meantime, our policy toward the argumentative branch of natural explanation has been, according to the vision of Bertrand Russell, to relegate it to a place-keeping role giving preliminary treatment to topics not yet treated by science, with the idea that science would get there sooner or later; or alternately, to the unification of natural explanation by means of reworking its language to be more and more rigorously observational, such that there would no longer be a distinction to be made between the experimental and argumentative methods. According to this ideal, the open questions treated in argument are just to be seen as more sloppy versions of more succinct observational questions which, once formulated properly, can be answered by science.

The attempt to reduce all language to observational language, though quite noticeable in the professions, never did quite lead to the abandonment of the argumentative enterprise, but has considerably weakened its operations, to the point where we now seek scientific explanation where such is either inappropriate or ancillary at best. This has contributed to trouble in human relationships, in mental health, in education, and in politics, not to mention other areas.

Such has the notion of natural explanation been narrowed to its experimental component at the expense of its argumentative component, that we ignore key concerns in the above mentioned professions simply because they are less amenable to being processed scientifically.

For example, attention to argumentative strategies of psychological care, especially such as those explored by Victor Frankl, has paled in comparison with physical/pharmacological treatments. Our attention to cognitive treatments in mental health has difficulty competing with the far more easily quantifiable physical treatments.

Regarding personal relationships, we are in dire need of deepening our idea of friendship not merely as the felicitous mutual meeting of quantifiable needs of each partner, but as a mutual, unconditional commitment to self-sacrifice through which we prove our love to one another.

As social animals, the bonds that bind us cannot be based merely on accidental conditions, such that those bonds are broken simply by the notice that needs are not being met. We are weak in our conception of friendship because we are weak on argument, which is where such knowledge is to be gained. Science can only tell us peripheral things about friendship, not what friendship is.

Although the ultimate purpose of education, as we well know, is long-term and intangible, educators more and more feel compelled to place their focus on relatively short-term and measurable goals. This, even though the relationship between these and the ultimate purpose of education is questionable. If education is to meet its purpose, some serious attention has to be given to maintaining an ongoing argumentative dialog and keeping our science on the matter in synchrony with that dialog.

Finally, although we recognize the need for good government, and that this ought to be the chief purpose of politics, so much of the political field is dominated by the more easily quantifiable science of manipulation. As a result, our efforts in that field are distorted in favor of malfeasance and governmental dysfunction.

In all these cases, what is lacking is productive argument. It is missing because we have lost confidence in argument as a key component of natural explanation. We must rehabilitate our notion of natural explanation to include robust argumentative dialog on matters that though not empirical in the strict, scientific sense, are still within our ability to move toward knowledgeable conclusions about them in ongoing dialog.

CHAPTER FIVE

Love and Natural Explanation

The words of the marital promise "for better or for worse" continue to confound so many of us, in that we recognize not only how difficult they may be to live up to, but also whether it even makes good sense to try to live up to them. Yet to do away with those words would surely deal a death blow to the meaning of love itself. We recognize, although not without trouble, that love is never proved as long as it implies no inconvenience. That lovers do their best not to inconvenience their beloved results in the common fact that most of the time, love is a convenient thing for us. In natural terms, convenience can be measured in terms of overall survival benefit, not just to the beloved or even to the lover, but to human society in general.

In ethological terms, the convenience of an organism is that which serves its felt survival interests. It is important to note that survival interests are not simply reducible to individual survival, and in fact some survival interests imply or even require the sacrifice of other survival interests. It is for this reason that we commonly see self-sacrifice among animals. The males of many species pursue their mating interests only at the risk of losing their lives. The same goes for animals protecting their progeny or worker ants protecting their queen. But none of these cases of sacrifice can properly be considered the acceptance of inconvenience, since in each of them the greatest felt survival interest is served, with the lesser impulses being sacrificed in pursuit of the greater ones.

It is easily arguable that love is the key to human survival, the specific human advantage over other species. (Moreover, since the beloved may well be other species of life, this survival advantage may even be conferred indirectly to them as well.) But the fact remains that we have no proof of love, that is, we don't even know that we ourselves are lovers or are beloved, until our dedication to others maintains itself in spite of the inconvenience—even and especially the overall inconvenience— which it entails.

One might think that this puzzle of love as a convenience that requires the acceptance of inconvenience for its own sake could be averted if we could allow that it is not important for us to know that we love or that we are loved, but just that we love. In that case, the embracing of inconvenience, even overall inconvenience, in the sense described above, could be thought to be a less than central and possibly even incidental feature of love. But this will not do for two reasons. First, because willingness to endure inconvenience, even overall inconvenience, for the sake of one's beloved cannot be less than a defining feature of love if love is to be anything at all other than an accidental alignment of individuals brought about by coinciding survival interests. If this is all that love is, then it is really nothing at all worth mentioning, any more than the coming together of animals at a water hole. As soon as it gets crowded enough, the watering animals will turn on one another, ending the temporary span of peaceful co-existence. Secondly, the benefit of love is not fully conferred to persons until it has been proved by the actual enduring of inconvenience. The benefit thus conferred is both to the lover and the beloved; the beloved in thereby gaining knowledge that she is a lover, the lover in thereby gaining knowledge that he is loved. It is the knowledge of loving and being loved that gives us the confidence to form the kinds of trust relationships required for prosperous and happy human existence.

Thus, the natural explanation of love proves paradoxical. For although the natural explanation of behavioral qualities is in terms of the overall survival benefit conferred, and indeed love does confer an overall collective survival benefit, it does so only by the experience of and the demonstrable willingness by us to experience inconvenience, even overall inconvenience. But according to the tenets of natural explanation, the intentional acceptance of inconvenience, especially overall inconvenience, is morbidly dysfunctional. On account of the at least implicit recognition of this paradox, human beings have never been quite sure what, in the final analysis, to make of love.

Brute animals are incapable of love in the sense described here because they are incapable of accepting inconvenience; that is, they are incapable of turning away entirely from their survival interests in pursuit of a greater interest which transcends these. Humans are capable of doing so thanks to their possession of rational awareness, whose felt end is not convenience, as in animal awareness, but the transcendent qualities of unity, truth, goodness, and beauty, to which realm love belongs. By our demonstrable willingness to forego our convenience for the sake of love, we create the context for our rational socialness, which unlike animal socialness, is indefinitely open and thus capable of embracing and realizing universal community.

This fact about love is no secret. There is nothing more distasteful to us than the thought of marriage or intimate friendship just for the sake of personal convenience. We consider this to be a case of false love.

Although we recognize Euripides's Medea to be a crazy witch, we equally scoff at Jason's rationale of overall family convenience as the motive for ditching her to marry the local princess. Euripides makes us realize that true love requires the foregoing of even overall convenience, and he managed to get this point across to an audience of men in a society that tolerated polygyny.

We are not sure what to make of love, because although on the one hand it seems so wonderful, even as the guiding force of life, on the other hand it seems altogether dysfunctional and wrongheaded. As a result, we lack confidence in romance itself—the kind of confidence required to make it succeed. That our rate of romantic failure is so high should therefore be no mystery to us, since this rate has been achieved by means of a self-fulfilling prophecy of destructive doubt.

And yet, at our best, we commonly celebrate this self-sacrificial aspect of love. We find it most uplifting, such that even if we don't see it evidenced in our own life, we long for and dote upon accounts of it in the lives of others, or even in fiction. We recognize that it is hard to do because it is hard to want to do; many of us wish for it but fail to want it. And although we recognize the great convenience of being loved, we have no sympathy for the unloving beloved and find the thought of such to be most despicable.

If love indeed is so eminently beneficial to us, and this benefit is based on the demonstrated willingness to suffer inconvenience—even great inconvenience—then one should think it would be easier for us than it in fact is to explain the sensibility of willfully turning one's back on one's felt survival interests —not one for the sake of another greater one, as is the case commonly with animals, but collectively, for the sake of love as a value altogether transcending survival. How is it, in other words, that our greatest survival benefit is conferred only by the willful renunciation of our own survival for the sake of something taken to be greater in importance than survival itself?

This is the point, I think we must admit, where natural explanation fails us. Regarding this one most important feature of human life, we are forced to go beyond nature—beyond survival logic—in search of a suitable account. Love simply has no suitable natural explanation.

A critic might deny this, saying that anything that confers a survival advantage in any term however long, and whether felt or not by the deliberating agent, thereby accords with survival logic. But those who argue this way ignore the way behavioral explanation works. Living things can only pursue their survival to the extent that it is felt by them in the form of some impulse. So the ignoring of one felt impulse can only be explained naturally by its being overridden by a greater felt survival impulse. This implies that there is no natural explanation for ignoring all one's felt survival impulses at once for the sake of something that is not a survival impulse, but a value of a different order.

Naturalists since Michel de Montaigne (1533–1592), and perhaps even as far back as Petrarch (1304–1374), have commonly been embarrassed by human rational awareness, reluctant to grant it a status autonomous from human animal awareness, which no one denies is based, as in other animals, on survival as its end. To the claim made above that rational awareness does not acquiesce in survival but in the transcendent values of truth, unity, goodness, and beauty, naturalists counter that nature is full of disguises, and that the apparent truth-orientedness of rational awareness is just a disguise.

But disguises in nature have a purpose: either to hide the collective survival advantage that one species has over others, or to preserve intraspecies competition. In this case, it seems difficult to avoid the conclusion that here, a natural motivation to deceive is not to be found, since in the first place, animals lacking rational awareness are thereby not in the position to notice the absence or presence of it, whereas those possessing it cannot imagine thek of it in them. The quality of rational awareness is already disguised as well as it can be, since it is at least directly unnoticeable by all but its bearers, to whom it is eminently noticeable.

To continue with this metaphorical speech, it is conceivable that rational animals might gain an advantage if their rationality could be read by other animals as brute animal awareness. But again, motivation is here too lacking, since the advantage has already been gained just by other animals not being capable of discerning in us the quality of rational awareness in the first place.

The advantage that rational awareness confers—and love, which comes along with it—is a social advantage, a rational social advantage. Therefore, disguising from one another the most fundamental aspects of our socialness, making it appear to be one thing when in fact it is quite another, would run counter to the purpose of being a rational animal, that is to say, of an animal whose socialness is perfected by its rationality and whose rationality is perfected by its socialness. Explaining away our rationality as a use of nature which disguises from ourselves our true nature, all to preserve a naturalist account of who we are, is good science only if the logic of natural disguise is tightly adhered to. But the logic is far from tight in this case, since there is no clear motive for there being a disguise in the first place.

Merely to insist that rational awareness, and love, which comes along with it, must be in the final analysis brute animal traits in disguise, rests on an unguarded assumption in favor of naturalism, and is bad science unless it is to be assumed that all science is naturalism. But we should never make such an unguarded assumption, so clearly reeking of the fallacy of argument by definition.

CHAPTER SIX

Zeno's Paradox and Our Experience of the Infinite

Zeno's paradox actually refers to a number of similarly constructed puzzles credited to Zeno, a follower of Parmenides, intended to support his master's thesis that being or reality is unchanging, that there is no real change or motion, and that all appearance of such is illusory. The idea behind each puzzle is that the assumption that change or motion is real leads to a vicious regress.

Those dealing with the puzzles of Zeno often refer to them collectively as if they were one. One collective label for them is the bisection paradox. In brief, the bisection paradox is that in order for there be motion or change from A to B there must first be passage through the midpoint between A and B. But in order for this to occur, passage must be made through the one-quarter point, and for that to occur requires first passage through the one-eighth point, and so on, ad infinitum. The puzzle is that going from A to B requires, as a precondition, transit through an infinite quantity of partial distances. This is assumed to be logically impossible.

Modern mathematics provides a definitive solution to Zeno's paradox according to one reading, but many think that it still remains unsolved according to another reading. The sense in which modern mathematics has solved Zeno's paradox is in the denial of the premise that necessarily the sum of an infinite set of finite quantities is infinite. It seems clear enough now that certain infinite sets of finite quantities yield a finite sum, in that the latter approaches a certain finite quantity as an asymptotic limit. So, for example, an infinite set that can be arranged into the following sequence has a sum that converges on 1 as a limit: 1/2, 1/4, 1/8, 1/16, etc. Even if one insists that the sum of such a set never quite reaches 1, the fact that it converges on a finite limit as its upper bound proves the sum of the entire set to be finite. This in turn refutes Zeno's paradox according to its most straightforward reading, by admitting that an infinite regress is implied but denying that it is vicious, since it does not imply the contradiction of having to travel an infinite distance in order to go a finite distance.

In another sense, however, perhaps modern mathematics has not solved Zeno's paradox. For although in the above solution recourse was made to an analysis of the puzzle by means of a function converging on an

Note: I owe much in the framing of the issue here to José Benardete, professor emeritus of philosophy at Syracuse University and brother of University of Hartford mathematics professor Diego Benardete. In particular, I refer the reader to José's book Infinity – An Essay in Metaphysics.(Clarendon Press, Oxford, 1964). In this book, he gives qualified support for the existence of the actual infinite. Here I do the same, although my argumentation differs.

asymptotic limit which by definition is never reached, Zeno's paradox is arguably teasing us about the notion of what might be referred to as a transit through an infinite number of finite distances to a symptotic point, i.e., a point that is reached—the terminus of the motion or change. This leaves us with a different problem: How can an action actually be executed which requires us first to complete an infinite number of steps and then arrive at a certain point? This seems to imply a contradiction, since an infinite sequence is by definition one which has no end, whereas in this reading of Zeno's paradox we are expected to get to the end of an infinite sequence in order then to accomplish something else.

As Leibniz himself conceded, there is no such thing as the infinitieth element of a sequence; the ordinality of every single step of an infinite sequence is finite. So if we have to get through an infinite sequence in order to execute any motion or change, it seems that no motion or change is possible.

The sense in which modern mathematics has solved Zeno's paradox is typically accepted as being based on the well-developed notion of potential infinity. In this sense, we can see the infinite both extensively and intensively—extensively, to generate infinite series such as the natural numbers, etc., and even uncountable infinities; intensively, to ground clear and distinct conceptions of infinitesimal quantities, i.e., quantities which, though technically greater than zero, are less than any specifiable quantity greater than zero. A prototypical example of such is the difference of 1 minus .999....

The sense in which Zeno's paradox has arguably yet to be solved regards the less well-developed notion of actual infinity, or infinity fully executed in act—in actual things, in our actual experience. Since mathematics is not about the actual but the possible, it necessarily remains neutral on this point. Solving Zeno's paradox in this sense requires affirming the existence of the actual infinite. So the question is left open for us to ponder philosophically: Is there in fact such a thing as actual infinity, or can we rule it out as impossible?

Right away we see trouble in this query, however. For we already accept potential infinity, that is to say the possibility of infinity is granted. So then if we then turn around and rule out the possibility of actual infinity, how can that not mean that infinity is not possible? If something is potential, that makes it not impossible. Conversely, if something is impossible, that should rule it out as potential. How can it make sense to affirm something potential but not potentially actual?

This is why actual infinity was so easy for Leibniz to accept. As an essentialist philosopher, he considered essence or possibility to have primacy over existence, which is to say he accepted that essence causes existence. In the first place, according to Leibniz, God's essence is the cause of God's existence. Unlike the medieval existentialist Thomas Aquinas, who insisted God was the uncaused first cause, Leibniz followed the essentialist tradition of John Duns Scotus in seeing God as self-caused first cause. Applying this notion to creation, that possible world will exist which has the most compossible essence. Therefore, there will be as much actual infinity in the actual world as can be fit into it. Actuality is nothing more to Leibniz than optimal possibility.

Of course, the affirmation of potential infinity X can be intended in at least two senses: one affirming that any of X is instantiable; the other that all of X is instantiable. Accordingly, without forcing a decision on whether essentialism is true or false, we recognize that we must be able to distinguish between Claim A: that anything is possible, and Claim B: that everything is possible. Perhaps, for example, our economy is one in which anyone can be rich, but this certainly does not imply that everyone can be rich. This applies to our topic in that potential infinity perhaps is nothing more than the potency implied by claim A, e.g. a line segment may be divided at any point along its length, but not at every point at once. Claim A possibility alone does not provide the grounds for actual infinity; only Claim B possibility does. Aristotle's combined acceptance of potential infinity and rejection of actual infinity seems to be based on his combined acceptance of Claim A possibility and rejection of Claim B possibility.

To be sure, we should all agree that some things are possible in sense A but not sense B. For example, a line could never be actually divided at all points, since that would imply that it is divided at any two adjacent points along the line. But there is no such thing as two adjacent points along a line; there will always be points in between.

But why should we reject Claim B possibility altogether, that in some cases the entire infinite potential of a function might be activated all at once? To the extent that we may take sensitivity to Zeno's paradox as a clue, might such a rejection be prejudiced by an inability to separate our imaginations from the constraints of time, so that we rule out the notion of a fully executed infinity due to time constraints? If so, we should recognize that a fallacy is involved here, which is the failure to take into account the infinitesimal interval. That is, in considering the execution of, say, an infinite convergence—which we recognize as a function endlessly converging on a limit which it never reaches—we might be failing to take into account that the infinite bulk of the temporal intervals involved in the process are infinitesimal, which means that they collectively would occur in practically no time at all.

In addition, to argue for an a priori impossibility of actual infinity would inappropriately force commitments on matters of fact, such as whether matter/energy exists beginninglessly or not. Modern science does not rule this out, and most who answer it in the negative do so on other than logical or metaphysical grounds. Perhaps the latest Big Bang was in fact preceded by a Big Crunch, and that by a previous Big Bang, with another Big Crunch before it, and so on. The truth about the matter may be for us an empirically undecidable matter from where we stand, but nonetheless it is a meaningful question whose answer, if it could be had, could only come from some kind of observation. It is simply not a question to be answered a priori, as even the great theist Aquinas conceded.

To decide on whether actual infinity exists, it will do us well to specify what we would be looking for when we are looking for actual infinity as opposed to potential infinity. The answer is discovered empirical or at least discovered noticeable content. The recognition of potential infinity is vacuous of content. It is merely an a priori logical, topological, or temporal analysis of the given. Nor could our awareness of infinity be merely by construction. We do have constructed notions of the infinite, but they are secondary in that our invention of them depends teleologically on prior intuitive awareness, so we would know what we were building toward. In this vein, there are two principle strategies: construction by negation and construction by mathematical induction. In the first case, we arrive at a constructed notion of the infinite by negation of our notion of the finite. This is most clear grammatically, as infinite is derived from the negation of finite. In the second case, we intuitively stipulate the existence of at least one element of a class, then provide for the production of the rest of the class by an iterative rule or rules. As such, for example, we define the natural numbers by first stipulating that 0 is a natural number, then adding the iterative rule that any natural number plus 1 is a natural number. It is psychological absurdity to think that our awareness of the infinite comes from our doing such things. Logic does not of itself produce content. We could only accomplish such constructions based on the direction given by an awareness of the infinite already present in us.

In short, to decide whether there is such thing as actual infinity, we have to notice whether here are content-rich cases of infinity in our experience. Here I will give three examples: one regarding human language, one regarding the (horizontal) continuity of actual detail, and the third regarding the (vertical) bottomlessness of actual detail.

Anthropologists have from time to time made attempts to see whether other animals can speak or meaningfully use human language at least in some rudimentary form. They have made considerable headway in some respects, but in one particular respect have been consistently stumped. Whereas they have been able to get various other animals to memorize and more or less consistently use arbitrary labels to refer to things and even actions in their experience, this has clearly been limited to their use as proper labels, not as common labels. The difference is that proper labels refer opaquely to a fixed, finite set of noticeables in the user's experience, whereas common labels refer through the mediation of meanings to infinite classes of noticeables. Human language, in short, is made possible only by our prelinguistic awareness of infinites. I consider this to be an awareness of actual infinity, since it is not a vacuous but a content-rich awareness. To be sure, the infinite classes themselves that we are recognizing pre-linguistically are not populated by infinite numbers of actual existents; but we spontaneously recognize that the meanings themselves are infinite in reference. We cannot really know what 'chair' means unless we understand it to refer to all chairs, the complete, infinite class of them.

We don't accomplish this awareness little by little, but all at once, which is the only way to grasp actual infinity. This awareness is infinitely rich, since we can never completely finish saying exactly what chairs are, and exactly how we can so competently distinguish chairs even from chair-like non-chairs.

If someone objects that ideas are not actual, I respond that here we are not focusing on ideas in the Platonic sense, or even in any other general or intersubjective sense, but in the psychological sense, as established in time in individual minds. (This point is made without prejudice against the viability of the other senses of the term.) In this sense, ideas are actual because they are acquisitions actually made in the world.

Whatever we notice or observe about the actual world, we recognize spontaneously that it is continuously detailed. As we delve into it, we discover always more detail in between other details previously noticed, in such a manner that we recognize it as infinitely rich. This is due to no mere inventive projection of the mind; for if it were, the result could not be continuous. What humans invent is finite and discreet. If I write a novel, my character development consists in a finite number of words and ideas; I depend on the reader to imaginatively fill in the gaps I inevitably leave. Even the reader will succeed only in filling them in a bit more than I have. But the result will be that there is no real chance for a sane mind with a sufficient, finite amount of time to devote to the task to confuse what we invent with what we discover. What we invent has discreet, limitedly rich detail; what we discover has continuous and therefore infinitely rich detail.

Not that our inventions are finite in all respects, since we do not invent ex nihilo. What we are doing when we invent, rather, is imposing a finite organization on some at least ultimately uninvented substratum, which in turn is infinitely rich in detail.

Our intuitive recognition that the actual world is infinitely rich in detail is evident in the absurdity of thinking that a science like physics can ever be finished in a finite amount of time.

Finally, we recognize that whenever we analyze some actually existing natural kind into its parts, we are left with a set of parts which are no less complex than what they compose. Chemistry does not get easier as we move from the study of molecule to atom to nucleon to quark. There is no sense in saying that quarks are any simpler in essence than are atoms or molecules. This can only be the case if our subject matter is bottomlessly rich in detail. Otherwise, each successive level would reveal simpler essences, and so on down to a bottom level of simple parts, as is the case in finite mechanical studies.

If then it is not legitimate to rule out actual infinity a priori, as Aristotle did—ostensibly to dodge Zeno's paradox!—we must leave the matter as to whether it exists to a study of what we notice and observe about the actual world. Here I have shown three aspects of our actual experience which have the markings of actual infinity: infinite richness in detail, which is something we can discover but not invent.

PART II
Epistemology

CHAPTER SEVEN

Unhealthy Skepticism

There seems to be a common if not prevailing notion among savvy people today that in order not to be naïve or credulous, we ought to practice a certain form of "healthy skepticism." This policy seems to apply more rigidly to some matters than to others, and I wonder whether the result isn't even less truth serving than the dreaded credulity we are trying to avoid.

The kind of skepticism I refer to involves avoiding the admission of the truth of certain key propositions unless there is no other conceivable option. Human imagination being infinite, the result is that there is practically no possibility that someone who adopts this policy would ever assent to any of these propositions. In other words, a negative decision has effectively been made in the name of skepticism, even though skepticism in this sense is supposed to indicate not a decision made, but an abstention from or delay in deciding.

This skeptical policy is certainly not applied across the board, which would be logistically if not psychologically impossible. However, such skepticism, by logical default, winds up still producing credulity in the form of an uncritical acceptance of the complementary proposition.

How we choose which propositions to target with this policy is another curious matter. It seems to be a certain class of what might be called good-news claims. Check these on your skeptical meter:

1. Humans are gradually learning how to live in peace with one another.
2. Politics without corruption is possible and plausible. Government can and usually does work effectively in the interests of the people.
3. The free market is not necessarily based on immorality, nor does it inevitably produce such.
4. Good ultimately prevails against evil.

The end result of this skeptical policy is that we are just as credulous as we feared we might have been by not being skeptical—but in the opposite direction. This bad-news credulity, in turn, tends to breed cynicism, which, in effect, as a form of surrender to evil, becomes a sort of a self-fulfilling prophecy!

The path from this kind of bad-news credulity to cynicism is clear enough. If in certain major ways there is nothing we can do to make the world better, then it is inane even to make the attempt. For cynicism is giving in to the evils of the world on the grounds that they cannot be avoided.

Is it right for us to be cynical? If not, then there is something wrong with our sadder-but-wider skepticism and we need to open our eyes to the exploration of the optimistic possibilities we have so far largely written off as naïve.

That humans are gradually learning how to live in peace with one another is not a preposterous claim. In fact, we are still in the first generation of human history in which ordinary people from all corners of the globe can meet, share their cultures with one another, and participate in the world community. Urban areas are actually less violent places per capita than rural areas, so the impression that people cannot live peacefully together may be based in part on a misinterpretation of the data. Of course, the more people you have in one place, the more crime there will be. But the suggestion that humans just can't get along would only be supported by data that violence per capita increases as population density increases. In fact, it does the opposite.

We decry political corruption on the one hand while on the other acknowledging it to be a practical necessity—that it's a game that needs to be played if one is to succeed politically. But if we need politics, and the practices we acknowledge to be corrupt are necessary to politics, then that corruption is not wrong but a necessary evil, and in fact something that ought to be done. Conversely, as long as we recognize the necessity of politics to human life, then anything we agree ought not be done ought also not be considered necessary to political success.

Moreover, politics is not corrupt to the extent that it accomplishes its rightful purpose. Now, politics still accomplishes some of its purpose, which implies that it is not completely corrupt. Moreover, its successes are owed to its non-corrupt aspects, whereas its failures are owed to its genuinely corrupt aspects. Furthermore, politics is also necessary to us insofar as it accomplishes its purposes. Therefore, genuine political corruption cannot be necessary, since it is unrelated to the accomplishment of rightful political purpose.

A similar argument applies to the free market. It is necessary to the extent that it achieves its rightful purpose. To this extent, whatever aspects of it are conducive to achieving its rightful purpose are not immoral. If we clearly see some practice to be immoral, we should see it by that fact as not necessary to economic practice.

This point only loses its force on the assumption that we cannot see whether economic activities are immoral until we see the economic result they achieve. But this is clearly false. We know, for example, that killing your business rival is wrong, or manipulating people in an inhumane manner, or cruelty to humans or other living things, etc.

Most surprising is our lack of confidence in goodness prevailing over evil. Evil is cast in our minds as strong and aggressive, while goodness is meek and passive. As a result, we tend to think the bad will inevitably corrupt the good. In response to this fear, we separate what we consider good from what we consider bad. But separating the bad unto itself only makes the bad worse, since it is thereby deprived of the influence of the good. The good, in turn, becomes prey to corruption by exclusionary biases attendant upon segregationist society.

In fact, what is truly good is inherently stable and reliable in cause and purpose, and is good on account of this, while what is bad is bad on account of being inherently unstable and unreliable in cause and purpose. Good, therefore, is inherently strong, while evil is inherently weak.

This does not imply that on any one occasion and in a short term, evil may prevail over good. But we should justifiably expect the opposite to occur in the indefinitely long term, since what is inherently stable survives well, while what is inherently unstable survives poorly.

CHAPTER EIGHT

Empirical Skepticism—Can We Not Think Outside the Box?

Skepticism generally is any theory that we cannot have knowledge at all, or at least cannot have knowledge of a certain kind. The rationale of skepticism can be based on quantity of evidence: that we can never have enough for knowledge; quality of evidence: that we don't have the right kind; disingenuity of belief, or inability to discern belief from prejudice; truth denial: that there is no truth; or the inability to define what knowledge is in the first place.

Empirical skepticism is one of those theories claiming that we cannot have knowledge of a certain kind, and whose rationale is based on quality of evidence. Simply stated, it is the theory that we cannot have knowledge of nonempirical claims on the grounds that the only evidence upon which knowledge can be based is empirical, or sensory and emotional.

Empirical skepticism is sometimes confused with another theory advanced by David Hume, himself a self-avowed empirical skeptic, that assuming the latter theory to be true, then we cannot have knowledge about the way the world really is, since such knowledge necessarily would have to rely on three kinds of nonempirical claims or assumptions: causation, substance, and the uniformity of nature. Hume's tack was to concede that we could not have theoretical knowledge of the world, but could still have practical knowledge of it; that is, we could still organize our observations into useful generalized predictive systems. This is what Hume thought science should consider itself limited to. Let's call this theory Humean skepticism.

In this paper, I consider whether Humean skepticism actually does follow from empirical skepticism. I will then turn my attention to whether empirical skepticism itself is true.

An empirical claim is a claim the determination of whose truth or falsehood is entirely a matter of observation. That I brushed my teeth twice yesterday is therefore an empirical claim—which, incidentally, happens to be false. On the other hand, that failure to brush one's teeth causes tooth decay is not, according to Hume, an empirical claim, and for three reasons. First, causal relations *per se* are not observable. Consider a simple case of a causal claim: that the cue ball hit the eight ball and caused it to move. All we really observe is a certain sequence: that the cue stick moves, makes contact with the cue ball, at which time a click is heard. The cue ball then moves, makes contact with the eight ball, at which point another click is heard. Then the cue ball stops or changes direction, while the eight ball begins its own journey. In short, all we see in any individual case is a sequence with one item following another. We don't actually observe any causal property.

Secondly, we don't really observe substances, but just manifolds. Our sense data do not present objects to us; nor do our emotions. Yet we somehow manage virtually on the fly to organize our perceptions into substances, or objects with functional unity and identity over time and change.

Thirdly, our causal judgment about dental hygiene is based on the processing not just of a single observed sequence, but is an inductive generalization based on many directly or indirectly (accepted by report) observations. Yet the credibility of induction itself as a form of reasoning depends on the assumption that nature is uniform. My confidence, for example, that stirring the pot after salting my porridge will eventually distribute the salt evenly throughout my porridge is based on the same aforementioned assumption: the laws of nature, whatever they are, are the same always and everywhere in the universe. If this is true, it means that, going back to my cooking example, I can be assured that if I can apply a continuous randomizing force to the distribution of the salt ions in the porridge, I can be sure that as I continue to stir, those ions will become increasingly more evenly distributed, moving toward an asymptotic limit of perfect distribution. This is in accordance with the law of large numbers, which states that the larger a random sample grows, the more closely it will approximate the probability of the occurrence or distribution of features as they occur in the larger universe, absent the influence of any local organizing principle. Now a random sample can be increased spatially or temporally; my continued stirring of the pot is a temporal way of increasing the size of the random sample.

In short, if Hume's reasoning is correct, then I cannot really know that failure to brush one's teeth causes tooth decay—or that smoking cigarettes causes cancer. I can only say with confidence that, however the world really is, these theories do a pretty good job both of covering observations already made and of predicting future observations. The reason for the gap between what we might call practical knowledge of the world and theoretical knowledge of it is due to the fact that we cannot observe causes, substances, or the uniformity of nature. In fact, Hume, Kant, et al. went on to claim these are patterns of sorts that we ourselves project onto our experiences in order to organize what would otherwise be a mere sensory manifold. Whereas Hume and Kant still allowed there actually is a real world that we could not know, some later followers of this way of thinking went on to deny the sensibility of asserting the existence of an unknowable world, thus masking their skepticism by denial. In the wake of this denial is left a world of our own invention, whose prime matter—sense data and basic emotions—comes out of nowhere.

But is Hume's reasoning correct? Is it really the case that modern skepticism implies Humean skepticism? Based on the modern skeptical conception of the empirical, then yes. For the modern notion does not allow for any gestalt-type perception or discovery of objects in our experience, and instead considers such intellective acts as cognitive invention or projection. Since awareness of causes, substances, and the uniformity of nature are all clearly products of gestalt-type intellective acts, they are not eligible to be considered as objects of sense perception according to the modern conception.

This is what makes modern skepticism so inconvenient: the limitation of knowledge to empirical claims ultimately rules out scientific knowledge, *per se*, which is supposedly the domain of empirical knowledge! Hume's proof of this almost reads like a *reductio ad absurdam* of empirical skepticism—except for the fact that he himself accepts the inconvenient consequences and as a loyal empirical skeptic nobly falls on his sword.

In short, if you want empirical skepticism, I hope you also like Humean skepticism, because that's what you'll be getting. On the other hand, if Humean skepticism really is not true, it must owe to the fact that empirical skepticism isn't true either. But how can empirical skepticism not be true? I see two ways.

The first way is the most straightforward: it is simply false that we cannot know any nonempirical claims. A nonempirical claim is a claim involving objects or qualities that are intangible, or irreducible to basic sensory claims. Nonempirical claims about intangible objects, such as God, angels, souls, etc., are most famously trotted out by empirical skeptics as examples of things we cannot know. But at least as important as those are claims attributing intangible qualities to things in our experience, such as that my mother is a nice lady, or that Karen is loving, or Marcia is trustworthy. As we have noted elsewhere, skeptics may try to accommodate such claims by creating empirical analogs of them, but the meaning will inevitably be lost in the transfer. There is simply no set of sensory observations that defines someone being nice, or trustworthy, or loving.

The second way is to argue that the modern skeptic's notion of the empirical is too narrow—so narrow that it excludes objects, or unities of any kind. Aristotle recognized this deficiency in pure sense perception, and this led him to conceive of intellectual perception, or the function of discovering patterns and unities in sense perception. He thus developed a dual-aspect theory of perception that resulted in a straightforward way of envisioning how we grasp objects in our experience—not just invented or copied representations of the objects, but the objects themselves.

It is interesting to note how close Hume and Kant were to Aristotle's view. In fact, the only difference is in whether to characterize what Aristotle considered intellectual perception as discovery or invention. Aristotle saw it as a type of discovery just as basic to perception as sensory perception, whereas Kant and Hume insisted it was invention, and therefore not to be counted as perception. Of these two positions, the latter is the more extraordinary, since it forces us to deny that we perceive objects or other unities in our experience, but rather that we project or construct them somehow for ourselves pre-consciously. This implies a whole lot of work for the mind to be doing—and doing imperceptibly, out of the range of our ability to observe. Modern empiricists—those who follow Hume and Kant in the matter just discussed—have never really given much of an explanation either for the necessity of their position—Aristotle's take was never refuted, but just ignored—or for why empiricism itself must ultimately be based on a most unempirical theory of mind.

As we haggle our way through these criticisms of empirical skepticism, we may eventually find that their common base is acceptance of the fact of intellectual discovery: that our intellect perceives or discovers patterns inherent in sense perception, grasping them as the unities of our experience, including causes, substances, and the uniformity of nature. We may still have to refine our understanding of just what these things are, but we don't have to doubt that they are.

CHAPTER NINE

Getting Clear on Justification and Belief: Another Shot at Gettier

A rather long-standing epistemological question is whether a justified belief that is but fortuitously true—that is, true only for reasons independent of those that justified it—should be considered knowledge. It seems the answer to this question should be that such a belief would not be knowledge, on the grounds it would be a matter of sheer luck if it were, whereas there is much reticence about admitting that one can know anything by sheer luck. Still, one encounters significant obstacles in the attempt to couch this response adequately within a theoretical framework.

This task has proven to be surprisingly elusive, something I will attempt to account for here by noting that the question itself is plagued by a confusion of three issues: whether there can be a justified belief that is fortuitously true; whether some apparent cases of such a type of belief are really cases where the appropriate justification is lacking; and whether other apparent cases of such a type of belief are really cases where the appropriate belief is lacking.

What is at stake, of course, is the platonic conception of knowledge, in recent times refined by people including Roderick Chisholm[1] and A. J. Ayer[2] and paraphrased aptly by Edmund Gettier[3] into the formula that knowledge is justified true belief. (Gettier points out passages at *Theaetetus* 201 and *Meno* 98 in which Plato seems to be committing to something quite similar to what Chisholm and Ayer advocate.) For if there is justified true belief that is not knowledge, then the definition fails. Of course, it might not be considered anti-platonic to go in search of a fourth element of the definition. This would not be necessary if it could be shown, and I hope to do so, that in the final analysis there is nothing really puzzling, paradoxical, incomplete, or incorrect about the knowledge formula; that it is, in fact, an adequate framing of the issue of epistemology.

To be sure, the question might be considered moot to those who would limit justification to possession of complete evidence by insisting that a necessary condition of justification is that it guarantee truth. These infallibilists may be disposed to write off the puzzle we are considering as one more reason not to embrace any incomplete evidence (fallibilist) theory of justification. But this is an off-topic response. If on other grounds one feels compelled to favor such a strong view of justification, then that is fair. But certainly one ought not

---

1   Roderick Chisholm. *Perceiving: A Philosophical Study* (Ithaca, NY: Ithaca University Press, 1957): 16.

2   A. J. Ayer. *The Problem of Knowledge* (Harmonsworth, England: Penguin, 1956).

3   Edmund Gettier. "Is Justified True Belief Knowledge?" *Analysis* 23, 6 (1963): 121–3.

adopt such a position just to skirt the present issue. The challenge we are faced with is to try to defend a moderate, fallibilist definition of knowledge against criticism from another faction of the fallibilist camp. To rebut the criticism of the latter by appeal to an infallibilist notion of justification misses the point altogether. If the traditional definition of knowledge is shown by Gettier's counterexamples not to work, that is no defense *per se* of infallibilism, nor of the universal skepticism that many see to be corollary to it.

The puzzle we are considering affects only a very small set of knowledge candidates, whereas if fallibility itself were the issue, this would affect a much larger set of knowledge candidates, arguably all of them. If one is to conclude the definition of knowledge ought to be adapted to an infallibilist notion of justification, it should not be on account of Gettier-type puzzles.

An interesting way of challenging the traditional platonic formula of knowledge is to attempt to point out as counterexamples cases of justified belief that are only fortuitously true, and therefore such that we would not be comfortable considering them as cases of knowledge, even though they fit the definition. Gettier, in fact, brought forth several such counterexamples, which many to date seem to consider as having thrown an unliftable fog over the platonic definition.[4] In this paper I will attempt to dismiss all Gettier-type counterexamples as cases where the appropriate belief is lacking. Since, according to the knowledge formula, something has to be believed in order to be known, such counterexamples would therefore fail to challenge it.

Similar to Gettier-type counterexamples are those that, I will attempt to show, play on a false idea of justification; i.e., cases of pseudo-justification. In this manner, this type of alleged counterexample would also fail to challenge the platonic conception.

After considering these two types of counterexample, I will return to the most general posing of the question: whether there can be a justified belief that is fortuitously true. If so, then either the knowledge formula is incomplete, or we would have to accept such cases—probably against our own rational instincts—as knowledge. I will argue, though, that there can be no such type of belief, on the grounds that they imply justification is compatible with irrelevance, which violates the core notion of justification.

Again, a "fortuitously true justified belief" is one whose reason for being true is unrelated to its justifying rationale. To give an example here is problematic, since at issue in this paper is whether there is such a thing. Those who hold there is would consider the Gettier-type and other examples below as cases of such.

Gettier argued that situations are imaginable in which someone believes a true statement *p* as a justified inference from a statement *q*, which is false. In such a case, *p* is a justified true belief; but we are loath to consider it knowledge, because the grounds for the belief—*q*—are false. Nonetheless, *p* is justified, since *q* is by supposition justified and *p* is a logical inference from *q* recognized by agent *s*. Necessarily, if we can imagine *q*, although false, to be justified, it would seem that we must extend the same justification to *p*.

Gettier gave two examples of this sort to challenge the platonic conception of knowledge: one depending on inference by existential generalization, the other on inference by disjunctive introduction. In the former, Smith generalizes from his justified, though false, belief in the particular claim:

Jones is the man who will get the job, and Jones has ten coins in his pocket.

to the non-particular claim, which, consequently, he also accepts:

The man who will get the job has ten coins in his pocket.

---

4   Gettier, 121–3.

The latter could still turn out to be true even if the former is false; namely, if Smith, who also, as it turns out, has ten coins in his pocket, happens to get the job—which, by hypothesis, he does. Yet we are loath to concede that Smith knows the inferred claim even though it appears to be a justified, true belief.

The example depending on inference by disjunctive introduction is that Smith infers from his justified, though false, belief:

Jones owns a Ford.

to the claim, which, consequently, he also accepts:

Either Jones owns a Ford, or Brown is in Barcelona.

Again, the latter could still turn out to be true even if the former is false; namely if, though Jones turns out not to own a Ford, Brown, by sheer coincidence, happens to be in Barcelona—which, by hypothesis, he happens to be. Yet we are loath to concede that Smith knows the inferred claim, even though it appears to be a justified, true belief.

It is important to note that the problems Gettier is posing here are not nearly as out of the ordinary as the examples may sound. They may just as easily arise in situations involving less extraordinary coincidences yielding predicaments perfectly analogous to Gettier's examples in all logical respects.

For example, suppose Maria has come to believe on credible evidence:

(1) Dr. Adams, whose office is at 234 Main Street, is the only dermatologist in the area.

This is ordinarily taken to entail:

(2) There is a doctor whose office is at 234 Main Street and who is the only dermatologist in the area.

So if Maria is justified in believing (1)—and there is no reason to think that she couldn't be—it seems she is equally well justified in believing (2).

Now suppose further that there has been a rare mix-up in the information Maria received from her credible sources. As it turns out, there is a Dr. Adams whose office is at 234 Main Street, but she is an oncologist, not a dermatologist. So (1) is false. But, as it turns out, (2) is still true: there *is* a doctor, named Dr. Eves, whose office is at 234 Main Street and who, in fact, is the only dermatologist in the area.

The odd result is that Maria apparently has a justified true belief—(2)—which we are loath to consider knowledge because the grounds for her belief—(1)—are irrelevant to (2). This case throws the platonic definition of knowledge in crisis, because it seems to include in its extension things we would not want to consider cases of knowing.

I think the problem will be solved if we note that Maria doesn't really believe (2) according to its proper reading, just as Smith, in the earlier example, does not really believe, according to its proper reading, that the man who has ten coins in his pocket gets the job. There is a reading of (2) according to which Maria does accept it, but admitting this would not challenge the knowledge definition.

This first kind of Gettier-type challenge in fact depends on a confusion of two readings of the inferred claim, in this case, (2). The first reading is what I call the proper reading, and the second reading is what I call the limited reading.

We can make this distinction in the following manner:

s believes inferred claim p according to its proper reading iff (if and only if)
s believes all recognized entailments of p.

On the other hand,

s accepts inferred claim s according to a limited reading iff
1. s does not believe p according to its proper reading,
2. s believes a particular claim q, and
3. s recognizes q as an instance or satisfaction of p.

Failure to accept the significance of this distinction between readings of inferred claims will lead to trouble in the notion of what a belief is. For if we confuse them, we get the absurdity that, provided the entailments are recognized, my belief in (1) commits me to believe that if Dr. Adams is not a dermatologist, then there is *another* dermatologist at 234 Main Street.

In the present example, the problem is, in fact, brought about by unrestricted use of existential generalization. I am arguing this is bad logic in inferring beliefs, on the grounds that it allows the entailment of extraneous claims as beliefs that would never on those same grounds be believed. To obtain an accurate account of belief entailment, we must restrict the use of existential generalization to limited readings of existentially generalized claims. Doing so would allow the knowledge definition to overcome Gettier's challenge. Of course, Maria doesn't believe (2) according to its proper reading on the grounds that (1). Proper belief in (2) could be paraphrased as saying that *some dermatologist or other* has an office at 234 Main Street and is the only dermatologist in the area. If Maria receives the information that Dr. Adams is not a dermatologist, that new information does not permit the entailment there is another dermatologist at 234 Main Street.

Altering the example slightly, we can dispense in similar fashion with the second Gettier challenge that depends on inference from disjunctive introduction. Once again, we have Maria believing justifiably the false claim:

(1') Dr. Adams, whose office is at 234 Main Street, is the only dermatologist in the area.

We then have Maria recognize the entailment by disjunctive introduction that:

(2') Either Dr. Adams or someone else whose office is at 234 Main Street is the only dermatologist in the area.

Now certainly Maria does not accept (2') according to its proper reading, but only according to its limited reading, just as, in Gettier's example involving disjunctive introduction, Smith does not believe, according to its proper reading, that Brown is in Barcelona. For if Maria did accept (2') according to its proper reading, then, on evidence that Dr. Adams was not a dermatologist, she would conclude based on that alone that there was another dermatologist at 234 Main Street, etc.

In fact, the unrestricted use of disjunctive introduction in the inferring of beliefs causes problems quite similar to those that the unrestricted use of existential generalization cause. The recognition that a belief satisfies the truth conditions of a more general claim does not imply the proper acceptance, in turn, of the more general claim as well, since it does not warrant our acceptance of any other claim that would satisfy its truth conditions except the claim we started out with.

Although I have treated Gettier challenges as belief problems, they could also have been treated similarly as justification problems. Where there is no cause for belief, justification is also lacking. But their treatment as belief problems takes precedence, because there is no reason to ask about justification where there is no belief.

Nonetheless, one other problem that can come up with the knowledge formula has to do more properly with a justification problem rather than a belief problem. Consider the following case.

John believes it hailed last Saturday afternoon in Toledo, which in fact it did. John has good reason to believe it: he heard about it on the Weather Channel. Unbeknown to John, however, was the report he had heard about hail was actually about hail in Topeka on the same day. The meteorologist misspoke herself, saying "Toledo" when she should have said "Topeka." John had turned the television on just after the meteorologist had finished her report on hail in Toledo, and, the city names being so similar, she switched one for the other.

In this case, John has a true belief that appears to be justified as well. This would force us to say, by the knowledge definition, that John knows it hailed in Toledo, which we are loath to do on the grounds that something about John's rationale seems unfit for our coming to such a conclusion.

In fact, although John may seem justified in his belief—since he consulted a credible, expert source—he is not really justified, since the evidence he obtained is, in fact, irrelevant to his conclusion.

It is rather customary to think that if someone has taken all due measures in coming to a conclusion, and in so doing obtains evidence that gives strong support to a conclusion, that such a person must be justified in his belief. After all, he has done all that could be expected; requiring more would seemingly suggest the extreme limit that only a state of omniscience would amount to a justification. As I have said before, to take such a position would take us out of the present discussion.

In fact, to deny justification to someone in John's position does not suggest any extreme theory of justification. For, albeit not due to any lack of diligence on John's part, an important quality is lacking in the evidence upon which John has based his conclusion: relevance. It is quite simple: for a body of evidence to justify a conclusion, it must be relevant to that conclusion. Data about hail in Topeka simply is not by itself relevant to whether it hailed in Toledo.

As long as one is set on defining justification in subjective, agent-centered terms alone, one will be vulnerable to this kind of puzzle. But justification is a function both of an agent's cognitive states and the quality of evidence on its own merits. Evidence gains its relevance from the latter, not the former.

For example, if after injuring my hand and going to have it checked I am told by the radiologist that there are no broken bones and I am even shown the x-rays. It should then surely seem that my belief is justified that my hand is not broken. I have consulted the most competent experts and inspected the photographs. I have been diligent and taken all expected measures to arrive at a warranted conclusion. But a key component of justification may still be lacking, despite all these favorable trappings. Suppose the x-ray photographs were mishandled and confused with those of another injured-hand patient. In this case all the radiologist's deliberations on the status of my hand, and my judgment based on her expertise, are irrelevant. Surely, a belief about whether my hand is broken cannot be justified based on an examination of someone else's x-rays! This is not a matter of margin of error; this is a matter of relevance. That is to say, despite all good-faith effort and credible expertise, a belief cannot be justified unless the evidence is relevant to the judgment to be made. If the evidence is irrelevant, then diligence and expertise cannot alone combine to justify the belief.

The opposition to looking at justification in the way I suggest is that it makes the definition of knowledge in question excessively remote from us, to the point of putting its very meaning in crisis. Since it is well understood that justification does have *something* to do with diligent effort, perhaps we should not give up so easily on the idea that it might be *wholly* a function of the agent. If we could understand justification in this way, the advantage would be the nearness, the ready applicability, of the concept. On the other hand, if applicability of a concept is considered to be a necessary condition of its meaningfulness, it is questionable whether a non-agent-centered concept of justification would be meaningful at all.

Before we go further, we should review the notion of applicability. According to some, saying I am six feet tall is meaningful only on the grounds that I can be measured by a measuring tape or by some other applicable standard to verify the claim. By these lights, saying one has a justified belief could only be meaningful on the grounds that one could, with diligence, do a double check. But if the standard upon which justification is based is remote, then that makes it more difficult to do a double check. The more difficult a thing is to verify, the more questionable, some would say, is its meaningfulness.

Now, requiring as a condition of justification that evidence be relevant to the conclusion and not just appears so to a diligent agent, *is*, in fact, a somewhat remote standard. But it is no more remote a standard than the one by which we are required to differentiate between a real belief and an apparent belief; or between truth and apparent truth. It is crucial to see that we are not putting any special pressure on justification here; the necessity of differentiating between the real and the apparent applies to all three elements of the platonic definition: truth, belief, and justification.

Of course, this makes the definition more remote. But it is a kind of remoteness we just have to live with, if the notion of knowledge is to have any sense at all. Provided that believing something is taken as being convinced it is true, and being convinced is taken as being persuaded by evidence, it follows that anything I think I believe—I think *eo ipso* to be true and justified. Add to that the possibility that I may think I believe things I really don't, and, vice versa, believe things that I wouldn't acknowledge. All this implies that once I decide that I believe something—even if I really don't!—I have decided that I know it. To achieve clarity in such a valley of delusion requires standards that are not entirely agent-centered. This will carry with it the consequence that evaluating belief will always be a troubled process.

The whole discussion we have had to this point ultimately comes down to the question whether a justified belief can be fortuitously true, i.e., whether there are true beliefs whose justified rationale is conceptually unconnected to the reason why it is true. The answer is that there is no such thing. For if there were, then it would have to be that there is also such a thing as an irrelevant justification. But there is no such thing as this, either. One of the necessary conditions of a justification is that it be—and not just appear—relevant.

As is often the case, the clarity of this answer appears to fade as soon as we ask for a definition of "relevant evidence." We think we know the difference between what is relevant to a judgment and what is irrelevant, but to put that difference in words is difficult.

One of the problems in gaining clarity on this matter is failure to distinguish between the objective aspect of evidence—its content—and the subjective aspect—its reference to particular observers. Given that our present concern is on the objective aspect, from now on we will be considering evidence according to its pure content, devoid of references to observers. If John judges from having seen Tom in Amherst that Tom was in fact in Amherst, the evidence we would then consider for Tom's having been in Amherst is not that John saw Tom in Amherst, but that Tom was seen in Amherst. If John possesses some trait that bears upon the quality of the evidence thus stated, that should be included in the evidence statement in a non-agent-centered way, e.g., that John was spotted in Amherst by someone with very good eyesight, or that John was well spotted, etc. Who makes an observation is irrelevant *per se* to whether or to what degree we are justified in believing something on that evidence. The problem with failing to attend to this distinction is that it forces us to focus on the subjectivity of someone observing something as opposed to the objectivity of what is observed. Here the challenge is to focus on relevance as an objective matter—a matter of coming up with a non-agent-centered definition of relevance—rather than as a subjective one.

For starters, we might try to put relevance in terms of necessary conditionhood, as follows:

Evidence e is relevant to claim p just in case if e is absent, p is false.

After all, a quality we want to see in evidence is that the truth of the claim it supports is contingent upon the evidence. But there are two problems with this. First, there are many necessary conditions of a claim that are irrelevant in that they are too generic. For example, a necessary condition of it hailing in Toledo last Saturday is that the earth has an atmosphere. So necessary conditionhood by itself does not confer relevance. Secondly, evidence may be relevant in any ordinary sense of the term without being or implying a necessary condition, e.g., in the manner that John's African ancestry is relevant to the likelihood that he has sickle-cell anemia. There are some people, though not many, who have this genetic disease but lack African ancestry.

The consideration of sufficient conditionhood as a marker for relevance similarly has two fatal flaws. First, it is too severe, in that evidence does not have to be completely convincing to be relevant. As addressed earlier, it is questionable whether even justification needs to meet this qualification.

Secondly, a sufficient condition may contain irrelevant elements mixed with relevant elements. For example, a sufficient condition to my being in France is that I am in Paris. But another sufficient condition of the same is that I am in Paris with a baguette under my arm. The baguette is superfluous: they are also made in Belgium, and from time to time people carry them across national boundaries. Yet, as irrelevant as it may be, my carrying a baguette under my arm is part of a sufficient condition of my being in France.

Going for something less than a necessary condition may put us on the trail to the answer we are seeking. We can say that:

e is relevant to p just in case e is a *restricting* condition of p,

where a restricting condition of p is one in whose absence p is less likely. (Note that a necessary condition is a special kind of restricting condition, in whose absence the likeliness of the truth of p is reduced to zero.) This has the benefit of capturing the notion that relevant evidence is evidence that narrows the search. But we still have a problem, in that opposite claims do share restricting conditions—so defined—in common. These are of the more generic type; i.e., in order to have sickle-cell anemia you have to be human, or an animal, or a living thing, etc. So it is clear that we need another limitation to adequately define "relevance."

The limiting qualification we are looking for is one that would exclude all and only those restricting conditions that are excessively "generic"; i.e., somehow indifferent to the claim. If I am asked why I turned left at the intersection between Main and Amity and I answer that it was partly because I was **at** the intersection, there is something irrelevant about the answer—despite the fact that for me to turn left at the intersection, I must be at the intersection. The irrelevance in this case lies in the fact that my being at the intersection is equally well a restricting (in this case, a *necessary*) condition of turning right—or of doing *anything else*—at the intersection. Giving that answer is silly, because it doesn't favor my turning left over doing anything else.

The same could be said about an answer such as I turned left because I only had the choice of turning left or right (or because two plus two equals four, for that matter).

This kind of irrelevant restricting condition can be excluded by using the notion of *pre-contextuality*. Some conditions have to be satisfied for there to be a context of inquiry, but play no role *in* the inquiry. For instance, the earth having an atmosphere is a pre-contextual restricting (in this case, *necessary*) condition to any (earthly) meteorological context of inquiry, e.g., to whether it hailed in Toledo last Saturday. But as a pre-contextual restricting condition, it favors no answer to the question(s) posed in the inquiry.

Let us express this qualification as follows:

> e is relevant to p just in case e is a *non-pre-contextual* restricting condition of p, where a pre-contextual restricting condition of p is defined as something that is a restricting condition of p *and all alternates of p*. An alternate of p is a rival claim to p, e.g., that instead of turning left at the intersection, I turned right, or stopped the car, etc.

According to this definition, coupled with the stipulation that no belief is justified unless it is based on relevant evidence, there can be no such thing as a fortuitously true justified belief. The whole notion that there might be such a thing derived from wholly agent-centered notions of justification. This definition establishes some non-agent-centered grounding for the theory of knowledge, which I believe makes better sense of knowledge—the way we talk about it, and the way we think about it. With this grounding, the platonic definition of knowledge—which provides so much clarity in framing the issues of epistemology—is no longer plagued by Gettier-type or other similar challenges addressed above.

CHAPTER TEN

Knowing Nonempirical Reality

Many today complain about the overemphasis in various sectors of human society on measurement as the way to judge or ensure ourselves of the quality of things. There are two types of complaint. The first is the cost-benefit complaint (CBC), in which, even to the extent that it is accurate, the costs of measurement outweigh the benefits. The second is the invalidity complaint (IC), in which measurement, in fact, does not lead to valid judgments about value. This essay focuses on the second type of complaint, after a brief review of the first, in which it is, in fact, revealed to be complicit in the second.

Regarding CBC, there are two ways for measurement to be harmful even to the extent that is accurate. The first is that it draws our attention and resources away from the production even of the qualities being accurately measured, and secondly, that it discourages our attention to unmeasurable qualities. In this second sense, CBC will tend to provoke IC, since it ignores whatever unmeasurable value exists. Measurement cannot be valid to the extent that it ignores one entire class of vital qualities: the intangible ones.

The relevance of IC is contingent, of course, on the reality of vital, intangible qualities. What made us go down this path in the first place is a tradition of skepticism or even nihilism regarding their existence. In fact, skepticism has been on the rise for a long time. Therefore, to address this problem head-on, we need to retrace our steps back to where the key conceptual commitment was made establishing this skeptical tradition. We don't have to pretend there was actually one time in history corresponding to this commitment, but that, over perhaps even a long period of time, there was an accrual of acquiescence in a certain way of looking at human cognition that led us to have less and less confidence in the nonempirical.

I consider this "key conceptual commitment," this "certain way of looking at human cognition," to be representationalism itself. After all, it is the single gauntlet through which practically all modern Western epistemology has passed. Representationalism is the theory that the given of consciousness is not actually the thing perceived, but a mentally constructed representation of the thing perceived. This creates a "bridge problem": to certify that our mental representations are accurate, we would presumably want to compare them with the things themselves. But if representationalism is true, this cannot be done. So we are left forever unsure of the extent to which our representations "correspond" to the real thing. After a while we grow tired even of imagining an unknowable, real world "out there," and are tempted to deny either its existence or its practical relevance to us.

Representationalism may have its medieval roots in the Thomistic dictum: *Nihil est in intellectu quod non prius in sensu*. Called the Peripatetic axiom (PA), and found in *De Veritate* (question 2, article 3, argument 19), it translates as "nothing is in the intellect which was not first in the senses." It is interesting to notice how this "axiom" came to be read more and more as a subscription to representationalism, when in fact Aristotle, the Peripatetic philosopher himself, was decidedly not representationalist. But more on him below.

PA, in fact, does not imply representationalism. It does not commit us to denying that the thing itself is or can be received by the senses or by means of the senses. Yet, heading toward the Renaissance, as a rift began to grow between empiricist versus rationalist trends of thought, representationalism, a common presupposition of both, quietly settled in as an unchallenged assumption.

At first blush and in spite of all the trouble, one might wonder what other option we have than to be representationalist. After all, it is impossible to deny that we fashion images of things from our senses and use those images in our deliberations about those things. Besides, if I don't have an actual chair in my brain when thinking of a chair, how can I have a real chair on my mind when thinking of it? Our best known sensory faculties are clearly geared for reporting images: auditory, tactile, visual, olfactory, and gustatory. Our memory is itself a conservation of those images.

But, in fact, none of the above forces the conclusion that we don't have direct awareness of the thing itself; merely that we also make and consider images of it, and perhaps we do both. In fact, that's what Aristotle thought. But somehow his enlightened opinion on the matter has been lost from philosophical tradition; it never made it through the representationalist gauntlet of modern epistemology.

Aristotle's elegant notion was that perceptual awareness was based on the cooperation of two faculties: sensory perception, on the one hand, and intellectual perception, or *nous*, on the other. He noted that sensory perception alone does not give us unities to grasp, but only continuous and therefore infinite sensory manifolds. But without unities there can be no objects, and without objects, no awareness. It is *nous* that provides the unity, by discovering intuitively, sometimes with the help of repeated experience, the pattern underlying the sensory manifold. (Later, this faculty became called the "common sense" but eventually this original meaning became lost, although the term remained.) This grasped unity is the thing itself.

Lest someone suspect that I am resurrecting an obsolete idea that has seen its day before being duly dispensed with by rigorous philosophical criticism, I dare anyone to find any record of such. To the contrary, this is an idea that just got lost in the confusion of the Middle Ages, even in the first millennium, when Aristotle was not taught for his own but for Plato's sake, or for the sake of his Neoplatonist successors, who had no interest in mundane things such as knowledge of individuals and who relied on the notion of a preexisting spiritual state to explain our knowledge of these forms, which Aristotle claimed we discovered here and now in the things themselves, and that our awareness of them constituted our knowledge of the things themselves.

Another criticism might be to ask how we know that representationalism is wrong, even if it is inconvenient. Certainly we should not abandon it just because it leads to skeptical conclusions about things; maybe those skeptical conclusions are true.

To this criticism I respond by saying that for representationalism to be true would require a virtually omniscient unconscious mind, since without any recourse to Aristotle's unity-grasping intellectual intuition, the only other course is to construct by some complex process, altogether opaque to the conscious mind, our objects of awareness out of the infinite sensory manifold itself. This would be an incomprehensibly monumental task, since we perceive the organized detail of our experience to be continuous—hence, infinite.

Immanuel Kant understood this, and for that reason argued that the unities of our experience were inventively, and in a certain orderly fashion, superimposed on our sense data. The only difference here between him and Aristotle is that Kant insists these patterns and unities are not discovered in the things, but superimposed on them by us. His only rationale for this insistence was the then unchallenged tenet of representationalism.

At least one follower of Kant's transcendental philosophy, Edmund Husserl, was frustrated by this denial of the possibility of mental discovery and the epistemic idealism that issued from it. In his later years he worked hard to make room for what he called transcendental realism, according to which by a disciplined process we are indeed able to discover the real unities in our experience.

If Aristotle is correct and we are thus able to knowledgably grasp intangible qualities, then how ought we deal with them in organizations? Measurement of tangible qualities is quite often intended as an indirect way of ascertaining what in themselves are intangible qualities: learning, intelligence, trustworthiness, etc. In the absence of confidence in direct apprehension of these qualities, we attempt to create measurable analogs of them either in whole or in part. But ironically, under the pall of representationalism we have to consider ourselves unable to know whether these analogs correspond to their intangible counterparts.

What might we be doing instead? First, I do not suggest the cessation of all measurement, but measurement in conjunction with a methodology appropriate to genuinely intangible qualities: continuously engaged dialogue. It's something we already do, and have been doing for ages.

One of the most sacred tasks in life is the education of children—by their own parents or guardians. Since their birth, we are in continuous dialogue with them on every vital matter; we want to be sure they learn from us what they need to learn. Yet we do not typically submit them to any kind of empirical testing to make sure they are learning from the parent-child relationship they have with us. I doubt that would even work.

But what does work is our remaining continuously engaged with them in dialogue, so that we are regularly receiving feedback from them as well as imparting new and repeated messages to them. This parenthood/mentor model should be the model we are using for the cultivation of intangible values generally.

It is not that we ought not try to measure measurable qualities, for the sake of ensuring their better development. But we should not on account of our so doing lose sight of the development of intangible qualities. Just because they are in a more narrow sense unobservable, still they are in a broader sense noticeable to us as vital aspects of human existence.

CHAPTER ELEVEN

The Direct Perception of Reality

A major motivation for skepticism—and also for a variety of attempts at avoiding it—in modern philosophy is what has been called the "bridge problem"—alternately, "The Problem of the External World." Based on acceptance of the theory of representationalism or indirect perception, we are tempted to lose hope that we can ever have knowledge of objects in themselves, since by representationalist assumption we have no way to compare the representations we have of things with the things themselves.

Much of modern epistemology has been in response to this problem, either in the form of accepting and elaborating on the skeptical limits this problem would impose, or by attempting to evade, solve, or dissolve the problem in a variety of ways. It is as if the character of modern epistemology itself is acquired by passing through this problematic gauntlet. Thus, we have tended to be dismissive of premodern epistemology, since it does not seem to show sufficient concern for this problem.

The motivating question here is whether a closer look at Aristotle's epistemology may result in a viable way to dissolve the bridge problem in a way that does not introduce the usual controversial infallibilist implications that typically encumber attempts to get around the bridge problem.

Briefly, my tack will be to notice that although Aristotle did in fact consider mental representations (*phantasmata*) formed by the faculty of *phantasia* (roughly: imagination) to be of central importance to the way humans acquire knowledge, it is not *phantasia* but the nonrepresentative perceptual faculty of *koiné aisthesis* (literally: the common sense) that is the primary faculty of our initial awareness of objects as such. Since *koiné aisthesis*, unlike *phantasia*, is a nonrepresentative faculty of discovery rather than an inventive or interpretive one, it gives us a way, though not infallible, of fruitfully comparing the *phantasmata* against direct awareness of the object and therefore stands as a reliable guide in the continued fine-tuning of our knowledge of things by *noûs* (intellectual perception) in the ongoing experience-building process of *epagogé* (induction).

Since I am anachronistically presenting Aristotle's theory of knowledge as a "new" solution to an older problem, in what follows I will precede my own case with a closer look at the bridge problem and modern responses to it. This will be followed by a brief discussion of other attempts at grappling with Aristotle's epistemology, which will set the stage for making my own case.

As cited above, the roots of the bridge problem are in representationalism. The history of the latter, in turn, traces back to medieval developments in the understanding of two notions in tandem. First is the so-called

Peripatetic axiom, culled from Aristotle himself and coined by Thomas Aquinas in the Latin dictum *Nihil (est) in intellectu quod non prius (fuerat) in sensu* (*De Veritate*, q2, a3, arg.19). Second is the concept intended by the Latin term *sensus communis*, also of Aristotelian origin, as a translation of his term *koiné aisthesis*. When Thomistic philosophy, at first considered too radical, eventually received its stamp of approval from the Catholic Church, Aristotle through Aquinas came to be accepted as "The Philosopher." Although there continued to be some disagreement in the interpretation of Aristotle, basic Aristotelian teachings came to be accepted as definitive and beyond controversy. The Peripatetic axiom was among such definitive teachings. But what exactly did it mean? Translated literally it reads: "Nothing is in the intellect which has not first been in the senses." The common understanding of this came to be that **our awareness of things is limited to what we have received through sense perception.**

Now what exactly counts as sense perception depends on how *sensus communis* is understood. But the understanding of this term changed drastically, devolving from that of a literal receptive faculty, one that would count as an additional sense alongside the other "five senses," to one of a faculty of constructive interpretation *on* sense data but which is not itself a sense. The devolution of this term continued until arriving at its contemporary meaning, which is even further removed from its original meaning.

The result is that the Peripatetic axiom now came to be understood as meaning that **our awareness of things is limited to what we have received through the five senses.** In other words, the original Aristotelian meaning of *koiné aesthesis* was now lost and was never recovered. This cleared the path for representationalism, whose possible skeptical implications were not to be felt as long as there continued to be a consensus that God's existence could be demonstratively known. Thus was born the tradition, which reached its pinnacle in no less a philosopher than Descartes, of employing God as guarantor of the veracity of our thoughts. Of course, once God's existence falls into doubt, or once the implicit circularity of this arrangement is noticed, the deal is off and representationalist epistemology falls prone to radical skepticism. And that is exactly what happened.

In the wake of the failed Cartesian attempt to use God as guarantor of the veracity of our ideas, the changed landscape suggested two possibilities: either our basic ideas are innate, or they are derived from sensory images. The former notion became the cornerstone of modern rationalism, while the latter grounded modern empiricism. In either case, Aristotle had become obsolete. Again in either case, the skeptical pressure of the bridge problem could be felt. For whether we obtain our "simple ideas" from sensory impressions or innately, the question of their correspondence with reality might still arise. Nonetheless, over time representationalism has become increasingly associated with its empirical form.

In the intervening time since then, while the thesis of innate ideas had a good run, the empiricist notion of ideas formed from sensory images has come to dominate philosophy as well as psychology. To be sure, rationalism itself has endured in nuanced forms, and in either case, the insistence on grounding our awareness on a repertoire of simple ideas has faded.

Moreover, various challenges to representationalism have been registered, but none so much as to be considered in the mainstream as an equally viable alternative. Counted among these are attempts by Wittgenstein and Husserl. The attempt of the former was grounded in his insistence on the public nature of language, which he took to rule out the possibility of private sensory ideas. This, in turn, would rule out the possibility of empiricist representationalism, evidently the only kind he countenanced.

Husserl's attempt, though it seems to have a seminal resemblance to Aristotle by admitting a confused presence in perception of the *noumenon* or thing in itself, places the bulk of the task of its effective recognition in a disciplined process of intellectual interpretation. In contrast, Aristotle considered basic apprehension of the object itself as an ordinary aspect of animal perception.

Other strategies employed in recent times to cope with the bridge problem can be roughly grouped into three categories: one metaphysical, and two epistemological. The former may or may not be combined with one of the latter.

The metaphysical strategy is to deny there is an external world, or at least that we are not justified in believing there is one. If we don't have to admit an external world, then there is no bridge to build.

The first epistemological strategy is coherentism. The leverage required to establish the grounds for this approach typically comes from the metaphysical approach, but this is not essential. Kant and many of his followers concede the existence of the *noumenon* but deny we can know whether our ideas correspond to it. Since coherence is widely accepted as a necessary condition of justification, once the decision is made to exclude correspondence as a viable criterion of justification, the choice of coherence to replace it is quite suggestive.

The second epistemological strategy is inference either to the best or most useful explanation. As long as "best" or "most useful" are interpreted as meaning best/most useful available, this strategy virtually guarantees a candidate will be chosen.

The merits and shortcomings of these strategies are debatable. At any rate, each is in a significant sense a capitulation to rather than a solution to the bridge problem. In the absence of correspondence, there is always coherence; whether or not we can have justification in a stronger sense, we can at least always have a best available or most useful available explanation.

It should also be said that each of these three strategies may be adapted to either an individualist or an inter-subjectivist formulation.

These strategies certainly seem to be plausible. One could even imagine settling for one or the other if one could do no better. The question of this paper is whether we can do better with Aristotle.

Any attempt to bring back into play, for contemporary consideration, elements of Aristotle's philosophy of knowledge has to contend with the claim that Aristotle's efforts on this subject—as with those of physics and astronomy—are obsolete. Against this suspicion, I argue that Aristotle's efforts in this area, though sometimes difficult to scrutinize, were never refuted—much less ever adequately understood—by modern philosophers. Aristotle simply faded away. Now, of course, Aristotle is back, with the renewal of interest in classical philosophy that occurred especially in the past half-century.

During this time period, notable efforts to shed light on Aristotle's epistemology were registered by J. H. Lesher, Martha Nussbaum, Jaakko Hintikka, C. C. W. Taylor, Bas van Fraasen, Murat Aydede, Michael Wedin, Terrell Ward Bynum, and Stephen Everson. Their attempts may be classified mainly into three types, which I will briefly address here: to certify scientific knowledge, to characterize perception within a constructivist framework, and to give a physical explanation of perception.

The majority of these authors, including Lesher, van Fraasen, Taylor, Hintikka, Aydede, and Wedin, came to Aristotle with concerns about scientific knowledge. The puzzle that motivates them is how scientific knowledge, which is demonstrative and necessary, can be based, as Aristotle insisted, on another nonscientific type of knowledge: intuitive or inductive knowledge of primary premises—which also has to be of a necessary character. Did Aristotle somehow think we had infallible intuition of the basic premises of science? How does induction (*epagogé*), which he speaks of often in this context, fit in with the intuitive faculty (*noûs*) that Aristotle, at the end of the *Posterior Analytics*, with apparent suddenness puts at the heart of his epistemology?

Nussbaum and Bynum studied Aristotle's theory of perception from a more or less constructivist frame of reference. "Constructivism" here means a theory of perception according to which we receive a manifold of qualities from our faculties of perception from which we imaginatively—and in large part pre-consciously—construct, by means of interpretative (i.e., non-perceptual) processes, the eventual objects of our awareness. Accordingly, they attribute the bulk of the achievement of object awareness in Aristotle to the faculty of *phantasia*. So much is *phantasia* emphasized and put to work that the reader is left with the question of what roles would be left to Aristotle's other two faculties of primary object awareness: *koiné aisthesis* and *noûs*? Should we in fact be considering *phantasia* at all as a faculty of primary object awareness?

Finally, Stephen Everson, in his work *Aristotle on Perception*, attempts to interpret Aristotle's theory of perception as an extension of his *Physics*, with the end of proving it to be in essence a physical theory of perception. Two questions are left by Everson's approach: first, why, if he indeed had a physical theory of perception, did Aristotle not simply express his theory of perception in the terms of his *Physics*? Secondly, how can Aristotle's account of perception be physical when his main organ of perception—*koiné aisthesis*—is itself evidently nonphysical?

The questions left by these three approaches set the stage for discussion of the theory of Aristotelian perception briefly given at the beginning of this paper. A guiding rule of the case I make is this: an adequate interpretation of Aristotle's epistemology has to account for and give meaningful and sufficiently distinct roles to the following key concepts: *koiné aisthesis* (sensus communis), *phantasia/phantasma* (imagination/image), *noûs* (intellectual intuition), and *epagogé* (induction). (The English translations are given here just for convenience; we need not spend time arguing over them.) I insist on this rule particularly because each of the above cited interpreters of Aristotle's epistemology got into trouble by failing to follow it. A difficult might seem that much easier to solve with the removal of some pieces, but the resulting picture at the end will be that much less clear because of it.

Some consideration will be given to the fact that the two principle texts referred to on this subject—the *De Anima* and the *Posterior Analytics*—have a difference in focus, the former being concerned with animal perceiving and thinking generically, and the latter specifically with human rational perception and thought. It is noteworthy, for example, that *phantasia* is not mentioned in the *A. Post.* (at all, but particularly in II, 19, where the emphasis is on synergy of *noûs* and *epagogé*). In contrast, *noûs* **is** mentioned in *DA* III, 3, where the topic is *phantasia*, but *epagogé* is not. An adequate explanation of Aristotle ought to account for these peculiarities as well.

My argument is that what Aristotle has given us is a cogent and plausible non-representationalist, non-constructivist theory of perception, though it leaves a vital role for representation while giving us reasonable grounds for a growing confidence over time in scientific knowledge. The cornerstone of his theory is *koiné aisthesis* (sensus communis), a pattern-/unity-/object-perceiving faculty that is nonphysical and forms the basis in rational beings for gradually refined knowledge (*noesis*) of primary concepts/premises (*noemata*) by means of the faculty of intellectual intuition (*noûs*), according to the reiterative process of induction (*epagogé*). The faculty of *koiné aisthesis* accomplishes this by "locking in the target"—i.e., by perceiving the rudimentary object/unity/pattern that to a rational mind serves as what G. R. G. Mure translates as the "rudimentary universal" (*proton men en tei psüchêi katholou*); (*A. Post.* II, 19, 100b 1–2). Once locked in, this rudimentary universal establishes a locus for further conceptual refinement by means of *epagogé*, allowing *noûs* to gain a more and more developed knowledge *noesis* of the more developed universal (*katholou*). *Phantasia* fits in as an intermediate function between *aisthesis* (which includes *koiné aisthesis*) and *noesis*—the knowledge acquired by *noûs*. Neither perception nor knowledge, it can be confused with either, and this is a chief source of error. Its role is to project possible developments of the rudimentary universal that might be discovered by *noûs*. What *noûs* eventually discovers by means of *epagogé* on repeated experience will either confirm those imaginative projections or contradict them. Knowledge (*noesis*) is thus gained by the mediation of *phantasia* in the process of *epagogé*. That knowledge is intellectual intuition, or *noûs* perceiving or apprehending the more developed universal. In this sense, *noûs* is the rational extension of *koiné aisthesis*, with the help of *koiné aisthesis* and the process of *epagogé*.

By this theory it is understandable why Aristotle did not mention *phantasia* in *A. Post.*, while not mentioning *epagogé* in DA III, 3. It is not strictly necessary to mention both at once, since the use of *phantasia* for gaining knowledge is couched within a process of induction (*epagogé*). As far as brute animals are concerned—the generic focus of *DA*—there is not much learning by inductive inference, hence less reason to mention *epagogé*.

To be sure, *phantasia*, as the faculty of forming mental images, has other functions (and malfunctions: hallucinations, etc.). At any rate, the main reason for its mention in *DA* seems to have been the explanation of mental error. According to Aristotle, *phantasia* is the ultimate locus of mental error. The senses (including *koiné aisthesis!*) technically don't lie; the error comes in our interpretation, recopying, and reorganizing of them, all of which are functions of *phantasia*.

A careful look at key texts in the *Analytica* and the *DA* should suffice to support the vision just presented. What follows in a discussion of the key texts.

The greatest lacuna in recent Aristotelian scholarship has been insufficient attention to the concept of *koiné aisthesis*. It is complained that Aristotle did not give us enough description of the concept. In fact, the following excerpt from *DA*, III, 2 426b 10–16 gives us a quite a bit to go on.

> Since we also discriminate white from sweet, and indeed every sensible quality from every other, with what do we perceive that they are different? It must be by sense; for what is before us are sensible objects. (Hence, it is also obvious that the flesh cannot be the ultimate sense-organ: if it were, the discriminating power could not do its work without immediate contact with the object.) (Translation: J. A. Smith in McKeon, p. 585.)

From this text, we can gather a few things:

1. That besides the particular sense perceptions, which are grounded in physical organs, there is a nonphysical sense faculty whose job it is to perceive the unified object.
2. That this unifying activity is not just for relating the distinct perceptions of different particular sense faculties (e.g., "white from sweet"), but also the distinct perceptions of the same sense faculties (i.e., "and indeed every sensible quality from every other").

In other words, a particular sense faculty such as sight not only fails to relate itself to the other senses, but it is also unable to relate one sight to another. Vision gives us no object, but only a manifold of visual data. Even the perception of white breaks down into a manifold of micro-perceptions of white. What gives us the perceived object clearly is what Aristotle describes here as the "ultimate" (and unfleshly) sense-organ. What here is called *to eschaton aisthetérion* is clearly the faculty of *koiné aisthesis*; it is ultimate in the sense that it alone yields object awareness, for without it our perceptions are but a scattered manifold—matter without form, as it were.

Bearing in mind that since the context of *DA* III is animal perception and thought, we conclude that this "ultimate sense-organ," the faculty of *koiné aisthesis*, is to be understood as a basic trait of animal awareness. Lest anyone worry that this attributes too much to the brutes, let us attend to the division of labor Aristotle alludes to in *DA* III, 4 429b 10. It is up to perception to give us "spatial magnitude" while *noûs* reveals to us "what it is to be such." Perception gives us water, and *noûs* gives us "what it is to be water." In both cases, the first corresponds to animal awareness, and the second to rational awareness. If perception gives us a universal, it is only in a "rudimentary" and not a developed sense.

How exactly *noûs* can yield knowledge (*noesis*) of the developed universal is explained in *A. Post.* II, 19 100a 15 ff:

> When one of a number of logically indiscriminable particulars has made a stand, the earliest universal is present in the soul. A fresh stand is made among these rudimentary universals, and the process does not cease until the … true universals are established. …
>
> Thus it is clear that we must get to know the primary premisses by induction; for the method by which even sense-perception implants the universal is inductive. …
>
> (Translation: G. R. G. Mure, in McKeon, p.186.)

What we learn here is that *noûs* is the rational extension of the *koiné aisthesis*, and that the rudimentary universal inherent in the latter is developed in *noûs* by an inductive process into a "true universal." Moreover, this whole process is considered as perceptual—as opposed to judgmental or interpretive—as revealed in Aristotle's summation at 100b, 5: "It is in such a manner that perception produces the universal" (my translation of *He aisthesis outo to katholou empoieî*).

In what has become a great trouble to interpreters, a few lines later Aristotle boldly declares that scientific knowledge (*epistemé*) and noûs are "always true" and that *noûs* is the "originative source of science." Nonetheless, our present analysis can render these claims as something less than an extreme form of infallibilism. In *DA* III, 3, Aristotle admits *phantasia* to be the generic source of mental error. He begins his discourse on *phantasia* at 427b complaining about earlier authors on the topic of the soul: "they ought at the same time to have accounted for error." (Translation: Smith, in McKeon, p. 586.)

I would only consider a theory of knowledge infallibilist if human knowledge were as a whole considered infallible; that one or several faculties involved in the process might be accorded a sort of intermediate infallibility is not enough for such a judgment. Indeed, it is common among contemporary philosophers to argue that sense perception *per se* is infallible, whereas error comes in the interpretation of sense data.

I think this is quite analogous to Aristotle at the end of *A. Post.* Perception—including, of course, *koiné aisthesis* and its rational extension, *noûs*—is infallible *per se*. So, too, is scientific knowledge (*episteme*), in the sense that the conclusion follows deductively from the premises. This latter infallibility is, of course, hypothetical; it cannot be read to imply the absence of defects in the premises derived from *phantasia*. Add to that the tacit confession that if deductive form is lacking, the deal is off. The infallibility conferred by *epistemé* is nothing more than deductive validity.

Another aspect to note is that knowledge by induction (*epagogé*) in Aristotle does not depend so much on complex probability equations as on the opportunity to improve *ad infinitum* on our animal perception of the object in *koiné aisthesis*, which gives us the object, to acquire by *noûs* what it is to be the object. This brings up the example of the old woman who thought dolphins were fish. Her grandson came home from school one day and reported to her that dolphins are mammals, that they breast-feed their babies in the water. The old lady grumbled a complaint about the crazy things they're teaching in the schools nowadays. Now, suppose this old lady accompanies her grandson to the big city marine aquarium one day. Need we wonder whether she would be any less able than her grandson to spot the dolphins in the tank? Certainly not. For whereas in her grasp of what dolphins are, which corresponds in Aristotle to the developed or "true" universal, she is far from the mark, in her recognition of the object per se, she may be just as capable as her grandson. What she has missed is the inductive investigations that would have led her reliably (i.e., infallibly), over time, to recognize the true nature of dolphins.

Thus *noûs* may be considered infallible in that it reliably leads over the course of time to more and more refined knowledge of things.

In short, it is unfair to consider Aristotle to be an infallibilist based on his comments at the end of *An. Post.*, since there he is merely discussing certain elements of human thought that are *per se* infallible. He attributes the cause of the fallibility of human thought to the faculty of *phantasia*, the discussion of which follows presently.

About *phantasia*, Aristotle makes clear in *DA* III the following:

1. *Phantasia* is not *aisthesis* (including *koiné aisthesis*): *DA* III, 3, 428a, 5 ff.
2. *Phantasia* is not *noûs*: *DA* III, 3, 428a, 15 ff.
3. *Phantasia* may be false: *DA* III, 3, 428a, 15 ff.
4. *Phantasia* may be incorrectly confused with either *aisthesis* or *noûs*: *DA* III, 3, 429a, 5 ff.
5. *Phantasia* is neither opinion (*doxa*), belief (*pistis*), nor any product of reason (*logos*): *DA* III, 3, 429a, 20 ff.
6. *Phantasmata* (the products of *phantasia*) are not *noemata* (the product of *noûs*),
7. though the latter involve the former: *DA* III, 8, 432a, 10 ff.

It is clear from these points that Aristotle is attempting to chisel out *phantasia* as a distinct cognitive faculty between perception and *noûs*, and that this faculty is both integral to *noûs* and a primary locus of erroneous thinking.

To sum up, Aristotle's theory of thought, correctly understood, is a form of fallibilist direct awareness that is not prone to the bridge problem in that it lacks the representationalist assumptions upon which the latter is based.

With all due appreciation for the vision of Aristotle thus presented, a critic might still threaten to sideswipe the conclusion thus stated by insisting the object awareness of *koiné aisthesis* is just another type of imaging. The recognition of the object cannot be direct, because the object is in a different place the apprehending mind. Notwithstanding the fact that he insists on the nonphysical, formal quality of *koiné aisthesis* itself, Aristotle does in fact consider the content of our perception to be physically gained through our fleshly senses. In light of this, how can the awareness gained be direct?

My response is that we can well note in our minds the difference between what we discover and what we invent. To be sure, there are cases where both invention and discovery are involved in tandem, such as in mathematics. But even in such cases we can with effort sort out the discovered elements from the invented ones. To deny the possibility of direct awareness is to deny the possibility of mental discovery. If we go in this direction, we shall have to recast the discovery/invention distinction as between two types of invention: viz. invention of the primary object of awareness vs. "creative" invention. I don't see what forces us to go to such an extent.

Another criticism to acknowledge is that the vision presented here does not jibe well with the declaration by Aristotle at *DA* III, 7, 431a, 15 ff.: "the soul never thinks without an image (*phantasma*)" (translation: Smith, in McKeon, p 594). This might turn out to be a problem I could not solve, were it not for the fact that it only exists in English and in this particular translation. In fact, when the Greek is consulted, the problem goes away. The verb for *think* in this passage is *noeî*, which is related to the *noûs/noema/noesis* cluster referred to in this paper. The root meaning, reported by Liddell & Scott, is "to discern, distinguished from merely seeing." Thus understood, Aristotle is speaking of that special type of thought related to the faculty of *noûs*. But we have already admitted above that *phantasia* is vital to the process of *noûs* in arriving at a more refined *noesis* of objects of awareness. In fact, this might be considered as Aristotle's depiction of the scientific process of theories being refined by hypothetical experimentation.

If this is the case, then perhaps we ought to rethink our common translation of *episteme* as "scientific knowledge." After all, *epistemé* carries the implication of knowledge gained by deductive inference, whereas modern science progresses not so much in that manner, but by creative theory formation followed by criticism through hypothetical experimentation. Modern science is much more what Aristotle would have to call a noetic process—related to *noûs*—than an epistemic or deductively demonstrative one.

CHAPTER TWELVE

Burden of Proof

A number of items come under the rubric of the logical topic known as burden of proof. The gist of the issue is that we ought to frame issues in a manner informed by a fair understanding of what the argumentative onus is for all positions that can be taken. In noncontroversial or settled matters, for example, the onus is clearly on anyone challenging the consensus, both regarding matters of observation and matters of argument. If an astronomy teacher is faced in the classroom with a denier of heliocentrism, the teacher is entitled to move on to topics which are based on the assumption that heliocentrism is true even without satisfying the denier, with the recognition that it is possible to conjure doubts ad infinitum for any claim, no matter how settled. Similarly, if the topic is the dangers of mixing sexual activity with intoxication, the presentation does not have to be stumped by the fact that someone in the audience actually recommends the mixture. In both cases, a minute or two of attention may be devoted to the objection out of courtesy; and perhaps in either case a forum could be arranged for more discussion of the matter among an audience for whom these matters are not settled. This policy could be thought of as analogous to that of controlling variables in experimentation.

The way burden of proof is handled in matters of controversy is another thing. In such a case, no one gets to sit in the catbird seat. Properly speaking, only matters of argument can be controversial, since any matter of observation is settled by whether or not certain observations can be made, not by the evaluation of arguments for and against a claim. Of course, both observational and argumentative enterprises are tentative, so there is never any final word on what has been proved and what has not; but in both cases, plateaus of consensus can be reached which deserve to be recognized.

It is regarding argumentative matters where some misunderstanding about burden of proof has crept up on us. Perhaps this has come in part from our failure to distinguish properly between matters of argument and matters of observation. After all, it is not that matters of argument have nothing to do with what we observe or notice; the distinction between them lies in what constitutes proof or disproof. In matters of observation, proof or disproof comes in the form of observational corroboration or falsification of theories. Matters of argument, on the other hand, are decided by the presentation, defense, and evaluation of arguments wherein a valid sensible argument whose premise stands up to criticism is taken as proving its thesis. Failure to attend to this difference leads to the misapplication of certain logical protocols proper to one field but not the other.

Here I focus on what I consider to be three kinds of misunderstanding of burden of proof regarding matters of argument about controversial matters, all of which are in some way related to policies appropriate to matters of observation, e.g., of science, but whose argumentative versions are fallacious:

1. That evaluation is tantamount to falsification or the attempt to falsify a claim.
2. That extraordinary claims require extraordinary proof, while ordinary claims require ordinary proof.
3. That the burden of proof lies solely with the one making the claim.

What I call the falsification fallacy is the misapplication of something that is proper scientific protocol to matters of argument. This is a touchy matter, because of course falsification of some kind plays a role in argument as well, but the protocol differs. In science, progress toward knowledge is made by means of the attempt to falsify theories through hypothetical experimentation. When the attempt at falsification of a theory in this manner fails, we say the theory has been corroborated; when it succeeds, the theory is thereby falsified. To be sure, even in science, falsification does not apply to the process of theory formation, but only to the evaluation of theories once advanced.

What is wrong with the attempt to apply this protocol to matters of argument is that here a claim or thesis is defended by a rationale or set of premises which deductively implies it, so that it is not appropriate to criticize or attempt to falsify the thesis directly, but only by criticizing one of its premises, i.e., showing a premise to be false or questionable. Yet if we make even this kind of falsification our sole mandate, we will fail to abide by a central policy of truth-oriented argument, which is charitability. Without charitability, all argument evaluation falls prey to the straw man fallacy, which is the refutation of arguments by taking them on in their least plausible form. In good argumentation, the rigorous criticism of premises should only follow an equally rigorous charitable defense of premises. This is the only manner in which we can be reasonably confident that any ensuing refutation is a good one.

I occasionally hear the dictum that while ordinary claims require ordinary proof, extraordinary claims require extraordinary proof. If we are to take this claim seriously, it implies we are to vet claims on their own merits before entering them into argument, deeming intuitively ahead of time whether they are inherently less likely (extraordinary) or more likely (ordinary). In the latter case, we can go ahead and support it with an ordinary amount of evidence. In the former case, we need to do better that that; we need to heap up more than an ordinary amount of evidence. If we don't do so, the implication is that the claim is not worth our serious consideration and we are thus entitled to dismiss it out of hand.

Now in some form, this policy might make sense in science, but it certainly cannot apply to argument.

In the first place, the notion of heaping up more or less evidence applies only to inductive argument, where there is no deductive connection between premises and conclusion, so arguments can properly be judged stronger or weaker according to how much evidence is proffered, e.g., how big the sample or evidence base is. To be sure, this can be seen to apply to science, since the process of hypothetical experimentation is an inductive one.

Another role this notion may play in science is to justify the advantage we give to currently accepted theories vs. their contenders. Since at no time are theories finally proved in science, there would be confusion if we did not have a standard of preference for current theories. Although this is somewhat a matter of convention, it makes administrative sense not to give equal consideration to all contending theories at once, since then the programs of hypothetical evaluation might become quite scattered. In this light, it makes sense that contending theories should have to show themselves to be stronger than currently accepted ones in order to warrant our making a change.

But none of this applies to the logic of matters of argument, which in the first place is deductive, and in the second place, on account of its deductive nature, requires that refutation and proof only come by evaluation of the premises. Thus the pre-vetting of controversial theses would be fallacious and biased. Validity forces engagement with the premises. Moreover, in matters of argument, proof is not by sufficient strength of argument, but by successful rebuttal of criticism of the premises. Thus, in argument, proof is not a more-or-less matter, but an either-or matter.

Another popular thought is that only the one making a claim has the burden of proof. Again, this may have its origin in the fact that in science, all criticism is focused on falsifying a proposed theory. Without proposing a theory, there is nothing to criticize in science. The result is that the only persons subject to criticism in science are those advancing theories.

As appropriate as this may be in science, it is inappropriate when applied to argument on controversial matters. For in argument, no one is in the catbird seat. Whether one is for or against a controversial thesis, claims it to be undecidable, or is just unconvinced either way, each of these represents a position taken on the matter and is thus subject to as rigorous a criticism as any other position. Doubt itself is a kind of conviction, and thus also demands an explanation; otherwise, there would be no difference between reasonable and unreasonable doubt!

Another problem with attempting to establish this as a rule of argument is that it fosters the impression that there are two camps: those making claims and those criticizing them, and that there is no rational mandate for all of us always to be in both camps. But in fact, if rationality is of any value to us, then surely it is the case that there is a rational mandate for all of us always to be in both camps. This means that the roles of the dialectic process are not to be separately distributed among us by choice or by historical circumstance, but that the whole process in its entirety is to be played out constantly in the minds of each of us. After all, if we set our minds to it, we are all equally privy to what the best arguments are for the various sides of any controversy. The only obstacle is the degree of our willingness to be fair-minded. Now, it may be difficult to be fair-minded, but it is not impossible, since it is possible to be moved by the recognition that we ought never be as committed to this or that being true as we are to the truth, whatever it may be.

That my third critique only applies to controversial matters of argument might lead to the objection that perhaps we have no dependable way of deciding what is controversial and what is not. Whereas I do concede that there is a gray area here that might be exploited, gray areas do not destroy distinctions, they only blur them. We still have this intuitive standard on which to rely, that a controversy is a matter of argument about which reasonable parties may disagree. Those of us who have responded to the rational mandate mentioned above of always being in both the camp of the proponent and the camp of the critic do not have too much trouble recognizing genuine controversy when they see it. Only those partisans who stubbornly limit themselves to one camp or the other in any given controversy are the ones ill prepared to notice such a thing.

CHAPTER THIRTEEN

Credibility in Science and Philosophy

Credibility is established differently in the sciences than it is in argumentative endeavors such as philosophy. In both cases, however, there is a common misunderstanding, at least among students and sometimes even among teachers, that credibility is established primarily by reliance on authoritative sources. In fact, to assume such leads to a vicious regress; since every authoritative source must first be established at some point in time, appeal to authority can at best be a secondary way of establishing credibility. Otherwise, there would be no way for credibility to be established in the first place, for there is no beginningless succession of authority.

Appeal to the authority of God will not avert this regress, since even appeals to divine authority must first be established by us as credible before we would be justified in accepting them.

Credibility in science is primarily established through observation; the more the empirical evidence behind a claim, the more credible it is. Thus, the establishment of credibility in science is an infinite, inductive process. As such, the number of observations establishing the credibility of a claim at any given time is probably too large for one person to have made, or even to directly confirm. This is what makes reference to the research of others essential for establishing credibility in science. For when we are doing science, we are pooling the work of many researchers, and it is largely this pooling that makes our own contributions credible. Moreover, consideration of the fact that scientific observations are made under such controlled circumstances and with such methodology and technology that it takes an expert to do it gives us yet more reason to depend on other scientists for the credibility of our own work. It is simply not something people can do either on their own or without having acquired the necessary expertise.

On the other hand, credibility in philosophy is established by quality of argument, by which is meant the quality of the presentation, defense, and submission to criticism of positions on controversial matters taken for the sake of argument. Here there is no pooling of the findings of previous researchers. An argument stands or falls on its own merits, as deemed by the judgments of each of us, which judgments, in turn, will subsequently be subjected to judgment by others. Moreover, unlike science, in which credibility is in large part a matter of the expertise required to make the necessary observations, philosophy is not a matter of expertise, for it involves no accidental or invented methodology or technology, per se. That is, whereas science is a historical activity, developing its manners and methods over time, philosophy is a perennial activity. A scientist from another era would not be ready to do contemporary science, but would have to be retrained first; whereas a philosopher from times past would still be qualified to philosophize with us today without being retrained.

This difference between philosophy and science is due to the fact that philosophical questions are open to argument while scientific questions are not. Philosophical questions are open to argument precisely because they are closed to observation and calculation. Questions which can be answered by observation or calculation ought only be answered in such manner and in that sense are closed to argument, while questions which cannot be answered in such a way can only be answered by a process of argument. Unlike with observational matters, a well-developed argument has credibility on its own without pooling together the work of previous philosophers on the matter.

Of course, a well-developed argument usually does have predecessors who ought to be acknowledged. If an argument of mine was developed as a reaction to the work of another, in that sense I owe a debt to that thinker and he or she should be credited. This, however, is clearly not for the sake of credibility, but merely for the sake of proper accreditation. There is also the matter of giving the audience a view of the landscape. Thus, in an argument essay on God's existence, I may initially refer the reader to the work of Thomas Aquinas, a famed author in the field, even if my own work has no debt to him. In this case, again, I do so not for the sake of establishing credibility, but just for the sake of clarity.

Science requires the pooling of the work of many largely because, as an observational endeavor, it makes progress only by making more observations. But the falsification of theories appears to be another matter. In this case, it seems falsification may be accomplished by one scientist making—or rather, failing to make—one observation. Yet in practice, we never see theories overturned so quickly, and it is good for us here to ponder why.

In science, we form theories T to cover the domain of observations O made collectively by all researchers in concert, then subject these theories to a process of attempted falsification according to the following deductive (modus tollens) format: we predict that if T is true, then a certain O yet to be made should obtain; if it does not, then T is false. Thus described, it sounds easy enough for one scientist to complete the task by one observation, in a manner similar to David slaying Goliath.

But in fact, it doesn't happen this way, and this is because of the physical complexity of science. If a scientist claims to have falsified a longstanding theory, discussion will inevitably arise about whether the falsifying experiment was done properly or some mistake had been made, or even if dishonesty may have been involved. All of these doubts will have to be assuaged before the scientific community trusts the falsification to be factual. This is not on account of undue stubbornness, but because science, due to its physically complex and expert nature, is hard to do and at times tempting to fudge. We are unlikely to accept dramatic or unexpected results in science until they can be replicated by other researchers to the point of becoming routine. This is what makes even falsification in science a team effort in practice.

The fact that no massive pooling of data, no physical complexity, and no expertise are involved in philosophy results in its credibility not depending on authoritative sources in the manner that scientific credibility does. When sources are cited in philosophical work, it is largely for reasons other than credibility: clarification of the subject matter, proper accreditation, or direct critical discussion. The first is to familiarize the audience with the background of a topic and is not essential to appreciation of the argument that follows. The second is for the sake of giving credit where credit is due; this is more a matter of ethics than anything else. The third reason for citing sources in philosophy is for the sake of direction discussion, either to challenge or to elaborate on someone else's work. These three reasons for citing sources also exist in science.

To be sure, proof in both science and philosophy is elusive. Both are tentative enterprises that do not achieve definitive or final results. In both cases, the task is infinite, while our capacity for answering questions is finite. General scientific theories are never literally verified by us, although they can be falsified. In the absence of accomplishing the latter, all we can do is corroborate them or increase our justified confidence in them by the ongoing accumulation of expert observations favoring them in an unbroken pattern over time. Therefore, reference to those who make these observations is essential for establishing credibility in science.

In contrast, philosophy meets its goal by well-developed argument shown to be sound over time by an unbroken pattern of standing up to criticism. Unlike science, this is not a collective process, but a distributive one. Unlike science, every participant in philosophical debate stands as autonomous judge over the whole process. This makes philosophy no less objective than science, however, in that all judgments made by everyone are themselves subject to ongoing criticism in the public forum. Thus, the credibility of any philosophical judgment consists in its ability to handle criticism in the public forum.

Who's to judge? We all are!

CHAPTER FOURTEEN

Our Common Grounds—The Public Forum and How to Take Care of It

In order to have productive dialog about any matter of controversy, we must establish such dialog on common grounds. Otherwise, both sides are bound lose track of where they are, each imagining the opposition to be more extreme than it really is. This will result in a downward spiral of confusion at the expense of friendship and reconciliation. An all too common bad habit of thinking is that we ought to advocate relentlessly for what we are convinced is true, engaging in polemic with the opposition in the manner of a war that needs to be won. Just as we are now learning the hard way that it is wrong-headed to think that we can establish peace by fighting wars, we should recognize that we cannot make progress toward truth by polemic argument.

As Aristotle noted, every genuine disagreement is based on a more fundamental agreement; disagreement can never be down to the bone. Aristotle's point, perhaps surprising to some, is no more than a logical tautology. This can be shown by example. In order for there to be a genuine disagreement between say, the theist and the atheist, there must be a prior and more fundamental agreement between them on what the definition of God is. Otherwise, if the theist's notion of God is Thor and the atheist's is Hera, there is really no disagreement between them at all.

To the cynical contention that it is not the case that, necessarily, any two conflicting human parties have any common ground at all, I point out two inescapable grounds: reason and humanity. Recognizing that these two overlap, let me rephrase to avert the redundancy: reason and human animality. If one wants to make this conversation more portable to prepare for the eventuality of our meeting up one day with other rational animals, we could rephrase a second time: reason and animality. Whereas accidental common grounds certainly ought not be ignored, these two need to be acknowledged as what constitutes our essential common grounds, the basis of all productive argument. But in order to be appreciated, the substance of both our rational and animal common grounds have to be noticed and felt.

The substance of our rational common ground is common truth orientation. Whereas polemic argument, which Plato referred to as rhetoric, cannot in principle be productive because it is geared toward winning arguments rather than to truth, in contrast, those engaging in truth-oriented argument are essentially not at odds with one another regardless of how vital the issue at hand or how hot the controversy. They recognize they are both striving toward a common goal: the truth, whatever it may be. In this manner, the way of productive argument Plato called dialectic or dialog reveals itself to be an activity engaged in between friends and which solidifies trust and friendship regardless of its proximate outcome. It is understood that the outcomes of dialog in this sense are always proximate, since as just characterized, the activity must now be seen as an infinite endeavor, which progresses through a series of proximate plateaus.

Of course, we often differ in what we believe is true, but we do not differ in our recognition that we ought to strive to know the truth. Even though temptations may lead us astray to the point of self deception, we still make our choices under the guise of truth: in good conscience or bad, each of our choices must be motivated by a rationale under the guise of truth. This is enough to keep us at the table in the public forum, since our rational thought is inexorably linked at least to the guise of truth. Unfortunately, we often disinvite from the table those we consider to be the bad guys, the animals, the ones you just can't reason with. As a result, deception more easily solidifies in the absence of the rigorous criticism they would have received in the public forum, and the world is much the worse for it.

As bad as a bad guy may be, he can't in full sincerity and without irony be opposed to the truth, whatever it may be. Our differences regarding truth focus entirely on disputing its content. Moreover, we recognize upon reflection that our greatest epistemic commitment ought never be to this or that as true—let's call these material truth commitments, as much as it is to the truth, whatever it may be—let's call this the formal truth commitment. This is the one common motto, the one mission of reason. It is exactly to the extent that my commitment to this wavers that I subject myself to the snares of self-deception. We may be able to contradict it, since we can contradict anything, but we cannot disavow it.

The public forum is only public to the extent that we keep it so by disinviting no one. Once we do, we are failing to live up to our formal truth commitment. For it is only material truth commitments which incline us to disinvite people from the table in the first place, whereas this very table is the only place well suited for the correction of erroneous notions, simply because, everyone being gathered in the name of one common formal truth commitment, all are equally called to justify their material truth commitments in the light of that commitment. Outside of the public forum, in contrast, one's material truth commitments may be held unconditionally, much in the manner of idols, with no compulsion felt to square it with one's formal commitment to truth.

Another essential component of our common grounds in the public forum is our common humanity or animality. Here is the ultimate material cause of our awareness of values: the basic inheritance in animal awareness of what is helpful and what is harmful to life, such that we and all animals intuitively pursue the helpful and flee the harmful.. The fact that our intuitions as well as the intuitions of other animals on such matters are imperfect is immaterial. At any rate, it is the stuff from which our awareness of values originates, transformed into such by the simple axiomatic, rational intuition that life is good. Our moral awareness, therefore, originates not from reason alone, but from an intimate collaboration between our animal and rational awareness. As such, the role our common animality has to play in the constitution of our common grounds cannot be ignored. It is something no one can change by reinvention. One cannot exit from one's own species. I cannot, for example, by fiat change in myself the basic commonalities of human nature, e.g., that we are social, that we are rational, etc. I cannot stop being human, nor change what it means to be human. The infinite leeway free will gives us to embellish our existence is within the limits of our common humanity. Just as we are bound in good conscience to be dedicated to the truth, whatever it may be, so, too, are we bound by our very chance for happiness to discover and live by what it is to be human, whatever such may be. Just as the former is a formal rather than a material commitment, so is the latter. No particular claim of what it is to be human is fit to dominate the public forum a priori, but solely the recognition that we do have a common humanity. I say this in principle, because much of the common conception of what it is to be human is uncontroversial.

In short, we take care of the public forum by disinviting no one from it, and by maintaining in our reflective awareness our formal commitments to truth and our common humanity/animality. Doing these things will make it least likely that deception will corrupt the public forum, which would be the abomination of abominations.

CHAPTER FIFTEEN

To the Truth, Whatever It May Be

As rational beings, we are given to the acceptance of certain ideals which guide us in our cognitive endeavors. Ideals are characterized by being impossible for us achieve, as least to perfection and at least in a finite amount of time. Some ideals are posited accidentally by individuals or groups in time. Other ideals are essential to being rational per se. Although these essential ideals may not be achievable by us to perfection in the here and now, they are indispensable to us in that without them, we cannot even reliably move in the right direction. The two such ideals we will discuss in this paper are devotion to the truth, whatever it may be, and devotion to universal community. I will argue that these two are, in fact, coextensive, mutually entailing ideals.

Our rationality puts us in a privileged position among living things, for not only are we survival oriented, as are the rest; we are also truth oriented. I consider vain any attempt to reduce the latter to the former. For even though, to be sure, being truth oriented does, indeed, confer to our species a decisive survival advantage, this does not constitute a reduction to survival orientation. Survival instincts that guide the behaviors and choices of other animals are responses to the organisms' immediately felt survival needs, whereas the survival advantages conferred by our truth orientation are typically remote from our immediate survival contexts—even centuries or millennia remote. It is easy to see, in fact, that in many cases our truth orientation is even a short-term liability to our immediate survival interests, in that it competes against the latter for our attention. Instead of emptying my bladder, I just keep on playing my video game so I can find out what happens when I get to the next level. Reportedly, when South Korea first installed high-speed Internet cable throughout the country, there was a spate of deaths from dehydration by those who could not step away from their online games even to eat or drink. (This kind of internet addiction is actually a worldwide phenomenon.)

However, the main reason why truth orientation is distinct from survival orientation is that the former, though it may confer a survival advantage in the long run, does not acquiesce in survival, but in truth, as its finality. Since all an orientation is, in the first place, is a finality, a difference in finality is a difference in function.

Our rationality, then, is a truth orientation, and as such, acquiesces in truth. Yet, clearly, not being an infallible function, it can stray from its mark, just as can other functions of living things. In so doing, it can stray innocently or culpably—innocently, if, despite our most diligent efforts, we arrive at judgments or choices that do not represent what is true, what is best, or what is right; culpably, if our error was guided by self-deception.

Self-deception occurs when our survival orientation, which is always active, surreptitiously enters into our rational processes and corrupts them into pursuing convenience instead of truth, based on the apparent inconvenience of the alleged truth under consideration. Our truth and survival orientations are always vying for our attention, and one tends to distract from the other. At key moments in our rational deliberations, our survival awareness distracts us in the form of temptations to accept biased conclusions subservient to our perceived short-term convenience. When we submit to these temptations, we are culpable for it.

If this is how rationality, our truth orientation, misses its mark, then how does it hit its mark? Well, the fact is that, even at its best, it never actually hits its mark, but moves ever doggedly toward it, as an asymptotic limit. For the truth, as apprehended by us, is, in the final analysis, infinite—both ontologically end epistemically. It is ontologically infinite, since what we have to know is infinite, and epistemically infinite, since our way of knowing is an infinite process.

What we have to know—for example, biology, chemistry, mathematics, ourselves, one another, morality, love, life—is intrinsically infinite, since the thought of completely knowing any of these in a finite amount of time is absurd. They simply go on and on, ad infinitum, as subject matters. The more we know, the more we realize there is to be known. The more we analyze them into components, the more we recognize that the components are just as complex as what they compose. The detail of all these natural kinds is, in other words, infinitely rich. We never get to pixels; the detail is continuous. Elementary particles are just as mysterious to us as the things they compose.

To the criticism that all these things are really finite, it's just that we confuse large finite magnitudes with infinite magnitudes. I respond that we know the infinite when we see it. To be sure, extremely large finite magnitudes befuddle us. They say that googol golf balls—or ping pong balls, depending on who you're talking to—can just about fill up the known universe. Now, a googol—its real name should be ten duotrigintillion—is 10 to the hundredth power. We have a very difficult time appreciating such a great finite magnitude. Were it not for the golf ball reference, I'd be totally lost. But what about googolplex? That's 10 to the googolth power. Wow! We have no chance of putting that in perspective.

On the other hand, our ability to grasp the infinite is intuitively immediate. It is this immediate apprehension of the infinite—which is not comprehensive or analytic, but nonetheless a real apprehension—that makes human language possible. Human language depends on our use of common terms: common nouns, verbs, etc. As opposed to proper terms, which (opaquely) label finite classes of things, common terms label infinite classes of things. Each person who learns/invents human language for the time must carry out this labelling process. In order to do so, the things to be labelled must be recognized. This recognition, though, must be ready enough so that it takes a child little time to intuitively grasp, in first learning the word 'dog', say, that the term does not only refer to the dogs he has already seen, but to all possible dogs. The same goes for our understanding of numbers. Children recognize that numbers just keep on going. To be sure, there are finite, mathematically inductive (recursive) definitions of such things as the natural numbers.; but even our ability to come up with those definitions depends on our prior intuitive recognition of the infinite sets to be defined.

The truth is also epistemically infinite, since our knowing process itself involves an ongoing critical process. Our beliefs are never comprehensively justified—that is to say, never justified beyond all possible doubt, but only, at best, beyond reasonable doubt. In turn, what constitutes a reasonable doubt is itself a matter that can only be settled beyond reasonable doubt. As such, we are never entitled in principle to close the door definitively to any matter of inquiry, though for practical purposes we often do and sometimes ought to do, at least for a time.

This is where the Pyrrhonian skeptics get their leverage for saying there is no knowledge, since that knowledge, to be such, must be infallible. But infallible knowledge is something only an omniscient being could have, and we are not omniscient. Essentially, what they are arguing is that since we cannot know everything, therefore we can know nothing.

But the Pyrrhonians are wrong, at least in this sense: although we cannot comprehensively know, we can make progress ad infinitum toward the truth, approaching it as an asymptotic limit, such that, the more we engage ourselves doggedly in the task, the nearer we come to comprehensive justification. Gradually along the way, the deficit between our level of justification and comprehensive justification becomes negligible for practical purposes.

Since, then, our search for truth is an infinite endeavor, what method must we adhere to best pursue it? It is here where we see the confluence of an epistemic ideal with a moral ideal. The epistemic ideal is unconditional devotion to the truth, whatever it may be. The moral ideal is unconditional commitment to universal community. These two ideals turn out to be extensionally equivalent, or coextensive.

Our rationality is not just an occasional function, but an unconditional mandate to know the truth. But since we never are in the position of being in full possession of the comprehensive truth, we must never allow ourselves to cling to any unconditional material commitment to truth; that is, to this or that as true. Our unconditional commitment must, then, be formal rather than material: to the truth, whatever it may be.

It is in this unconditional formal commitment to truth that we find our ultimate common grounds with other rational beings, with other human beings here on earth. Human community finds its ultimate grounds here and nowhere else. We cannot afford to allow certain material truth commitments, no matter how well thought out, well researched, or impeccably argued, to stand as necessary conditions of our communion—our engaging, our conversing, our being in dialog—with others. For if we do, we are in principle setting an arbitrary, finite limit to our truth endeavor, which is what defines us as rational beings. Our truth endeavor is common to us all qua human, since we are a consummately social animal: our knowing is social, our intelligence is social, even our surviving is social. Our advantage as rational social animals is lost, then, unless we doggedly pursue the infinite endeavor of achieving universal community. For universal community is the grounds for the possibility of the open forum, and the open forum is, in turn, the grounds for the possibility of doing philosophy, which is productive and therefore nonpolemic dialog.

The upshot of this is that if I, in principle, give up on anyone due to a certain difference in our material truth commitments, I am thereby turning my back on the two unconditional ideals that both define and perfect us as rational social beings: that to the truth, whatever it may be, and that to universal community. I say "in principle", because there are many prudential considerations which in practice may require us to cut ties with one another, either temporarily or indefinitely. But even in such cases, our commitment in principle to these ideals must remain intact if we are to remain on the path of the human truth endeavor. Giving up on any of my fellow human beings on account of some material difference in our truth commitments is giving up on my unconditional commitment to truth, whatever it may be.

PART III

Metaethics

CHAPTER SIXTEEN

What's Wrong with Hedonism?

Enlightenment philosopher Jeremy Bentham (1748–1832) opened his work, *An Introduction to the Principles of Morals and Legislation*, with the following powerful declaration:

> Nature has placed mankind under the governance of two sovereign masters, pain and pleasure. It is for them alone to point out what we ought to do, as well as to determine what we shall do.

Thus were born two enlightenment traditions, still influential on present-day thinking: psychological hedonism and ethical hedonism. Coupled with the other standards of empiricism, psychological egoism and utilitarianism, these together formed the "deposit of faith" of the British Enlightenment, which led directly to the development of capitalist theory (economic liberalism) and political liberalism as well as forming the underpinnings of modern social science.

I say "deposit of faith" for several reasons. First, these theories, though with one exception conceptually independent, have for ideological reasons proven hard to pry from one another. Utilitarians tend to be ethical hedonists by default, which in turn for similar reasons has proven difficult to disentangle from psychological hedonism, which almost always occurs in tandem with psychological egoism; all of which are protected by the embrace of an empiricist tradition that takes pleasures and pains as if they were givens of sensory perception.

Secondly, though these theories have from time to time each been subjected to rigorous criticism—albeit the bulk of this has come more recently—modern science and popular attitudes, especially in Anglo-American culture, have largely built on them as if they were uncontroversial.

My aim here is to offer a critical appraisal of ethical hedonism, first by taking due notice of its remarkable resiliency in responding to some classical criticisms, and then by subjecting it to some more serious challenges.

But let us begin first with a discussion of terms.

Psychological hedonism is the theory that pleasure and pain, or their anticipation, are ultimately the only things that can motivate us to act. Here we are particularly concerned with humans, but this would presumably count for all animals as well.

Ethical hedonism is the theory that, ultimately, pleasures and pains are the only things of worth—the former positive and the later negative. Thus its formulation in the claim:

GP. Goodness is defined as pleasure.

More on this formulation below.

Psychological egoism is the theory that any human or presumably any animal can ultimately only be motivated by its own self-interest.

Utilitarianism is the theory that only those acts that maximize utility are right, i.e., that produce the most net good. By default, utility is typically hedonistically defined as the balance of pleasure over pain, assuming they can be compared on the same scale.

Finally, (modern) empiricism, apart from analytic claims based on deductive conceptual inference, is the theory that only those claims can be known whose component concepts can be shown to be derived wholly from sense impressions. Typically (and curiously!), allowance is made for emotions, pleasures, and pains, which are presumed either to be basic data of sense perception, or wholly derived from such. That this is a curiosity is all the more evident from the fact that these are all generously rather than narrowly defined in empiricist tradition, such that even things we would call higher joys are accepted as sense data, whereas our recognition that the frog in front of us is either a single organism, or the same one that we saw last year, is not.

In spite of the close almost conspiratorial association of these five theories, there is only one probable entailment relationship among them, and it is unidirectional. Psychological hedonism can be seen as implying ethical hedonism as long as we accept the "ought-can principle," that we have no obligations we are unable to keep. If the only values to which we are constituted to attend are hedonistic ones, then it should follow that ethical principles governing what we ought to do be couched entirely in terms of those same hedonistic values.

In the past century or so, however, since psychological hedonism has fallen out of favor among philosophers, ethical hedonism—which still enjoys popularity—no longer draws much support from it. But it does draw support from empiricism, thanks to the empiricization of pleasure and pain in terms of the *hedon* and the *dolor* as perceptible units of pleasure and pain. It seems also, in what might be called the "bundling fallacy," that the fact that these theories have been fitted so well together makes any one of them seem more difficult to refute.

Nonetheless, ethical hedonism has taken its share of attacks over the years, and has proven itself to be quite resilient. The first two shots across the bow are derived quite clearly from GP above:

1. There are bad pleasures.
2. There are unpleasurable goods.

After all, if A is defined as B, then accordingly it follows both that all A are B and that only A are B. But 1. implies that not *all* pleasures are good, while 2. implies that not *only* pleasures are good. If either is true, then ethical hedonism is false.

The good news for the opponent of hedonism is that it is easy to give examples of both claims. The bad news for them is that it is just as easy for hedonists to explain those examples away. The result is that this approach ultimately fails to quash hedonism.

I will illustrate with one example for each.

One case of a bad pleasure would be if some chemicals company made a brand of ammonia that looked, smelled, and tasted like grandma's lemonade. Surely this should be counted as bad pleasure.

But hedonists will, with legalistic relish, point out that it is not the pleasure of the taste and smell of fresh homemade lemonade that is bad; no, that is always good. What is bad is the association of these goods with something evil: the consumption of ammonia, in such a manner as to encourage the evil. The ultimate source of the evil, therefore, is right back where hedonists say it should be: with the pain that comes from the consumption of ammonia.

One case of a non-pleasurable good is knowledge of something dreadful—say, the looming destruction of humankind. Surely, this example contends, it would not be pleasurable to gain knowledge of such a thing, yet many will insist it is still something worth knowing, i.e., it is a good.

Here hedonists will note that even if there is no pleasure to be had from the utility of the knowledge gained—in this case, by hypothesis—there is nothing anyone can do to stave off destruction. And even if we prescind from the spiritual utility of preparing for one's own death, etc., tthis will only count for believers. We might still note it just happens to be a psychological fact for humans that there is pleasure in knowing, regardless of how disturbing the subject matter.

These two classical objections aside, let us move on to consider other challenges.

3.   Not pleasure but joy makes us happy; but joy is not pleasure.

The idea behind this is that the kinds of things we typically call pleasures are things we can reliably and directly procure for ourselves. But these things can be procured without contributing to our happiness: "empty pleasures." Whereas the kind of things we typically call joys, while always contributing to our happiness, are arguably not pleasures, since they do not belong to that class of things that we may reliably and directly procure for ourselves.

The hedonist will deflect this criticism by insisting on the one hand that joys, though not reliably and directly procurable, indeed are a type of pleasure—higher pleasure—gained indirectly by virtuous living, etc. While 3. may be favored as according better with the way we commonly talk about pleasures, it is not a death blow, since hedonists are prepared to acknowledge that our common talk about such things may be faulty.

4.   If hedonism is true, pleasure would be the greatest good. But clearly it is not the greatest good.

If I ask a member of the Boston Red Sox now which is the greater good: A. the winning of the World Series, or B. the pleasure of winning the World Series, what do you think he would say? If he ever got past the confusion of the question itself, one must assume he would answer "A", based not only on the fact that the goodness of the pleasure of winning the World Series is based on really winning the World Series, but also on the fact that the goodness of the pleasure of winning the World Series is an abstraction the contemplation of which does not bring much pleasure, whereas the contemplation of winning the World Series brings great pleasure. If we accept as reasonable the definition of "greater good" as that the contemplation of which brings more pleasure, then, clearly, winning the World Series should be considered a greater good than the pleasure of winning the World Series. If this is so, then pleasure is not the greatest good. But if pleasure is not the greatest good, then hedonism is false.

I think this objection may be a fatal blow to hedonism, but it is based on such an abstract consideration that it may be hard for us to duly appreciate. So let's try another way to say basically the same thing.

5. If hedonism is true, then there is ultimately no cognitive reason why things give us pleasure; but in fact, there are cognitive reasons why things give us pleasure. Therefore, hedonism is false.

A cognitive reason is a reason present and available in conscious thought, as opposed to a reason present only mechanically in the body, or in the opaque machinations of the unconscious mind. If hedonism is true, then the ultimate reason why the things that give us pleasure give us pleasure are mysterious to us as rational agents, lurking rather in the mechanical functions of the body or in the inscrutable recesses of the unconscious—if such a thing really exists!

Going back to the example of the celebrating baseball player, what do you suppose his answer would be to the following question:

What is the cause of your pleasure?

Of course, the answer would be: winning the World Series!

But if hedonism is true, then this answer is incorrect. For it would suggest a vicious circle: winning the World Series is good not in itself but only because of the pleasure it brings. But the pleasure of winning the World Series is caused, in turn, by winning the World Series.

Typically we track down greater goods from lesser ones by recognition of (teleological) causal inferences: the greater pleasure is the end for which the lesser pleasure is the means. If this is true, then hedonism requires here either that there should be no cause at all for why winning the World Series is so pleasurable: it is just an opaque mystery that it is pleasurable, or that the reasons are ultimately only to be found in the minutiae of the sciences of psychology and physiology. But both options are plainly absurd. We know very well what causes the pleasure of winning the World Series: winning the World Series! This implies that winning the World Series is the greater good, and that hedonism is false.

CHAPTER SEVENTEEN

Life Is Good

Earlier on we discussed the nonexplanatory character of ethical hedonism as its Achilles' heel, noticing that it forces us to accept as opaque mysteries why certain quite ordinary things, especially what we would call higher goods, give us pleasure. We are permitted, of course, to say those things are good because of the pleasure they bring. But we are to remain mute on why they bring pleasure—for it would be circular now to give the routine answer that they bring pleasure because they are good, or even because we recognize they are good. To avoid such circularity, we are forced at best to defer these questions to psychologists and neurologists; but even to them, these questions would be arcane indeed, if answerable at all.

This shows that hedonism makes the mistake of putting the cart before the horse. Supposing even that it be true that all good things ultimately bring pleasure, their bringing pleasure is not because they are good. It is our recognition of goodness that brings pleasure, especially higher pleasure. As for pleasures that come to us on their own, even they are not good on that simple account—but, if at all, on account of the goodness of the context in which we recognize them to occur.

If this reasoning, summarized from a previous discussion, is correct, then it is incumbent on us to produce a non-hedonist axiology, or theory of goodness, which, like hedonism, is lacking neither in objectivity or universality. We need not interpret this as a task to produce an anti-hedonist axiology, according to which pleasures cannot be good; we shall only require that wherever it is the case that pleasures are good—even if they are always good—they are not good on the simple account of their being pleasures. (Similar remarks go for pain vis-à-vis evil.)

Briefly, an axiology is objective if the goodness or badness of a thing is based on reasons to be discovered in things and their contexts, rather than imposed on them from without by arbitrary preference. Objectivism is nothing more or less than the simple denial of subjectivism; in other words, it need not be interpreted as anti-subjectivist. Of course, there are more or less subjective goods, as in the goodness of the flavor of chocolate. Yet even this is not completely subjective, but only in a sense. For all humans who perceive flavor do so through their human sense organs mediated by human experience. If someone hates chocolate, there is usually a special reason for it—physiological, psychological, etc.—that could eventually be found if we thought it worth the bother. Still, no one should deny that, in a sense, the goodness of the taste of chocolate is subjective.

Also, an axiology is universal if it gives a competent criterion for why all good things are good to the extent that they are good, and bad things bad to the extent they are bad. I call a theory competent if it does not lead to explanatory gaps—such as the hedonist one cited above—or contradictions. Universalism is nothing less or nothing more than the simple denial of relativism. It need not be interpreted as absolutism—or anti-relativism—which is the notion that moral truth is ultimately expressible in the form of exceptionless laws of conduct. A universal axiology does not imply exceptionless laws of conduct.

Instead of looking to the proverbial heavens for the ultimate roots of our moral awareness, I look instead to animal awareness; not just human animal awareness, but animal awareness generally. For there we notice an acute inclination to pursue what is helpful and flee from what is harmful. It should not bother us that this inclination, either in us or in other animals, is neither omniscient nor infallible. It's enough that it is darn good; good enough, at least, to have effectively promoted the survival of all the species now extant. Whether not just animals but all living things ought to be counted here is a good question, but we will avoid it now as unnecessary to our purposes.

It should be noticed that this underlying awareness in animals of what is helpful and harmful is not limited to themselves, nor even to members of their own species, but extends also to all other animals with whom they interact: as predators, prey, or in some other relevant capacity. For to carry out these interactions requires some degree of competency in recognizing what would be helpful or harmful to the other animal(s).

I consider the animal awareness of what is helpful and harmful to be the roots of moral awareness, yet not constitutive of it, since as such it lacks evaluative force. What is missing from it, however, is supplied by the appreciation—which humans possess—of the axiomatic truth that life is good, which in turn spawns two corollaries: that whatever is helpful to life is (to that extent) good, and whatever harmful (to that extent) bad.

Although we can and sometimes do pretend to doubt this axiomatic conviction, it is, in fact, indelibly ingrained in us; a fact made evident by the observation that every complaint about how bad things actually are only gains leverage from the recognition of how such evils mar the basic goodness of life. Unless life is good in the first place, then "how bad things are" can't really be bad at all, since there would be no underlying good for those allegedly bad things to spoil. In short, there is no better reason to conclude something to be true than that we cannot fail to believe it and cannot without contradiction even pretend to doubt it.

Therefore, because of these things, even if we cannot say we share our moral awareness with other animals, we ought to acknowledge we share with them the roots of that awareness. But this leaves us in a tough spot. For no sooner do we gain our appreciation of this moral awareness than we recognize how easily the same thing that is good for some living things may be bad for others. So our moral awareness forces us to seek criteria by which to properly calculate or judge net good despite evils incident in it. The most difficult or embarrassing part of this calculative process is coming to grips with the necessity of somehow quantifying life itself, i.e., prioritizing life forms. After all, if there is something that presents a net good to a higher life form but a net evil to a lower one, we recognize that all else being equal, we ought to favor the interests of the higher life form. Thus, I ought not use a fertilizer to make my grass green, which sickens my cats and dogs. Similarly, Europeans who want productive vegetable gardens with which to nourish their families have to devise efficient ways of ridding their gardens of slugs, which bodes poorly for slugs.

In fact, we do quantify life, and we do it intuitively. And though the results of these intuitive prioritizations are far from fine grained, they do give us a working framework for judgment, albeit with plenty of gray areas, as one should expect.

But how do we quantify life? Some have settled on sentience as their answer. According to this view, the consideration we owe to another living thing is proportionate to its ability to feel, to suffer, etc. (Of course, this is not to be confused with ecological questions about the worth of an entire species, etc., to the environment.)

To be sure, there are critics of the evaluative prioritization of life forms. Some charge there is a "speciesist" bias that will inevitably corrupt the process. But these critics are divided among themselves as to the nature of this bias. Some claim that humans will inevitably more highly appraise those species more useful to us. To them I respond that if such were the case, then humans would consider the chicken one of the highest animals, since it is hard to think of another animal more useful to human survival. Others insist that our bias points in the direction of human likeness: animals more like us are considered higher life forms than animals less like us. To these critics I respond that humans are readily able to recognize higher life forms—e.g., the octopus—even among animals taxonomically remote from us. Perhaps it has taken more study to notice such things, but sooner or later, given enough exposure, we seem to notice.

Another line of criticism is presented by what might be termed the "zooegalitarians," who insist—or at least try to—that all animal forms ought to be equally valued. To them I respond that anyone who lets a human being die to save an amoeba is surely guilty of some form of unjustified homicide.

I don't enjoy silly games such as this, but those who take such positions should be able to handle the hard cases. And it is clear to me that they can't. Let's suppose the theory of transmigration of souls is true, which claims that souls live many lives, even possibly passing through a variety of life forms. In such a case, we might have to admit that those souls passing through the life forms were equal to one another in value. But this would make it no less true that the life forms themselves were in much the same prioritized order of value as we now see them. If not, then either killing a human being in cold blood should be no crime, or I should deserve to be imprisoned for killing an amoeba.

CHAPTER EIGHTEEN

What's Wrong with Psychological Egoism?

Although many do not recognize it by its name, just about everyone is familiar with the theory of psychological egoism. One of the pillars of Enlightenment thought, it maintains considerable influence in political and economic theory and the social sciences. Although it strikes many as *prima facie* counterintuitive, as a theory psychological egoism has proven remarkably difficult to criticize effectively, since much of the eponymous force that by its lights holds sway over us is claimed to be exerted unconsciously. Here I will argue that psychological egoism fails us as a theory not so much by being false as by not really saying much at all; certainly not what it has been claimed to say.

In brief, psychological egoism is the theory that humans, as animals, can only be motivated by self-interest, and that even our apparently altruistic behaviors reveal themselves on closer analysis to be self-interest-motivated.

The basic credibility of the theory is that it is based on the ethological principle that survival is the basic instinctual motivation of animal psychology. As such, humans being animals, we cannot expect to be free from this determining influence of nature. Proponents see a direct connection between the survival impulses we experience and our perceived self-interest. But as we shall see, this connection is faulty.

The gist of the theory is twofold:

1. It is vain to expect humans to be genuinely moved by the interests of others, *per se*; and
2. The management of human behavior and activity ought to be keyed to self-interest.

Therefore, if this theory is true, then everything from child-rearing and education on the one hand to political and economic science on the other, as well as the study of ethics itself, should be grounded in psychological egoism; and largely, it has been.

As I hinted above, the theory has done well in handling at least its most obvious objection: that there is much altruistic behavior among humans. Psychological egoists counter this by insisting that none of this behavior would exist without an underlying self-interest payoff either in the form of a hoped-for return of favor, or shared self-interest of some other sort. If I help you, no matter how altruistic it may seem, it is only on account of a perceived gain in self-interest.

The revolutionary change in thinking that this theory brought about was the refutation of pure altruism, or caring for others with no thought of one's own reward. Previously accepted as noble, it now became more often dismissed as an inanity.

To be sure, psychological egoism is a descriptive theory, so it does not have the force of recommending the preference of self-interest over caring for others. It exerts its force more in management theory, as discussed above: motivational strategies are to be couched in terms of self-interest theory.

The effectiveness of psychological egoism as a theory depends on the distinctness of the experience of self-interest, such that it can be conceived as a constant of sorts, which in turn depends on the distinctness of the experience of the survival impulse, such that it, too, can be conceived as a constant of sorts. But in fact, neither of these experiences, as it turns out, are distinct, or at least not nearly as much so as they would need to be. In particular, the survival impulse is multiply ambiguous, and in ways many of which belie association with self-interest theory; while the experience of self-interest is doubly vague, varying widely over two spectra of variability: scope and term. Because of this ambiguity and vagueness, the theory of psychological egoism is rendered practically toothless, if not mute, lacking even the power to speak against the possibility of altruism.

The multiple ambiguity of the survival impulse in nature is so obvious that I wonder how theorists ever saw fit to associate their notion of self-interest with it. In fact, it can hardly be called one single impulse, but is several; I see four as predominant: individual survival, genetic survival, progeny survival, and pack survival. I suppose the assumption must have been that all these impulses really just boil down to the same thing; but to that I vehemently object, on the grounds that they typically conflict. Motivated by the impulse of genetic survival (i.e., sexual desire), the male spider gingerly strums the outer web of his desired mate. But to do so he must ignore his individual survival impulse to steer clear, since he recognizes her as a threat to kill him. Similarly, the female spider, motivated by progeny survival, will ignore her own survival interests to protect her egg sac. Single ants will run from danger, and yet will gladly sacrifice their individual survival for the sake of the colony. Nature is full of self-sacrifice for causes higher than individual survival.

These considerations might lead to the thought that the concept of self-interest required for psychological egoism might be salvaged by divorcing it from association with survival impulses. Instead, we could see it as the ultimate aim of rational cognition. To be rational can now be seen as to be self-interested. The rational order of human society can then be seen as a sort of self-interest calculus, grounding our political, economic, and social realities. Society itself can be seen as originating from a contract whose motivation is the maximization of mutually preserved self-interest pursuits. What did not accord with this calculus would be considered irrational. Society would be improved by being reconceived as an efficient machine running on self-interest.

What is wrong with this project is that for it to make sense, human self-interest would have to be conceived as a constant of sorts; but as experienced, it is widely variant along two separate spectra: scope and term. In scope, it varies from wide—or generous—to narrow—or stingy. In term, it varies from long—"enlightened self-interest"—to short. Moreover, it seems both variations are fickle and unpredictable. Why I perceive my self-interest now generously and later stingily—now in the long term and later in the short—is not itself a matter for self-interest to decide. If I attempt the response that I perceive my self-interest widely or narrowly, or in the long or short term, according to my perceived interests, then I am guilty of circular reasoning, for the perception of those interests are themselves constituted by those particular self-interest "settings."

My judgment that S acts on self-interest at time T, therefore, gives me very little predictive power if any, since in order to predict I would need to know not only whether S's self-interest at t will be wide or narrow in scope, but also whether it will be long or short in term.

Yet it is not the case that one has no deliberate control over the scope and term of one's perceived self-interest. It is possible through self-criticism for one to come to recognize he has been too stingy or shortsighted, and to resolve to change to become more generous or more enlightened. Perhaps these changes will not come overnight, but it seems silly to deny their possibility. After all, what does it take for me to develop a wider scope of self-interest but to reflect on the ways in which I identify with others? The same can be said for adopting a longer term view: just knowing that I ought to do it is enough to get started.

In the end, I think it may well be conceded that humans are only motivated by self-interest. But the fact that we have deliberate control over both the scope and term of our self-interest implies that this concession is of little if any theoretical import. It is surely no limit on our ability to be genuinely altruistic, as long as we conceive this not as an act of self-alienation, but of genuinely identifying with the interests of others, making their interests ours.

CHAPTER NINETEEN

Do Plants Think?

Ethical theory is largely built on the notion of community, one way of defining which is the collectivity of those to whom consideration is due in our moral deliberations. The two dominant notions of community in play are the community of moral agents, roughly corresponding to Kant's "Kingdom of Ends", and the community of sentient beings. Another version of the latter is the community of conscious beings. Although what exactly it is to be a moral agent may be disputed, this is typically restricted to beings with rational awareness, capable of bearing moral praise and blame. Similarly, although what it means to be sentient or conscious may be disputed, it typically excludes non-animals such as plants, fungi, etc., and is proportionately applicable to the extent of the sentience or consciousness of the animal.

We have reason to wonder whether our sense of community thus conceived is in fact too narrow.

This paper explores whether community ought to be defined as the collectivity of all organisms, or living things, on the grounds that all living things, to the extent they are organisms, have awareness at least in the form of the struggle to survive, to pursue what appears helpful, and to flee what appears harmful. Instead of basing community on the notion of moral agency, perhaps we should be basing it on the notion of moral patience, a moral patient being any subject worthy of intrinsic consideration by moral agents. Instead of our focus being on the sentient community, perhaps it should be on the organismic community of all living things struggling to survive.

Of course, this will leave gray areas. We are not sure exactly what to count as living; biologists typically exclude viruses as living things, based on the absence in them of continuous organismic activity. We also will have to cope with our troublingly vague but persistent intuition that some things have more life than others. But gray areas and vagueness equally affect the notions of sentience and consciousness. Some might even prefer to consider being an organism, being sentient, and being conscious as coextensive terms. If so, we ought to take care to notice that observational primacy should be given to being an organism, since the literal observation of the sentience or consciousness of other subjects is something we cannot do, or at least not nearly as reliably as we can determine whether something is an organism or not.

The main work of arguing for organismic community will be to make the case that organisms such as fungi and plants in their own ways share the same fundamental signs of awareness that animals exhibit. Although we may not be able to give evidence that they experience pleasure and pain, they amply exhibit pursuit behaviors and, in more subtle ways, even avoidance behaviors characteristic of what we have considered the defining distinction of animal over non-animal life. While the claim that non animals exhibit pursuit behaviors has drawn little if any controversy over the years, the claim that they also exhibit avoidance behaviors has only been gaining ground in the last thirty years or so. Gradually, as our powers of observation improve, the evidence is mounting that we ought to be calling into question any categorical claim that non-animals lack survival awareness.

To be sure, it is generally accepted that all organisms have built-in faculties for promoting survival and hindering or fending off organismic failure. But only some of these count as behavior. The beating of the heart, for example, does not count as animal behavior; it is for that reason called involuntary. It does not require thought to do, and in fact it is not even something we are conscious of making ourselves do. It is only what we can call voluntary action that can be considered behavior in the sense of something whose doing requires or implies some kind of thinking. Traditionally, we have written off plant behaviors as involuntary and therefore not indicative of an underlying awareness.

A second caveat will be that a skeptic might persistently choose to deny that an activity implies thinking on the grounds that it is supported as well by underlying mechanical, chemical, and involuntary organismic activity. But since this is true of all organismic activity, we ought to avoid making this move as it can easily lead to the slippery slope of denying all awareness per se. Although at first this might seem like an easy and clever way out of trouble, this perch on the catbird seat is short lived upon the realization that its justification will require explaining away how organisms such as ourselves can explain away the appearance of awareness we really don't have. As Augustine once said, si fallor, sum: if I am deceived, I exist; even if I have false awareness, it is still awareness.

So it comes down to this: if we can recognize clear cases of voluntary behaviors in non-animal organisms such as plants and fungi, we could justifiably assert that they do have awareness of some kind. But how can we recognize voluntary avoidance behaviors in non-animals? Is it that we are so much less like them that we lack the empathy to notice the kind of awareness they have even if they have it? Or is it that we just have not been looking intently enough? After all, organismic behavior usually involves bodily movement of some kind, and whereas animal movement usually occurs fast enough for us to easily notice, that of plants and fungi typically doesn't.

A criterion for distinguishing voluntary from involuntary behavior would have to be something indicative of nonautomatic deliberation: some kind of weighing of circumstances; some kind of transit from being less sure to more sure about how to respond to a situation; some indication of a learning process, or of a process of trial and error; or even of some kind of social interaction. Examples of such are being found more and more in the plant and fungus kingdoms.

Along general lines the cases in the plant kingdom involve dealing with predation and parasitism by sending out volatiles, or airborne chemicals to discourage predation, attracting the enemies of their enemies, and warning other members of their own species so they can take action. Sometimes the warnings sent out are effective even between species. Among fungi, the cases most currently under consideration focus on pursuit strategies—how fungi can figure out and remember more efficient ways to get to their food sources.

Of course, some of these plant and fungal behaviors might be involuntary, but others are hard to write off so easily. Certainly we should not be writing them off simply on account of their being non-animal behaviors. Momentarily, we will be discussing two cases: the case of coyote tobacco, or Nicotiana attenuata, and the case of the yellow mushroom, or Physarum polycephalum.

But first let us consider the American wisteria vine, Wisteria frutescens. I often did battle against it in my mom's back yard, where it grew as a weed. Since it is a vine, it requires the support of other objects, typically other trees and bushes, upon which to climb and establish its own canopy of leaves. From time to time, when gardening for my mom, I would look over to where I expected to see her lilac bush, briefly noting that it seemed the lilac had been replaced by a different bush. Upon closer examination, I would find that the lilac was still there, but its entire canopy of leaves had been systematically covered over by the leaves of the wisteria, which had accomplished such by a meticulous and highly complex winding of its own spindly branches around the lilac branches in such a manner that, the more leverage was required to climb, the more times the vine had wrapped itself around the branch it was climbing, never choking itself off or blocking any of its own leaves from the sun. Choosing to save the lilac, I would then spend hours unwinding the wisteria vine from the poor lilac, in the process coming to appreciate how complex the process must have been, with so many difficult decisions to make. If someone had given me a long rope of artificial wisteria with the same physical traits as live wisteria, I would have been hard pressed to accomplish the same feat. How did the wisteria so carefully manage to avoid ever having its own leaves blocked from the sunlight? How did it manage to establish so perfect a canopy of leaves for itself, never wrapping its vine around any of its own branches, while so aggressively and completely dominating the lilac? How did it know or learn how many times—once, twice, three times, or even more—it would have to wrap itself around a certain lilac branch in order to continue its upward climb?

Coyote tobacco grows wild throughout the mountain west, both to the north and to the south. It often grows in the wake of forest fires and has to deal with a wide variety of survival conditions. Accordingly, it has developed a number of distinct lines of defense at least some of which are difficult to dismiss as automatic or involuntary.

In the studies of J. C. Cahill and others (see especially http://taxusbaccata.hubpages.com/hub/Nicotiana-attenuata), these lines of defense are listed and described. The first, of course, is its production of nicotine, a toxin which wards off all but a few predators and parasites. In particular, there are two species of hawkmoths it has to deal with whose larvae feed on the plant and are immune to the effects of nicotine. But its relationship with these moths is complicated by the fact that the adults are the plant's most effective fertilizer. So in ordinary cases, the plant's life cycle is set up to maximize fertilization by these moths by blooming at sunset, when the moths become active. In response to the predation by the larvae of these species, coyote tobacco sends out volatiles, airborne chemicals which attract insect species that prey on the larvae. But since there are times when these species preying on the larvae are too few in number or too vastly outnumbered, it appears that the coyote tobacco plant has a decision to make: whether to alter its life cycle to accommodate a fertilizing species which, although less effective at fertilizing than the moths, does not harm to the plant. It does this by opening its flowers at dawn rather than at dusk, thus no longer attracting the moth species and instead attracting a species of hummingbird. When it makes this "decision", it sends out a chemical message to the other coyote tobacco plants in the area thus coordinating a social shift in fertilization strategy of the whole patch of plants!

In the above paragraph I put the word "decision" in scare quotes, but perhaps I should not have. Is this not clearly a case where a nonautomatic decision has to be made? Would we hesitate to deny cognitive status to any similar decision-making situation faced by an animal?

Toshiyuki Nakagaki had been studying the yellow mushroom for some time when he finally decided to test the cognitive powers of the organism (http://ronbarak.tumblr.com/post/9087600886/what-do-mushrooms-think-ofn). So he submitted it to the same kind of intelligence test used on rats: the maze. In step one of the experiment, he placed the mushroom at one end of the maze and a cube of sugar at the other and then waited. After about one full day, he observed that the mushroom, sensing the presence of the food source nearby, had sent its feelers in through the tunnels of the maze. In a manner similar to you or me, the feeler would do a U-turn and go back when it came to a dead-end. After a while its feeler found the sugar and attached it.

In step two, he took that same mushroom with its same feeler intact and placed it in a new maze of identical design, with the sugar cube again at the other end of the maze. This time, what he found the next day amazed him. First, the mushroom this time had sent its feeler straight through the maze without any dead-ends to the food source. Then, the mushroom sent out a new feeler in a straight line to the food source following the maze cover. It had actually cheated in order to find an optimally efficient way to its food source!

I don't think it is plausible to deny that these two examples offer ample evidence justifying the conclusion that we ought to take seriously the claim that non-animal organisms have cognition, and that perhaps just being an organism should be the standard we use in deciding who and what we should care for and care about in our moral deliberations.

PART IV

NORMATIVE Ethics

CHAPTER TWENTY

What's Wrong with Utilitarianism?

The ethical theory of utilitarianism is perhaps the main pillar of the British Enlightenment, which included a closely associated package of core theories including psychological egoism and hedonism, as well as theories derived from all of the above, such as capitalism. The close association of these core theories is by and large not, as I have emphasized, logical, but accidental in nature. Nonetheless, it is even today difficult to find a utilitarian who is not also a hedonist. Still, a proper critique of utilitarianism *per se* should ignore its accidental association with hedonism; the two ought to be evaluated each on its own merits: hedonism as a theory of metaethics, and utilitarianism as a theory of normative ethics. For this reason, I shall ignore further mention of hedonism in this paper and shall treat the term "utility" as denoting net good and not necessarily net balance of pleasure over pain.

Typical of Enlightenment theories, utilitarianism has a built-in flexibility that allows it to absorb much criticism without being dealt a fatal blow. I will go over some of the classical criticisms and their rebuttals before addressing what I consider to be utilitarianism's fatal flaw: its inability to countenance inestimable values.

Whereas metaethics is focused on the task of defining goodness, normative ethics is famously trained on the question: What makes right acts right? The following logical relationships between the concepts of rightness, wrongness, and obligatoriness suffice to extend the import of this question to all three, where p is any act:

1. that p is wrong means that p is not right.
2. that p is wrong means that it is obligatory not to do p.
3. that p is obligatory means that p is the only right thing to do.

Thus, as we directly depend on utilitarianism to give us the criterion of right action, we extend its domain to the other normative terms as well by means of the above.

> (Act) Utilitarianism may be stated as the theory that:
> AU. An act is right if and only if it maximizes utility.

This means the theory requires that only the best act among alternatives is right. If there is a tie for best, then all best choices are right. If there is only one, then that choice is obligatory. In any case, it is always obligatory to choose from among those best alternatives. In short, the theory states that all and only those acts that bring the greatest net benefit are morally right.

Before going further, it is important to note that it is possible to construct versions of utilitarianism that don't judge acts directly but by means of some intermediary devices, such as rules. Thus, "rule utilitarianism" is stated as follows:

RU. An act is right if and only if it conforms to a rule that maximizes utility.

RU and AU can be seen to be looking for quite distinct things in an act. In the case of AU, the utility it brings as an individual "act token" is all that matters. In RU, it is the "act type" that matters; i.e., the individual act's coverage by an optimal rule. But in both cases, it is the individual act that is being evaluated.

Not that utilitarian theory cannot be trained to things besides acts, but such uses will be extrapolations from the analysis of acts; e.g., institutions considered as act patterns, etc.

Our treatment here will focus generically on "act utilitarianism," with an understanding that the points made here will be applicable to other derived forms of the theory after due allowances have been made such as those discussed above.

Utilitarianism offers itself up as an intuitively plausible theory, a type of cost-benefit deliberation. It seems to accord quite well with the way we think we ought to shop and make business decisions. But in other areas it may seem to yield disturbing results. Here I will first review four classical objections to utilitarianism that I believe have failed to strike a fatal blow: calculative impracticality, the denial of supererogatory acts, indifference to distributive justice, and indifference to classical virtues. Then I will move on to consider the more serious objection that it fails to countenance inestimable values, whereas moral life routinely involves them.

At first blush, AU seems a silly theory in that it seems to require us to do quasi-mathematical calculations on the fly. To this, proponents reply that AU does not claim to be effective as a rule of thumb, but just as a theory of normative ethical truth. Rules of thumb need to be practical to be easily applied in everyday experience. They need not even be literally true in meaning, as long as they are effective at predicting. Newton's theory is still commonly used for some this-worldly physics calculations even though no one today takes it seriously as a theory. Its advantage is that it is easier to apply, coupled with the fact that in some this-worldly situations the added margin of error it produces is negligible.

Similarly, utilitarians might recommend that we not lose time making calculations in the field, since doing so may itself be counterproductive by the theory's own lights. According to the theory itself, our preferable means of deliberation is contingent upon what is most effective for us, and may even vary from time to time.

Still, there is a more profound question related to calculating: What are we to calculate? Is it the eventual utility that by hook or crook—even by accident—comes trickling in as a result of the act chosen, going even into the remote future? Or is it only the utility that could reasonably be expected to follow from the act? If it is the reasonably expected utility that determines rightness, that gives us an advantage in that it is foreseeable, but gives us the disadvantage that it is not real-life consequence; whereas actual utility has the actuality advantage at the expense of not being foreseeable and possibly even accidental.

The way utilitarians have responded to this criticism is by splitting into various camps, covering just about every plausible response to this puzzle. So, at best, it seems this criticism becomes an internal matter for utilitarians, since it may turn out in the end to rule out all but one version of utilitarianism, but not all versions at once.

Another criticism against utilitarianism is that it is too severe: it denies the possibility that an act might be right even though it is not the best choice. Thus it denies the possibility of supererogatory acts, or acts above and beyond the call of duty. Some consider this quite a problem, since they see moral heroism as a real dimension in human affairs. In fact, there are two key ways to finesse this objection. The first is to insist that we honor more those who take considerable risks to their own well-being in order to carry out their obligations; that is, we understand that some obligations are harder to keep than others, and we show more appreciation for the keeping of our more difficult obligations. This is a reasonable point, since I don't think there is a common expectation that each of our duties will be of equal degree of difficulty.

The second way is to argue that risk itself is a liability, which in moral deliberation counts as a disutility, such that the more heroic alternative in a decision-making context may actually not yield a greater overall utility, due to the liability of the added risk itself. It may then be one among several right alternatives—the rest of which are less risky, though yielding less utility than the heroic act minus the risk liability. Still, we respond appreciatively to the one who chose to take the risk, even though it was not actually a better thing to do. This maneuver has the added advantage of positioning us to explain why sometimes a certain risky act may, in fact, be wrong even though it would yield by far the greatest benefit if the risk were averted.

The third criticism against AU is that its judgment of right action is based on net utility as a quantity alone, without any consideration of how that utility is distributed. The result is an apparent lack of consideration for how well or how *fairly* goods are distributed. Some critics of this ilk argue that many goods unfairly distributed is a greater evil than a lesser quantity of goods well shared. The blind spot of this criticism is that for utilitarians, utility is not necessarily material in nature. For example, sense of social belonging can be a utility. Therefore, utilitarianism may at least indirectly favor just distribution of goods by the fact that this promotes the utility of social belonging. On a more mathematical note, many defenders of utilitarianism have pointed out that since some goods, particularly material ones, show a diminishing return of utility when distributed poorly, this allows that optimal distribution might turn out to produce greater net utility.

A fourth criticism is that utilitarianism can yield apparently heartless results in the form of indifference to what many of us consider basic moral virtues: honesty, promise keeping, just judgment, etc. This is because utilitarianism eschews action based on principle in favor of action based on consequence. Therefore, the following types of commitment are hard for a typical subscriber of AU to accept: I shall never steal, I shall never murder, I shall never lie, I shall never render false judgments in the name of the law, etc. Utilitarians are so committed to maximizing utility that they are willing to do anything, including breaking any rule or law, provided it maximizes utility, which seems to fly in the face of moral virtue. This criticism may even apply to rule utilitarianism itself, in the case that a rule to break laws under certain conditions may also be judged to maximize utility.

In this case the utilitarian may adopt the strategy of insisting that apparent maximal utility in the short run or in a narrow scope is often eventually outdone by greater utility in the long run or in a wider scope. Imagine an unruly frontier town in the Old West whose inhabitants are very upset by a recent killing. The public consensus concludes Clem Collins, a notorious man of violent crime, is the culprit. After Collins is arrested and set for trial, the investigating sheriff has a break in the case and discovers that the real killer is beloved Sunday School teacher Suzanne Appleworth, who has just unexpectedly died from a massive stroke. The sheriff, recognizing the town would erupt in chaos if he attempted to follow the principle of never rendering false judgment in the name of the law, and recognizing also that everyone was better off with Clem Collins behind bars, keeps silent about his findings. As a result, Collins is found guilty of murder and is given life in prison.

The charge of critics is that in such a case, utilitarians would have no choice but to agree that the sheriff ought to keep quiet about the truth, thus enabling a false judgment in the name of the law. Nonetheless, this is still immoral, therefore utilitarianism is false. But in fact, the utilitarian still has the choice to set his scope more widely and argue instead it is important for us to maximize utility by accepting a short term and local deficit in utility for the sake of maximizing utility in the long run and in society at large by rendering a truthful judgment even when it is evidently inconvenient to do so. This may be argued to maximize utility in the long run by eventually engendering more popular trust in government. By being truthful even when it was inconvenient, the sheriff will have proved his trustworthiness to the community and thus solidified social bonds.

In short, the above criticisms of utilitarianism all seem to fall short of dealing it a fatal blow. But now let us move on to consider another that I believe does: utilitarianism's failure to countenance inestimable values.

Utilitarianism relies on the premise that every value can be weighed and compared against every other in such a manner that all values may thus be estimated and entered into a sort of arithmetic calculation, to produce the output of a net utility for every alternative act in a decision-making situation. This implies that all values be estimable. Now, what if some values in fact are inestimable? In that case, utilitarianism fails, because it has no decision-making procedure for inestimable values. Utilitarians are aware of this vulnerability and so steadfastly deny there is such a thing as an inestimable value. The most common form of doing this is to deny the existence of rights. Indeed, rights, if they exist, are inestimable claims on moral agents; inestimable in the sense that they are not considered eligible to be bartered.

But what is really the case? Are there really inestimable values? The test of an inestimable value is that there is no imaginable finite value than which it can safely be judged to be less in value. Is it not the case that human beings pass this test, and thus human values may be considered inestimable? We love our pets, but it is not unheard of to trade them, formally or informally. Leaving your pet cat with the new owner of the house when you move is a trade of sorts. Would it be permissible to do the same with our children?

On the other hand, are we sure that adoption is not a type of trade in humans? Or that euthanasia or the death penalty is a case of bartering away human life? Of course, the latter two are controversial, but adoption really is not. We know that those who adopt usually have to spend a considerable amount of resources in return for their child. How is this not a trade? We can't put utilitarianism on the ropes with the present criticism unless we have an answer to this question. For if we don't, we should concede we are not so sure that human life is an inestimable value, and thus lose our strongest case for the existence of such.

To begin, we can perhaps concede some types of adoption are in fact cases of human trade, and that these are the types we consider wrong. Then we can insist that legitimate cases of adoption are not a form of trading; that what we are paying for are services, not the child itself. After all, much administrative work is required to process an adoption, and also intermediary child care, legal fees, etc. I suppose the key insight on this matter might be that we would certainly not think it right to trade one child for another, whereas tradable commodities generally are considered tradable for items of the same class: one car for another, one house for another, etc. If all this is true, then adoption—at least in the best of cases—ought not be considered as human trade.

If trading humans, bartering away human rights, and the like are indeed unconscionable, this should imply that human values—at least some human values—are inestimable. If this is the case, then utilitarianism as an all-encompassing normative ethical theory can't be true, because it can't process such values. This does not imply, however, that utilitarianism will not remain true for all situations it can handle, namely mundane situations in which no inestimable values are at stake. For we have really been able to detect nothing unworkable about the theory in the absence of inestimable values.

Even if we have cleared enough space for a nonutilitarian envisionment of normative ethics, this does not warrant the anti-utilitarian attitude taken on by so many, including Immanuel Kant, who despised the utilitarian focus on consequences as fundamentally disrespectful. This exaggeration may have been due to Kant's almost complete lack of concern for mundane things. But mundane decisions are still moral decisions, since they, too, involve values. We really have no reason to deny utilitarian sovereignty over mundane matters. The theory does indeed prescribe for us the correct way to do our everyday shopping, etc.

Unfortunately and often tragically, and even in the absence of a good reason for doing so, human policy often becomes most obstinately utilitarian when tough decisions need to be made regarding human life and well-being on a large scale. For on that scale, we tend to despair of the possibility of doing things otherwise. How is a battlefield general supposed to effectively attend to the inestimable claim on his conscious of each of the soldiers in his command when planning his next battlefield maneuver? It seems that once we choose to fight battles at all, we are forced to be utilitarian about it. Maybe that's an argument for pacifism: that any institution is wrong that forces us to barter human values as if they were mundane values.

At this point, utilitarians might offer the rebuttal that not only their theory but no ethical theory can effectively process claims to inestimable value. But in fact, the medical profession gives us an example of how this may be done in the way it processes requests for receiving organ transplants. Whereas a utilitarian approach might recommend giving the organ to the most worthy recipient, medical professionals recognize this to be outrageously inhumane. Instead, they employ a combination of factors in their decision making: first come, first served; magnitude of need; and the likelihood of a successful transplant over time. These approaches are nonutilitarian in that they abstain from judging one human life to be more important than another. Yet, they are nonetheless objective criteria. All else being equal, it is unfair to pass over someone in the front of a line to serve someone in the back. This value will be overridden by more pressing concerns, such as greater need. Finally, concern for efficient distribution of the resource itself permits us also to consider lower the likelihood of rejection as a criterion. To the objection that this is just, in the end a disguised form of utilitarianism, I repeat that the case against utilitarianism does not call us to be anti-utilitarian, but simply nonutilitarian. The difference is that the latter denies utilitarianism is always true, while the former denies it is ever true. It's okay to barter over organs to be donated by minimizing the likelihood of rejection. What's not okay is to barter over humans themselves.

CHAPTER TWENTY-ONE

A Proposed Reconciliation between Utilitarianism and Its Opponents

The original title I had projected for this paper was "What's Wrong with Nonutilitarian Moral Theory?," intended to match the title of a previous essay, "What's Wrong with Utilitarianism?" But I scrapped the title, realizing it might cause some confusion, as if I were suggesting the logically impossible: that both of two contradictory pairs were false. Because, literally speaking, for any meaningful claim p, necessarily either p is true or not-p is true. Applying this to our topic, literally speaking, either utilitarianism is true or nonutilitarianism is true. I am convinced it is the latter, and will review my reasons for this judgment below. On this point, the reader may also refer to my earlier aforementioned essay on utilitarianism.

So why then, if this is to be an essay on the truth of nonutilitarianism, would I have ever thought its title should be about what was wrong with it? The fact is, the opposition to utilitarianism is divided between those who proclaim diametrical and therefore contrary opposition to it, and those who assert the simple denial of the theory. The former really ought to be called anti-utilitarians, since their contrary opposition leaves a whole spectrum of unexplored territory between their position and utilitarianism itself. The latter, on the other hand—the simple deniers—are taking the contradictory stance, leaving no middle ground between them and utilitarianism. This is a key distinction to which we ought to attend regarding all matters, especially matters of controversy: the difference between contrary and contradictory opposition. Two contrary claims may not both be true, but can both be false; whereas of two genuinely contradictory claims, necessarily one is true and the other false. That is because contradictory opposition divides the logical universe in half exhaustively. It is upon this principle that Aristotle based his method of division, which is the basis for taxonomic categorization of all kinds.

The sciences heed well this method of contradictory distinction. Oddly, it is in philosophy itself where we seem to have gotten sloppy. That is how the term "nonutilitarian" came typically to refer to theories that are in fact anti-utilitarian, in that they deny that consequence ever has to do with the rightness of our decisions, in contrast with utilitarianism, which claims it always and exclusively does. Genuine nonutilitarianism, on the other hand, simply denies that what is right is always and solely a matter of consequence.

Another terminological problem is that whereas utilitarianism is a catchy, universally accepted label, there is no convenient universally accepted title for its contenders. "Kantian ethics" is often used, but that is too narrow, since it commits us to one specific author. Here I will use the term principle-based moral theory to refer to the anti-utilitarians, and to be fair will accordingly refer to utilitarianism more generically as consequence-based moral theory. These will be understood throughout as contrary opposites. My claim is both are false, but that a theory intermediate between them that incorporate both extremes in a coordinated manner is true. That theory is neither anti-consequence nor anti-principle—although it is non-both—but recognizes the role both ways of thinking play in the way we make correct decisions about what is right and wrong.

One other *caveat* is that despite the common historical association, we should avoid making the assumption that consequence-based theory is, or implies, hedonism, or the theory that goodness is reducible to pleasure. However strong the association, it is an accidental one.

Consequence-based theory claims that what is right in any situation is entirely a matter of consequences: in any decision to be made, that option is right that contains or produces the most net good. This answer is obtained by weighing the estimated values of the goods and evils contained in or produced by each option against one another in a manner analogous to finite arithmetic. Thus, consequence-based moral theory is committed to the assumption that all values are estimable. The proponents of this way of thinking are aware of such, and therefore bite the bullet and take on the task of denying there are any such things as inestimable values. Accordingly, they deny the metaphysical reality of rights, since rights are claims of inestimable worth.

It is this one feature of consequence-based moral theory that chafes its opponents most, the criticism of which became the launching point of principle-based moral theory, whose kernel notion is that there are inestimable values that we may routinely encounter in our decision-making situations—and these, not being estimable, are not subject to be bartered, traded, or even calculated over, simply because nothing analogous to the process of finite arithmetic works on them. Therefore, they are to be treated as infinite values, or as ultimate ends in themselves. Thus did Kant describe his vision of morality as a "kingdom of ends," the ends being rational subjects, or moral agents.

The brand of moral philosophy eventually worked up by principle-based theorists is one that provides a negative mandate: it tells us what *not* to do. Contrast this with consequence-based theory, which gives us a positive mandate: it tells us what *to* do. Thus, taken as a comprehensive theory, principle-based moral theory gives us a map, so to speak, of where the mines are, but the business of planning our steps across the minefield is up to us; all we have to do is not set off any mines. Setting off a mine would be the analog of disrespecting someone, or neglecting or abrogating someone's rights; in other words, failing to honor an inestimable value. This leaves us with a conceptual gap to fill: now that I have an idea of where the mines are, I need another principle to help me decide, within the limits imposed by principle-based theory, which course to chart. Otherwise, my moral decision making from that point on and within those limits would be intolerably arbitrary.

Arbitrariness in decision making is tolerable when it is finite; e.g., when we are left with a finite, manageable quantity of items to choose from. But infinite arbitrariness is intolerable; intolerable in the sense that it is irrational or absurd. Decision making is a matter of boiling down infinite and unchartable options to a finite and chartable few. Without achieving this, rational deliberation would be a failed operation.

This lacuna of principle-based moral theory—that it does not provide a positive mandate, but leaves that aspect of moral decisions arbitrary—suggests not that this way of thinking is just plain throw-it-out false, but that it is incomplete. Whether it is altogether false depends on whether there are really no such things as inestimable values. Let's try to answer that question first, and then come back to the question of how to complement principle-based theory.

Let's face it: to deny the reality of human rights is counterintuitive. Moreover, to deny rights just to make one's favored theory come out true seems backward thinking. In matters of conflicting notions, it is the things we are more sure about that we ought to save, at the expense of what we are less sure about. But outside this particular discussion, our acceptance of the reality of rights is simply not a matter of controversy at all. That is why the burden of proof should be considered to be on the consequentialists.

Moreover, it is clear we are not comfortable treating human values in the manner in which we treat mundane values. Three boxes of Cheerios are worth one and a half times the worth of two boxes of Cheerios. Are we comfortable the same is true of humans? I think not. And although we love our domestic animals, we sometimes see fit to trade them for various reasons. Cats hate moving; I have friends who have simply left their beloved furry friends with the next occupants of the house they moved from. They took the time, of course, to do proper introductions, etc. Moreover, we buy and sell cats, dogs, and other animals. To be sure, we may decry the manner in which animals are treated when they are traded and sold, but the opposition is one of practice, not principle. All the while we recognize these are things we ought not in principle do with humans. It is unconscionable even to trade one human for another human, or for several. Clearly, then, human things are of inestimable worth.

Once satisfied with the notion that principle-based moral theory provides us with the essential insight of setting aside inestimable values as not subject to barter, trade, or the like, how shall we proceed from here? I think the answer should be clear: we go back to consequentialist reasoning and make our choice based on the remaining calculable values, without disturbing, abrogating, or ignoring—as much as is logistically possible—the inestimable ones. In fact, this is what we actually do in the best of cases, though it may have escaped our notice.

The fact is, consequence-based thinking works fine with mundane matters. It tells us how to shop and do everyday things, for the most part. (Of course, since humans are involved in just about everything we do, there are always peripheral concerns of respect to attend to. But these hardly come into play when deciding whether to spring for the discount single-ply toilet paper.) It therefore seems an extreme case of overkill to completely deny consequentialist reasoning, or to deny it at all in situations in which no inestimable values are at stake.

From this, it should follow as well that consequentialist reasoning should also be appropriate for making decisions in areas involving inestimable values, once those values have been duly noted and "quarantined," or taken out of play for bartering and such.

Let these few examples elucidate my point.

The first example is a classical thought experiment. Suppose I am in a contingent of three people hiking in the Grand Canyon. We come to a precipice that partially gives way, leaving the other two hanging on for dear life. One of them is a three hundred-pound renowned pediatric surgeon. The other is a one hundred fifty-pound methamphetamine addict. Let's just say I am of average strength. The situation is such that it is clear I will only be able to save one. One thought—along utilitarian lines—is that I ought to save the surgeon, since his life is of more value to humanity. But I shun that notion, on the grounds that every human life is of inestimable worth. Instead, I calculate over the estimable values that remain in play: my limited physical abilities, the respective weights of the two men, and the resulting odds of my saving either. Judging correctly that my odds of saving the addict are much better, I reach out and grab him, pulling him to safety, while the surgeon falls to his death.

This is analogous to my second example, which is taken from actual decision-making protocol in the health-care profession. The manner in which decisions are made on how to use donated organs involves several weighted parameters. But in no case are they given to the most valuable person to society, or to the person with the best moral character, etc. All else being equal, the organ is given to the next person on the waiting list. But that person may be passed over if there is someone on the list below him who is in more dire need. A third interesting criterion, also used as a tiebreaker, is that the organ is given to the person least likely to reject it.

It is the last two criteria cited that interest us here. Although it may be unconscionable to calculate in a consequentialist manner on the value of human lives, it is acceptable to calculate over the value of how badly the organ is needed, or over the chances of a successful transplant. After all, the organ itself is a calculable value, which the medical profession correctly does not want to waste, but rather wants to maximize: either by giving it to the person most in need, or to the person least likely to reject it. This still is consequentialist reasoning, but framed in a context duly pruned by principle-based moral reasoning.

PART V
SOCIAL MORALITY

CHAPTER TWENTY-TWO

Compromise and Obedience—The Virtues of Social Morality

Although often scoffed at in modern times, the keys to successful and happy human life, especially organizational life, are the indispensable virtues of compromise and obedience. Here I lay out my case for these two great and underappreciated virtues.

Despite the modern obsession with individualism, the key to human happiness and prosperity is our socialness. I take this as indisputable based on biological evidence. We human beings can make no more of ourselves on our own than can individual ants or honeybees. Just as they, we are born helpless and entirely at the mercy of our adult caretakers. In a way, we are even more indebted to our social contexts than either bees or ants, since their instincts eventually kick in to script their adult behavior, whereas our eventual adult behavior and inner life is to a very large extent dependent on what we learn. Learning, by and large, depends on social relationships. Even that learning that might be called individual is arguably dependent on previously established social learning contexts, eventually stemming all the way back to infantile parent-child interactions.

This makes it difficult and probably futile to try to identify anything purely individual about the human being. Psychologists should be able to press this point even further, to the affirmation that even identity formation itself is a social process.

Notwithstanding the evident primacy of our socialness, we seem to have a difficult time gaining a clear picture of the socialness of morality itself. We tend to envision moral values as pertaining mostly to contexts of individual rather than social deliberation, vaguely considering contexts of social morality as constructs of individual morality contexts.

I consider this tantamount to trying to learn football by studying the actions of only one player at a time and never bothering to take in all the action as a unity. To be sure, there is such a thing as blended individual action, such as a crowd of cheering fans. But even there, one can see the difference between a concerted action—the fans chanting something in unison or cooperating to perform some patterned action—and plain cheering. The latter is largely just the result of many spontaneous individual vocalizations. (Not to press the point, but even this could be considered social action, in a sense, since it occurs within a socially established context.)

It seems clear then, if we are to have clear moral vision, we need to have a clear understanding of what social morality is, and how it is distinguished from individual morality, or "general morality" as it is traditionally called.

The good news is that this in not a difficult thing to do. Since social morality is, after all, morality, we don't have to introduce an entirely different set of basic values. Social morality inherits all the content of general morality (not that specifying this is easy). The task then is limited to specifying the content peculiar to social morality.

We can see what the special content of social morality is by examining the difference between individual and social morality. Individual morality is the morality of choices deliberated over, made, and carried out by individuals. Social morality is the morality of choices deliberated over, made, and carried out by groups. (We don't need to unpack "morality" here, because its content is not at issue.) The relevant difference here is that between how individuals deliberate over, make, and carry out choices, and how groups do the same.

This comparison yields an obvious difference—that groups making and carrying out decisions have a problem that individuals don't have: how to deal with disagreement between individuals within the group. Moreover, it seems clear that disagreement may arise at two distinct points: at the point of making a decision, and at the point of carrying it out. It is at these two junctures where the special virtues of social morality—compromise at the first juncture and obedience at the second—are necessary for successful and happy human life.

Compromise is the virtue that processes disagreement in group decision making toward a group decision. It therefore only applies to the deliberation phase. Obedience is the subjugation of the individual will to the will of the group to enable group action. Obedience only applies to the execution phase and not to deliberation.

Without compromise, groups would stalemate in the deliberative phase and cease to exist at the moment unanimity does not spontaneously arise in the decision-making process. The existence of a group consists in action; if decisions cannot be made, no action can be carried out.

Without obedience, groups would not be able to execute action effectively and therefore would put their existence in jeopardy. Most groups exist for good, even vital reasons. To risk their well-being at the altar of the primacy of the individual would ultimately harm groups as well as individuals.

Calling compromise a virtue does not imply that any particular compromise is good or right. It implies only there is no time when the effort to compromise ought to be refused or neglected.

Calling obedience a virtue does not imply that obedience on any occasion is right. It only implies that even in situations in which the unjust action of a group morally requires us technically to disobey, our disobedience on such occasions ought to be itself "obedient"; i.e., in submission to the group's well-being and for the sake of the group, even to the point of individual sacrifice.

Compromise is important not just because it is logistically necessary to group existence and functioning, but because it cultivates mutual respect between disagreeing parties, which sets the stage for future negotiations. If we followed the oft repeated but poorly conceived dictum not to compromise on our moral values, we are not only setting ourselves up for an impasse that threatens the group's continued effective function, but we make no progress toward the values we ourselves are striving for. The insinuation favoring the dictum is that such compromise would be a form of hypocrisy, as if compromise implied selling out on our values, or watering them down. But in fact, those very values are better served by compromise, since not only does compromise achieve some immediate progress toward those values, but also cultivates a mutual respect with those on the opposing side, which bodes well for the prospects of further progress in future negotiations. It is nothing short of rash to negotiate as if there will be no tomorrow. To win more now by bullying at the bargaining table is just plain bad business. Not only is it disrespectful to other conscientious beings whose goodwilled cooperation we require in our ongoing social pursuit of truth and goodness, but it also surely will have negative repercussions on future negotiations.

Another obstacle to compromise is that it ought to be confined to goodwilled parties; that we should not compromise with "bad guys." The idea is that bad guys will only exploit our own good will at the bargaining table to their own advantage, and that therefore we ought to respond in kind by exploiting whatever brute-force advantages we may have over them in forcing our will upon them.

We should note first off that there is a slippery slope here; for what is more likely to make us doubt the goodwill of our opponent than that they oppose us on an issue of vital moral importance?

In recognition that this one point may, if accepted, lead to a general collapse in commitment to the value of compromise, we should not consider it a minor concession. Nonetheless, unless we have an adequate rebuttal, we should concede.

The fact of the matter is that in none of our dealings are we quite sure of the purity of the intentions of those with whom we are dealing—nor of our own! But human socialness is not possible without trust—there is no such thing as a trust-free social process. We cannot therefore survive without establishing some basis of trust with those with whom we must deal, even though we are not able to precisely judge their moral character (or our own!). To be sure, the grounds for trust may be greater or lesser, but they are never nil; our common humanness and existence on the same planet as rational animals provides the default backdrop for trust when all else fails. As bad as Hitler was, he was only human—and he was, yes, fully human. We need to admit that if we are to move forward from the mess that he and the rest of us made of recent history, lest we slip back into the same mind-set that enabled it in the first place. If instead we choose to continue to scapegoat the bad guy by isolating him conceptually from the human race and heaping the blame exclusively on his shoulders, then we fail to see our own complicity. Hitler himself was a product of non-compromise—the confluence of decades and perhaps even centuries of bullying on so many social levels and in so many institutions in which he was involved, from family through national to international arenas. For us now to treat evil in the world by the same non-compromising, bullying methods would only bring more such evil into the world. Instead, we need to turn these processes around, and in fact it needs to begin with the way we treat our "bad guys."

Lest someone take issue with my argument against "scapegoating the bad guy" by arguing that bad guys are just the guys we ought to blame and that by not doing so we take them off the hook, I respond that the problem with scapegoating is not that we are blaming the bad guy, but that we are *limiting* the blame to the bad guy. In such a way, the processes that generated the bad guy in the first place remain entrenched in our social processes and institutions, ready and disposed to churn out more trouble.

The question of whether we ought to compromise with "bad guys" comes down to this: Should we address our evils in such a way that will only produce more? Not compromising is bullying; bullying produces bad guys. Moreover, bullying bad guys only makes them (and their associates and loved ones) worse.

Good compromise is a process of goodwilled, truth-oriented dialogue that will at least temporarily declaw if not convert ill-willed participants. All bad will is based on self-deception, a purposeful ongoing denial of truths inconvenient to one's worldview. The result is a mind-set tailored to enable the ill-willed person to act in the manner he had with prejudice preselected. If we do not challenge this very process, we are then complicit in the evil that comes of it. Bullying does not challenge the self-deception of the ill-willed person, but enables. The only effective challenge to self-deception is ongoing, rigorous truth-oriented dialogue, which itself is the process of virtuous compromise.

If then we recognize that we must, without exception, always strive for good compromise in all our social deliberations, should we say the same about obedience? If compromise, as we have argued, is an unconditional virtue of social morality, and that any attempt to hedge it would only undercut it, are we to conclude the same of obedience?

Yes and no. Or better: no and yes. No, in the sense that there is an asymmetry between obedience and compromise, and it consists in this: compromise applies to decisions not yet made, so is guided by—and guides—the hope in a virtuous decision being made; whereas obedience applies to decisions already made, so therefore is necessarily colored by the moral quality of that decision. We have finally come to a clear consensus—let us not ever lose it!—that we ought not obey unjust commands. This is the basis of movements of civil disobedience from Socrates to Marin Luther King Jr. and beyond. Our clarity on this matter is sufficient for us to consider it a settled matter, and makes one wonder why we could not have settled it earlier.

Of course, I am speaking in principle, and not in practice. In practice, it will always be exceedingly difficult for, say, a fighter pilot to disobey a commander's order to drop bombs on a city or a village, and that is why we should recognize that whenever we have wars, we should have to expect such atrocities; in such cases, disobedience requires individual sacrifice, sometimes even of one's own life. Here is where the "yes" part of the answer comes in. Civil disobedience of this kind really is a deeper form of obedience. It is sacrifice for the sake of the good of the group or organization.

In ordinary obedience, we subjugate our own individual will to the will of the group to enable the execution of group action. As dramatic as that may sound, it is something we do routinely. Since obedience only applies to instances in which there is a conflict between our own will and the will of the group, it is a type of self-sacrifice made in goodwill for the sake of the good of the group. It implies a sacrifice of one's own intellectual convenience, since the one obeying senses a disagreement between himself and the group, but considers it not momentous enough to be worth the breakdown in trust within the group caused by disobedience. Similarly, virtuous civil disobedience is also a kind of self-sacrifice, in that now the one disobeying has judged that he must endure the negative consequences of breakdown in trust relationships within the group, owning them openly and absorbing them permanently within his own life, accepting all of the attendant suffering, danger, and inconvenience—not for his own sake, but for the sake of the group. To obey in this instance would have been only for his own sake, since he too recognizes that what he is doing is unjust. Therefore, obeying would in a deeper sense be an act of disobedience, since the motivation would not be for the sake of the group, but for the sake of his own convenience. In fact, obedience to a command one recognizes to be unjust is selfish and even disloyal—i.e., disobedient—to the group.

So superficially, obedience is not an unconditional virtue, since we are called to disobey unjust commands. But in a deeper sense, virtuous civil disobedience is itself a more profound form of obedience.

CHAPTER TWENTY-THREE

Economic Pessimism

Despite the fact that the human species is clearly at its apex of economic productivity, a sense of economic pessimism looms as a dark cloud in the minds of many. This sentiment is motivated in large part by clear evidence of a persistent and in some respects worsening gap in the distribution of economic goods and services, which at the very least offers a strong suggestion of gross injustice. Perhaps equally ominous is the threat that our world economy will soon outstrip its own resource base, and that, in the meantime, our fossil fuel economy is leading us into the additional crisis of global warming. There is also a growing worry about increasing water shortages around the world. These concerns in tandem now present to us a credible threat of an impending catastrophic cultural decline. It is vital, therefore, for us to make a sober assessment of how much trouble we are really now in, and whether, in spite of these looming concerns, there is adequate reason to hope that we can manage our way through these momentous challenges and move decidedly toward a world economy that is both just and sustainable in the long run.

Yes, we have seen cultural decline before, and we speculate to what extent the causes have been political, economic, or just due to the forces of nature. Most probably, it has been a combination of these factors. Many causes have been posited for the decline of the Roman Empire. It was politically top-heavy and overextended, and its development of far-reaching areas of the globe enabled resistance movements to spawn and develop there. But Romans themselves famously decried as perhaps the chief threat to their continued prosperity the problem of the greed of the wealthy.

It is now coming to light due to the excellent work of researchers that the pre-Incan civilization known as the Moche, who had arrived at a fully agricultural mode of existence on a well-irrigated desert coastal valley eerily reminiscent of present-day California, declined back to a decentralized horticultural existence largely due to their inability to cope with a disastrous long-term change in weather patterns. But politics and economics helped exacerbate the decline considerably, as the poor were forced into increasingly more dire conditions to buffer the loss in productivity for the wealthy, until the harsh treatment itself became cause for revolt.

It is widely accepted that Aztec society was already headed for trouble before Europeans had arrived due to their near exhaustion of their lumber resource base for fuel—exacerbated by extreme increases in human sacrifice in response to their increasing economic woes. Many of the surrounding peoples under the thumb of the Aztecs, who had served largely as the ultimate source for human sacrifice victims, were only too willing to team with the Spaniards against the Aztecs, without whose help and manpower the Spaniards would have had no chance at victory, since they would have been vastly outnumbered.

Karl Marx had famously argued that capitalism, roughly the form of economy in the developed world, contained the seeds of its own destruction in a variety of ways, mostly related to the fact that its very maintenance relies on the continued credible promise of indefinite future growth, whereas the world in which we live is, at least in certain key respects, inescapably finite. One of these respects, of course, is our natural resource base. To be sure, not all markets sell physical products or services, but ultimately all wealth derives from the surplus of vital physical goods, especially food, without which the values of all other nonphysical and non-vital products are nil. A bar of gold is of no direct service to anyone, nor can online video games sustain us through a time of famine. And even online gaming requires fuel for the electricity.

In some respects, the behavior of markets may have proven more resilient than Marx had predicted. He may have underestimated, for example, the infinite capacity of the human imagination to dream up new markets as well as to renew old ones, thereby staving off the predicted monopoly effects to which he argued markets inevitably tend as they age. But I am still waiting for us to disprove his prediction that capitalist economies develop a greater gap between rich and poor as they age. While it is true that this phenomenon is worse in some places of the world than in others, the decisive variable in the equation seems to be the extent to which the people of a place have enacted or evolved laws and customs to curb that capitalist tendency. The less effective the public oversight, the worse the gap, it seems.

We ought to keep in mind here that something happened to capitalist ideology along the way from Enlightenment thinkers such as Adam Smith, who envisioned capitalism as a sort of economic democracy that was to be well-regulated to ensure it produced the best result for society as a whole, to twentieth-century figures such as Ayn Rand, who more brazenly hailed it as a type of social Darwinism that lionized the economically strong while accepting that the weak needed either to pick themselves up by their own bootstraps or be weeded out.

Regardless of which version of capitalism we choose as our paradigm, it would be rash for us to ignore Marx's warnings at least with respect to capitalism outstripping its natural resource base and to its eventually producing a socially untenable gap between rich and poor. The latter point can most clearly be seen in the international arena, in the gap between rich and poor nations. Although we might want to believe that the devastating poverty that exists in the world, which is the cause of starvation, rampant disease, and in some places a way of life inferior to what it would be in the "state of nature"—the avoidance of which even pessimistic political philosophers such as Hobbes argued brought us to accept social organization in the first place, in the form of a "social contract"—is all caused by bad government and local corruption, economists know it is largely a matter of some countries getting into the game of modern economic development later than others. Imagine what your chances would be of winning at Monopoly if you enter the game after all the properties have been bought up. You wouldn't have a fair chance to compete.

We know also that the earth does not now have the resources for the entire population of the planet to consume at the rate Americans now consume. This implies we cannot even reasonably hope for a continuation of our present-day consumer economy, which would have to accept the aforementioned future possibility as its asymptotic limit. This being so, we could only hope for a transition to an economy not based on ever-increasing consumption, but on sustainability. The big question: How?

To borrow a page from Aristotle's *Metaphysics*, there are actually several "how" questions to answer. One is of efficient cause: How can we even gain control of the world economy to bring about such a transition in the first place? Another is about material cause: What will our future fuel base be? Our consumption problems now are largely a matter of fuel consumption of nonrenewable fuels. A third question is about formal cause: Do we even have an idea of what the form of economy is that we ought to transition to? Finally, a fourth question is about final cause: What kind of uniting social purpose can we imagine that could motivate us to jointly embark upon the appropriate course of action that would lead us in the direction of accomplishing all of the above?

Regarding the question of efficient cause, one thing we have to recognize is that we can create an entire economy from scratch no more than we can create a brand new species of vegetable from scratch. The economy about which we are speaking is the world economy, which is too big for us just to scrap and replace with a newly invented one. But exploiting the vegetable metaphor further, just about every vegetable we now eat is considerably altered from its original wild state. Over the centuries, we have gradually transformed these various plant species to be the tasty, nutritious, chewable, appealing, digestible items they now are. Wild carrots cannot really be chewed and swallowed; they can only be gnawed on, and doing so burns the lips. So while we cannot create new species of things from scratch, we do a very good job of tweaking existing species to serve us better and better. It is not a perfect process, but it has allowed us to prosper for hundreds of thousands of years.

Another analogy is tree pruning. We cannot from the outset of a tree's life decide exactly where each of its branches will eventually go. But what we can do is prune trees, and we have developed the art so well that we obtain much more out of, say, our fruit trees than nature would have itself provided.

So it must be with the world economy. We cannot simply scrap what we now have. But we can prune it and breed it in the direction we need it to go. We can prune it by dropping the false ideal of *laissez faire* capitalism and, instead, accept our role as stewards—not servants—of the economy, according to which it is our duty to look ahead and plan out the aspects of the economy that can be effectively planned—some can!—while elsewhere keeping a close eye on economic growth and behavior with an eye to optimal—not minimal—regulation in more fine-grained pursuit of justice and sustainability. Even now, some countries are doing these things better than others, so it is not entirely a matter of inventing something from scratch.

Regarding the question of material cause, i.e., our fuel future, we first must see that there are no home runs to be hit, so we must be willing to play "small ball." Let's first review some of the "long fly-ball outs" we've had to suffer through.

The first was nuclear power. On the plus side, it is a "clean burning fuel." One big minus is that it creates a potential for catastrophe and represents a thorny hazardous waste problem. But even if we could trust ourselves to manage nuclear fission safely (a nuclear fusion economy is but a pipe dream), we need to remind ourselves that it is not a sustainable fuel. Even at present consumption rates, we have much less than a century's worth of known uranium resources remaining. A breakthrough in this arena could only come if we were to develop a fuel-efficient way of extracting trace uranium from ocean water. Perhaps we can't afford just to stop using it altogether, but at present it cannot be considered part of the solution, since even at best, its increased use would only hasten its exhaustion as a resource.

A more recent flash in the pan was the hydrogen economy. In fact, we have hydrogen fuel-cell technology up and operating. But we have no fuel-efficient way of obtaining the free hydrogen we need as the fuel. We need to burn roughly enough non-hydrogen fuel to free the hydrogen that would be energy-equivalent to the hydrogen freed. The most concrete proposal to free hydrogen more efficiently would be to cultivate on a massive level genetically altered bacteria that would produce free hydrogen as a waste product. But no one is close even to conceiving of an energy-efficient way of doing that, since it would have to be done on a massive scale.

In fact, we are hurting ourselves by waiting for a home run to be hit in the fuel economy game. Instead, we ought to be chipping away with increased investment in known sustainable fuels such as solar, water, wind, and geothermal. Solar technology, in particular, is still a growth industry. Until recently, we have directed our efforts here on a small scale: solar panels on residential and commercial roofs, etc. But there are also large-scale applications that we ought to be exploring, such as environmentally sound ways to establish large solar farms on nonarable or desolate land. There are also other more efficient ways of harvesting the power of the sun than by the use of panels, ways that may be better suited to large-scale products.

We ought not ignore the use of cultivated plant matter as a source for fuel. To be sure, this requires good economic planning to prevent the skyrocketing of food prices due to increased competition for arable land. To this end, innovators are looking in two directions: the use of inedible portions of edible crops for fuel, and the use of plants, such as Argentinian switch grass, which thrive on nonarable land. Both of these ideas have a distinct, plausible future in our economy.

Whether all of the ideas just cited will collectively solve our fuel problems or not should not be the test question by which we determine whether they are worthwhile to pursue. This is a logical fallacy that in the past has hobbled our best efforts. The fact is that each of these directions distinctly contributes to the solution, and that is all the justification they need. Humans have proven time and again that we solve our worst problems not all at once, but by faithfully chipping away at them over the decades, even centuries. The advent of the industrial era got us thinking big, and maybe regarding our most difficult problems we have been thinking too big.

As to the question of formal cause—what should we expect our future economy to look like?—here, too, we have long been hobbled by a fallacy; in this case, the fallacy that a fundamental choice needs to be made between capitalism and socialism. In fact, this is not only a false choice, but a non-choice. It is a non-choice because there is no such plausible thing as pure capitalism or pure socialism. We cannot have the latter, because we could not proactively plan a world economy from scratch if we tried. Besides, it would require a level of behavior control that is ludicrous and would be catastrophic to human culture even if achieved. As far as pure capitalism is concerned, that would be tantamount to a universal black market, which would be equally catastrophic to human culture.

Moreover, the socialism-capitalism dichotomy is a false choice in that it fallaciously presents the two as contradictories rather than as what they really are, which is contrary extremes on a spectrum. Even though the United States hails itself as a land of capitalism, it is in large part socialist. Socialism is economy proactively planned, managed, or run by or in the public sector. By that definition, the largest single socialist institution in the world is the US military! In fact, all laws and regulations are in the same sense socialist, as is the public sector as a whole: police departments, public parks, schools libraries, the interstate highway system, and the economic infrastructure as a whole.

Americans who still suffer from the illusion of a capitalist promised land sometimes bemoan the fact that not all nations and states have income taxes, or this kind of tax or that kind of tax. But every single government in the world has its way of getting the revenue it needs for the functioning of its public sector and for the establishment and maintenance of its economic infrastructure. In Saudi Arabia there are no taxes because the government gets its revenue directly from petroleum. In Hong Kong there are no zoning laws because the government owns all undeveloped land and so is able to set favorable contractual terms for its use at the point of sale to developers, which inevitably will include some provisions for low-cost, mixed-income housing. Greenwich, Connecticut, can afford to keep its property tax rates very low simply because, thanks to its lucky proximity to New York City, its property values are very high. And by the way, Greenwich also enjoys a good amount of revenue derived from land donations by some of its wealthier residents from the past.

So the question ought not be whether the future economy should be socialist or capitalist; the question ought to be whether here or there a socialist mechanism or capitalism mechanism is called for. This question needs to be asked over and over with respect to every area of the economy. The two should be seen as tools in our tool kit, neither of which we should blush from using when appropriate.

Regarding, at last, the question of final cause—what it will take to get the whole world on the same page to work effectively for a sustainable and just economy—this question is being gradually answered before our eyes now. The world cannot act in tandem until and unless it is—unless there is—a world community. A world community cannot be established merely by mechanical or formal means, such as creation of the United Nations. It is established simply by ordinary people from around the world—and not just the ruling classes—getting to know one another, befriend one another, mingle, and share their cultures and lives with one another. This is happening now. We cannot do much to make it happen any faster other than to recognize that it is a process we ought to be welcoming and rejoicing over, rather than mourning the loss of our more culturally homogeneous pasts. We need to see that our destiny involves a universal community and internationalism. Even if we refuse to welcome it, it is coming. The more we welcome it, the more peaceful and less painful the transition will be. We therefore have the duty to reinterpret our political notions of patriotism and even our theologies to accommodate a future world community. Only pain and suffering will come from resisting the process.

So is there cause for optimism? Of course there is! But it is an optimism that needs to be embraced, and embraced now. If we fail in this regard, then and only then do we make prophets of the pessimists.

CHAPTER TWENTY-FOUR

Failed Relationships, Identity Confusion, and Altruism

When I was a boy, before our present-day culture of obsessively organized after-school programs, when you came home from school your first duty was to change into your play clothes. You weren't supposed to get your school clothes dirty, so that you could wear them more than once. Then you were to do one or two simple chores, and then do your homework, which was never that much. Then you went out to play until you were called home for supper. Sometimes you played first, then did your homework after supper.

This play was entirely unscripted. Sometimes you played in groups of two or more, and sometimes you played alone. On many of those occasions when I was alone or with only one or two playmates, play consisted of observing—and interfering with—nature, particularly spiders, insects, and other bugs. To be sure, this play may have been in part driven by idle curiosity and even a touch of cruelty, but nonetheless it has since yielded for me important lessons that apply to human life.

The games I played with bugs were nameless. One type of game I played could have been called Confuse the Bug. I would interrupt the life of a spider or insect in some way, then watch and see what happened. For example, I would see a spider just putting the finishing touches on a web, then I would break the web—carefully, so as not to hurt or lose track of the spider. Then I would wait and wait to see what would happen. Usually the spider would settle down, stunned, make some false moves, then finally start the laborious process of rebuilding. If I came back later, I would see the web back in pretty much the same place. But if I disturbed the spider a second time, the spider would seem less sure what to do. I never followed through completely on this particular experiment, but noticed at least that individual spiders and insects can get confused when their life activity is suddenly, and especially stressfully, interrupted. The effect, particularly if this is done repeatedly, is that they seemingly "forget who they are" and cease their activities, sometimes permanently, but at least for a time; a sort of animal identity crisis.

My more usual subjects of study were ants. I would take some carpenter ants and "fight" them by shaking them together in my hands until they engaged. This was easy to do with ants from different colonies, as one would expect. With ants from the same colony, you had to shake them quite a bit more until they engaged. Once engaged, though, they would not let go. So with enough disorientation, you could make two sister ants "forget" their sisterhood; an ant identity crisis.

I typically found I was able to put these poor little individual creatures into identity crisis by isolating them and applying some sort of interruption of their daily activities. But one thing I was never able to do, though I tried, was to give an entire colony of ants—or yellow jackets, for that matter—an identity crisis. I could never even break up an ant food line, unless I simply kept sweeping the entire line of ants away indefinitely. Otherwise, the line would faithfully reform and continue after a brief delay. As long as the individual ants remained in communication with one another and did not get isolated from the colony, they would not be swayed from their activities. But if I took a bunch of those ants away from the colony—say, in a container with plenty of soil and food—they would at first show a little interest in the food, and would briefly make inchoative efforts at digging tunnels, but with no coordination. Then they would just stop. They weren't yet dying, mind you; they still had plenty of energy. But no motivation. They didn't know what to do any more, so they just did nothing.

Although I actually do feel remorse for my cruel childhood spider and insect experiments, there are important lessons to glean from them, which we will discuss briefly. But first, one more bug story.

As an adult, I more recently made a series of observations of a wasp I now know is called *Sphecius speciosus*, or the eastern cicada killer. I was working out with my son practicing baseball skills, and I would notice that sometimes the baseball rolling over the infield dirt would attract a type of wasp. So I began to take closer note, and saw that this type of wasp was typically at work this time of year—when the sound of singing cicadas filled the air—dragging the paralyzed body of an adult cicada over the ground. It was a laborious task. After a few weeks of observation I had it mostly figured out. First they would go into the infield dirt and dig a burrow. Then they would go fetch and fly in their paralyzed host—another laborious task—and land somewhere near the burrow, where they would then drag it the rest of the way.

By now, of course, I have lost my cruel streak and try my best to be an unobtrusive observer. We were still interrupting their activity, mind you, but this time it was inadvertent, due to the baseballs rolling near them. The fact is, those baseballs somehow attracted their curiosity. For the most part, they were not being harmed or forced from their activity by the balls. Even a nearby stationary baseball might be enough to make the wasp drop its hulking host to investigate. But once its activity was thus interrupted, it would never go back. Instead, it would eventually just fly away, after thoroughly investigating the baseball. And there the poor, paralyzed cicada would remain, day after day, only inches from the burrow where the wasp would have nestled it inside its own little alcove and laid one of her eggs upon it. This showed me how destructive interruption of life activity can be in nature, even when that interruption is not traumatic or particularly stressful.

As I later learned from researching the matter, it turns out that *Sphecius speciosus* typically is able to carry out this laborious process several times in one laying season, so the interruption of just one egg laying probably did not doom its reproductive efforts entirely.

Although we humans are rational, and, unlike spiders and insects, our lives much less scripted by fixed instincts, we are still animals. To that extent, I think the observation of these creatures is relevant, and we can draw some meaningful comparisons.

Once upon a time, a friend who was a single mom with one teenage child revealed to me that her child was the product of a failed relationship with a troubled man, a drug addict who was unreliable. She had been so traumatized by this failed relationship that after cutting ties with him, she had never again even tried to have a relationship with another man. In her words, she wouldn't even know how to go about it. She was utterly mystified and stumped by the thought. I remember looking into her eyes and being able to tell that she cried all the time. Although the relationship had long since ended, it was still quite an open wound for her. She told me that, on a regular basis, she would take long walks and just pray and cry for hours. Then she stunned me by saying this: "I don't even know who I am. Can you please tell me who I am!"

At the time, this comment just didn't make sense to me, but over the years I've had more time to reflect, As such, I think that, unfortunately, this may well be a common experience. People whose lives are interrupted by failed love relationships—whether family or romantic—can forget who they are, forget the humanness that guides their activity, just as the individual creatures cited above forgot who they were—forget their "ant-ness" or their "wasp-ness" or their "spider-ness." This woman went on to describe her life as if she were in a communicative cocoon; she could try to describe to others, even those who loved her, the nature of her suffering, but they just couldn't understand why those unfortunate things that happened could just stop her in her tracks, why she couldn't just pick herself up by her own bootstraps and get on with her life. Consequently, she just kept it all to herself, which isolated her even further.

In fact, it looks as though that is just the way things are in nature. Interruption—particularly traumatic interruption of basic life activities—can be fatal. If so, then what is a woman such as this to do?

First, let's rephrase the question: What are *we* to do? I think nature shows us that individuals in this situation may not be in the condition to resolve the problem on their own. So the first thing we need to do is notice that this is the way creatures are by nature, and be on the lookout for individuals traumatized by relationship failure.

Second and even more important, we need to take a lesson from ant colonies, which by virtue of their consummate socialness are collectively immune to this kind of alienation-from-life activity. We should keep in mind that we, too, are social animals, and therefore our socialness is our cure for this condition. But unlike ants whose social behaviors are fixed by instinct, our social behaviors are freely chosen, our social attitudes freely formed. So how well socialized we are is a matter of choice and freely formed moral character. This is where the danger lies, and why people can fall through the cracks.

The term "altruism" has fallen out of favor in the past half-century or so, due to suspicions it has no basis in nature, where, after all—or so the thought went—reigns the "law of the jungle." But this whole line of thinking ignores the prominent level of socialness found in nature. In fact, socialness may well be a specialization that came into existence to counteract the "interrupted life" phenomenon described here. Far from following the so-called law of the jungle, social animals, in fact, follow a law of altruism, in which the members of a colony or pack live for one another. Yellow jacket females are all perfectly fertile; at any time they can just fly off and mate, if the drones are swarming, and begin their own colonies. And for various reasons not well understood, some in fact do. By far most don't, but instead sacrifice their own fertility to this year's queen. Consequently, most of these females will never mate and never reproduce. Only those who survive the winter and retain their health go on to be next year's queens.

During each mating season, a female crow has a decision to make: Am I to be a mother, or am I to be an aunt? And each mating season, many of these females, again for reasons not well understood, choose to be aunts. Crows have long-term memory of sibling relationships (mostly the females; the males, as usual, are considerably less social), and somehow are able to make a kind of animal "greater good" calculation leading them often to sacrifice their own fertility for a season.

As for humans, our socialness, unlike in the rest of nature, is open and universalizing. We tend toward a degree of socialness that is maximal for what our resources will permit. The more resources available, the more social we are. Hunter gatherers group in numbers that are the most their environment will permit. When food and water are plentiful, their groupings are larger. The move to agriculture greatly boosted our socialness for the same reason, so that the agricultural sense of socialness keeps expanding, to the point that today we are living in the first generation of the world community.

The reason for this—and the biological purpose of our rationality seems to be this—is that the greater our socialness, the more stable, prosperous, and happy we will be. The less social we are, the more enemies at the gates, the more easily we can be ruined by isolation. Socialness is the antidote for this ruinous isolation that comes from that scourge of nature, "interrupted life syndrome."

Oddly, there is a dangerous force of isolation that lurks as a countertrend in modern society, and that is alienation. It occurs when, on account of our isolation, we feel as if we no longer belong, and cease to take proprietary interest in our world, our society—either in part or as a whole. When this occurs, we are doomed unless rescued by the altruistic efforts of others.

But in fact, altruism has a remarkable feature, in that it can work in both directions. Not only do my altruistic efforts work to restore others to social and mental health, but they can help cure me as well. That's right—we can help ourselves *by helping others*. If I am in a hole so deep I cannot pull myself out, I may yet be in a position to help someone else out of their hole. By doing so, I am resocializing myself and, thus, rehabilitating myself. Moreover, having helped that person back to safety, I can now expect help in return.

The point is that our socialness is so dense and so thorough that we do not have to, and ought not, focus on first helping ourselves in all or even in most cases. Quite often, the person we are most able to help is not ourselves, but another. So that's exactly what we should do. Doing so helps reintegrate us and typically gives the one we are helping notice of our need, so that they, once helped by us, will be able and most likely willing to help us in return.

Life itself depends on continuity; it is *defined* by continuity. No wonder then that interruption is inimical to life. What is death, after all, but the final interruption? We must, therefore, be diligent in our social processes to keep life going. This is not something we can do alone, but only in groups.

That's the way it works with ants. And with humans.

CHAPTER TWENTY-FIVE

Is It Dangerous to Be Rich?

On its face, to be poor is not a desirable thing. For poverty implies the absence of sufficient resources to assure a full and happy existence in the absence of accidental misfortune. Poverty means powerlessness, which in turn, implies being at the mercy of others. This would not be so bad if those who are not poor were both individually and collectively generous enough to provide for the poor. But such is not reliably the case in human society. The recognition of this fact gives grounds to the suspicion that there is something bad or at least dangerous—morally dangerous—about not being poor, and especially about being rich. Yet in spite of this suspicion, we are stymied by contending doubts; first, that wealth may be the natural and just reward of one's efforts and the efforts of one's forebears and therefore to impugn it would be both unfair and counterproductive; secondly, that poverty might somehow largely only have itself to blame—that the causes of poverty lie not in wealth, but in poverty itself.

These contending suspicions lead to a schism in the way we think about poverty and wealth, a schism which not only exists between persons and classes of people, but within them as well—within each one of us. The most convenient response to such divisions is to simply cast one's lot with one side and ignore the claims of the other, according to the greatest social convenience. Thus we see a class divide, with those who identify themselves with poverty blaming the problems of society on the wealthy, and those who identify with wealth blaming society's troubles on the poor. This makes genuine dialog on the question difficult, so thoroughly has it been booby-trapped by social polemics. Triggers are set off to explosive results whenever the name Karl Marx is mentioned. On the other hand, we complain about big box stores and big business as if one would be defiled by doing commerce with them, and carefully tailor our criteria of wealth so that we ourselves are not wealthy by those standards.

As a result, those on opposite sides of the divide may see the same things very differently. For example, some progressive Catholic friends of mine consider it to be a plain fact that the recent resignation from the position of Speaker of the House of republican Congressman John Boehner, who happens to be Catholic and was the one who led efforts to get Pope Francis to speak to Congress in the first place, was on account of his having been privately told off by the pope for siding politically against the poor. On the other side of the church aisle, Boehner is being extolled by conservatives as a martyr for the cause of effective government at the hands of liberals who promote entitlements which bloat and corrupt government. In my conversations with both of these groups, I was treated with incredulity just for having had to ask. Both sides felt their view was obviously the correct one.

We have a love-hate relationship with wealth. Whereas we waver over whether or not it is tasteful or immoral to flaunt wealth, it is hard to imagine, all else being equal, someone turning away from the opportunity to become more wealthy. I might turn down a higher salary because of the inconveniences of moving, because of the changes that job would force on my family life, or because I just don't like the job. But I certainly could not imagine turning down a raise just for continuing to do what I do now, on account of the moral danger of wealth! In spite of this, there is a persistent tradition in human culture that wealth is morally dangerous.

Nowhere is this more forcefully expressed than at the beginning of Chapter 5 of the Epistle of James in the New Testament:

> As for you, you rich, weep and wail over your impending miseries. Your wealth has rotted, your fine wardrobe has grown motheaten, your gold and silver have corroded, and their corrosion shall be a testimony against you; It will devour your flesh like a fire. See what you have stored up for yourselves against the last days. Here, crying aloud, are the wages you withheld from the farmhands who harvested your fields. The cries of the harvesters have reached the ears of the Lord of hosts. You lived in wanton luxury on the earth; you fattened yourselves for the day of slaughter. You condemned, even killed, the just man; he does not resist you. (James 5:1–5, The New American Bible, 1971)

Now, James, presumably James, the first bishop of Jerusalem, who at the time was the de facto leader of the new Christian sect (which was still largely a Jewish movement), was Jewish himself, and was speaking not only from his position as church leader but in the name of the Tanakh (Old Testament) and longstanding Jewish tradition. Judaism since ancient times is rife with stern warnings against the evils of wealth, and yet also extols it as a blessing. This makes it difficult to know how to properly contextualize the above excerpt. Clearly, the message of James cannot be that everyone who has wealth is damned, since father Abraham himself was a man of great wealth and yet blessed. On the other hand, we cannot possibly stray too far in the other direction, since it is clear James is not mincing words.

Unlike Marx, whose indictment against the wealthy is collective and not personal, focusing on the entire class of the wealthy, the diatribe of James is largely personal: wealth has a corrupting effect on persons. What kind of corruption James had in mind might be better revealed by the last sentence of Chapter 4, just before he lashes out against the rich: "When a man knows the right thing to do and does not do it, he sins." (James 4:17) This gives us assurance that James is not affected with some kind of proto-Marxist determinism according to which the corruption of the wealthy is an inexorable social condition, but that the object of his indictments are the wealthy who freely choose corruption. For the notion of sin just offered by James involves a free and deliberate choice against one's conscience. So James's concerns about the corrupting effect of wealth are largely about personal sin.

But James is not blind to the concerns of social justice that motivated Marx. In speaking of harvesters crying out for their withheld wages, he alludes to the position of unchecked power the wealthy enjoy in setting the wages of the poor who work for them. The presumption seems to be that people endowed with such an unmitigated advantage will be hard-pressed to pay out a fair wage. Their wealth buffers them from the consequences of their own greed and stinginess, which to the non wealthy would come in the form of criticism, scorn, and shunning at the hands of their defrauded peers. But the wage earner is not the peer of the wealthy, so is not in a position to perform this corrective socioeconomic function.

What we can draw from both James and Marx, even if dismissing the latter's socioeconomic determinism, is that the wealthy are likely, individually or collectively, to perpetrate injustice and lose their moral perspective on sole account of the unguarded power their wealth affords them. For we are wealthy—or at least dangerously so—to the extent that we enjoy unguarded power, while we are poor to the extent that we lack power. Who is in position to mediate this gap? The wealthy are. But how will they be motivated to do so fairly, both individually and collectively?

This rich-poor gap thus described is not something we ought to accept as a simple fact of life, since it is and creates social dysfunction by its very existence. The only operant natural check on it, apart from our own deliberate intervention, would be the overall loss or destruction of wealth brought about by wars and natural disasters. What a horror to have to depend on such things as our only corrective functions!

Democratic theory assumes the possibility of an equitable public forum in which all perspectives can receive due attention and be hashed out accordingly. Based on this assumption, we might have reason to hope that the unbalanced relationship between rich and poor just described might be balanced out by democratic processes, which presumably would duly empower the poor while checking the unguarded power of the rich. This is the ideal justice demands, but is it realistic to believe that such a forum is available to us? Who would monitor its processes to assure its healthy functioning? What human social agency has the power to check the unguarded power of the wealthy?

As awkward as it may sound, there is only one possible answer and that answer is us; not any exclusive us, but the all-inclusive us. There must be a table at which we all sit in universal community, rich and poor, as brothers and sisters belonging to the same family. Nothing less than this will allow to emerge the social vision and motivation to address the dysfunctional gap between poverty and wealth.

What stands in the way of this happening is nothing other than social alienation; not only the alienation of the rich from the poor and vice versa, but alienation in general. Alienation is the engendered attitude of our not belonging to one another, either generally or based on some class or demographic difference. As social animals, we have progressed over the millennia of our existence on earth to larger and larger social forms and now are facing the grandest challenge of all: universal community. In every stage of our existence up to now, our social belonging has always been defined as much by exclusion as by inclusion. To the extent that we forge our identity, our sense of belonging, by exclusion, we create the grounds for social alienation, i.e., we create alienation as a by-product of our own identity formation. Identity being a need for us, we are tempted to secure it, our sense of belonging, in the easiest possible way. Exclusion being the shortcut to identity, we are tempted to forge our identities by exclusion, and that is where all our troubles lie.

The other way to identity, admittedly more difficult, is inclusion—ultimately universal inclusion. The difficulty of it lies in the amount of effort we have to put into making all things human—even all things living—our own, rather than other. For the first time in history, we are in a position in which common folk from all around the world can meet and become intimate with one another, either in person or electronically. This gives us so much work to do in order to achieve a genuinely inclusive common identity. But it's work we have to do, and it's work we can do. As humans, we have been doing it our entire existence, albeit kicking and screaming, always moving toward a broader and broader sense of community over the millennia, until we now have come to the point at which the process can feasibly be completed.

The dysfunctional gap between the rich and poor only exists because of the mutual alienation felt between the two, which was built on the bad habit of exclusionary identity formation. This is why James, representing the best of Jewish religious tradition, chides and condemns the rich: for their false sense of independence from the poor, for their nonidentification with the poor. We might chide the poor on the very same account, except for that when we are breaking up a fight between a bully and a weakling, we must focus the bulk of our efforts on the bully. Only after the fight has been broken up do things have a chance to be sorted out equitably.

Yes, there may always be poverty, but only transitory poverty here and there; the poverty of those recovering from natural disasters or the death of a parent; the poverty of students who sacrifice work for study; the poverty of immigrants moving to new lands for the sake of economic opportunity or political liberty. But we must not accept dysfunctional, generational poverty as an indelible reality of the human community.

PART VI
Political Morality

CHAPTER TWENTY-SIX

Non-Manipulative Politics

Many of us have come to the conclusion that politics, especially elective politics, is all about manipulation: if you want to win, you have to manipulate public perception. In this essay I explore whether it is possible to conduct a successful election campaign without depending on manipulative tactics, and whether this is what we ought to recommend.

Before going further, let me clarify that I do not consider all of modern politics to be manipulative. But I think manipulation is winning out as the recommended strategy of those who advise those who run for office. Any recommendation of non-manipulative politics here should be read not as a battle cry for the formation of a brand-new movement, but as an exhortation for us to take up with renewed vigor the good traditions of honest political action already with us in some form or another.

Accordingly, the two claims I am exploring are as follows:

i.   Manipulative campaigning is not a necessary condition to winning elections.
ii. We ought to recommend non-manipulative politics.

These claims really amount to an evaluation of one argument, since the first claim is subsidiary to the second. If winning elections *per se* is not immoral and the only way to win one is to manipulate, then manipulation could be considered morally acceptable as a necessary evil. The first claim (i), of course, denies this, and so will take its place as a premise in the argument favoring the second claim (ii).

My reasoning is as follows:

1. A manipulative means in human affairs is evil to the extent that it consists in the impersonal treatment of persons, which is disrespectful, offensive, and harmful to future social relations. It can also be said to set up politicians themselves for eventual failure while curtailing the genuine political process.
2. An evil means even to a just end is wrong if there is another equally effective means to that end that is less evil.
3. In the case of elective politics, a non-manipulative campaign is a lesser evil *per se* than a manipulative campaign.

4. A non-manipulative campaign can be at least as effective as a manipulative one.
5. Therefore, manipulative election campaigns are wrong.

Manipulation in human affairs is the attempt to elicit a desired behavior from a subject not by appeal to the intrinsic merits of the behavior, but by means of threat of punishment, promise of reward, or deception. Key to this concept is that the rewards and punishments do not naturally emanate from the desired behavior or its absence, but one would expect them to be provided by the manipulating party.

Manipulation, moreover, unlike rational persuasion, is not aimed at eliciting a change in belief or attitude, but rather at eliciting observable behaviors that are deemed to be favorable or convenient to the manipulator.

Manipulation can be classified into two types: overt and covert. Overt manipulation makes no attempt to hide the fact of what it is. It is just plain bullying. Covert or deceptive manipulation, on the other hand, depends on a feigned non-manipulative front. Overt manipulation is common when the manipulator determines he has an overwhelming power advantage extending into the foreseeable future. In other cases the manipulator is forced to do his work covertly.

This paper focuses on covert manipulation. I narrow my focus in this manner for three reasons: (1) it stands in need of being exposed; (2) the opportunities for it in our society seem to be more common; and (3) in recent times people have taken up defending it as a proper way of doing politics.

The evil of manipulation in human affairs lies in the fact that it ignores human personhood. Manipulators do not appeal to us through our conscience. Nor do they engage us in free rational deliberation. Bypassing these things, manipulators seek to control our behavior by means of our animal impulses, desires, and fears. It is disrespectful to ignore a person's conscience, especially when one is seeking a favor from that same person. Once a person comes to realize that she has been treated thus, she is bound to be offended. To treat someone impersonally, especially while seeking a favor, is tantamount to denying that person's existence as a rational being. In manipulating, the manipulator considers his subject not as a person at all, but as a brute animal.

When the subject becomes aware of all this, he will surely recoil from trust relationships with the manipulator, and it will be difficult for that lost trust to be restored. As we know, much manipulation—the deceptive kind—comes in the guise of friendly, respectful relations. The difference lies in the fact that unlike in truly friendly relations, the ultimate goal is not the relationship, but the obtaining of the desired behavior or favor.

In this manner political manipulation cannibalizes the social relationships required to sustain political activity. This is bound to lead to the ultimate failure of the manipulator, while stymieing the political process for everyone.

The well-known political theorist William Riker makes clear the manipulative ideology so common in our times. As many others, he defines our rationality in manipulative terms, leaving no conceptual space for any non-manipulative rationality. According to Riker, for people to be rational is for them to induce, by rhetorical art "other people to join them in alliances and coalitions" and by marshaling circumstances "in such a way that other people will want to join them—or feel forced by circumstances to join them—*even without any persuasion at all* [my emphasis]."[1]

This way of conceiving of politics, which has become the prescriptive attitude in many circles, shows well the disregard for conscience that is the earmark of manipulation.

The recommendation is not to waste time trying to persuade people by an appeal to conscience when it is much easier to manipulate them in the manners described above. There is a promise of greater control and predictability of outcome. But how long can these "coalitions" last? Only as long as the deception, the promise

---

1   www.nap.edu/html/biomems/wriker.html; http://rhetorica.net/heresthetics.htm

and desirability of the reward, or the threat and fearsomeness of the punishment. Soon enough, the deception will be discovered, and a new deceptive scheme will need to be introduced or the reward will lose its appeal and have to be increased, or the punishment will lose its fearsomeness and will have to be made more severe. The maintenance costs of this method of management skyrocket ad infinitum.

In the end, the only thing left in its wake is destroyed opportunities for the formation of trust relationships, from which true alliances and coalitions are built. Trust relationships can be developed only in the context of mutual respect for one another as autonomous decision makers. Although this assertion is not denied, proponents of manipulative politics seem willing to trade away the possibility of the formation of true alliances and coalitions for the sake of greater control of outcomes, on the grounds that politics is competition, and success in competition is measured by outcomes.

The fact that the covert manipulator must appear in a non-manipulative guise reveals something important about us: we are attracted by non-manipulativeness and disgusted by manipulativeness. Political statesmen are loved and admired for appearing to be non-manipulative, while scorned for appearing manipulative. There is a big political payoff in maintaining a non-manipulative guise, while it is a death knell to appear manipulative.

I expect this fact is well known by all. What surprises me is how we fail to take it as strong evidence that perhaps one could succeed better just by not being manipulative. After all, if it is so important to maintain a non-manipulative guise, what better way is there of doing that than by not being manipulative in fact? In this manner, one would avoid the constant risk of having one's schemes exposed.

Of course, the non-manipulative politician would not be admired simply for not being a schemer. She would have to have views people could both relate to and be considered viable. This, in fact, is where the urge to scheme probably begins. The politician's recognition of the reward of telling people what they want to hear, coupled with her uncertainty in the popularity of her own convictions, may easily bring about the temptation to go the deceptive route for the sake of a successful campaign. If she trusts the soundness but not the popularity of her political convictions, why not hide them until the election is over and, in the meantime, deliver the message that has the best chance of winning people over? The thought may be that the deception will only be subservient to—and not corruptive of—a just cause.

At this point, one might ask about the purpose of politics, as well as the purpose of an individual vying for office. Every profession has a purpose to provide for a social need or demand. This fact is not obscured by the fact there may be phonies in any profession who are not professionally motivated by the purpose of their profession. Apart from these individuals, those who are drawn to a profession are in some sense responsive to its purpose, if not drawn to it for that purpose.

Whatever social good politics is supposed to procure is certainly not compatible with social destruction. Deceptive methods, as argued above, are socially destructive. Once I deceive, I have to hope the deception will never be exposed, if I hope to avoid the harm to my future relations with the deceived. Not only is this a bad bet, but it would only avert part of the damage, leaving intact the damage done to my way of viewing the public. Now I have habituated myself to viewing them not as peers whom I am called to serve, but as animals whom I must steer. This, in fact, is the worst part of the damage of manipulation, that done to the manipulator. Once I begin down this road, I am very likely to keep on it—especially if my (apparent) political success is now defined by my taking that road. I am no longer a peer of the people, so I cannot be their political servant. I am no longer their peer, because I now have a dirty secret I must keep from them forever: that I now consider them as brute animals. Thus, the purpose of politics—whatever that is—has been thoroughly circumvented. Moreover, I have alienated myself from my own purpose in entering politics—unless my purpose was false to begin with.

If manipulative politics is ultimately a sham, as I've just argued, that is reason enough to explore the possibility of non-manipulative politics,

What is non-manipulative politics? It is friendship, love, argument, and representative stewardship—all based on the principle of rational persuasion. This, in turn, is based on the acceptance that every human being is my peer as a political agent; that political action is owned by everyone, and that therefore everyone has the rights and duties of its ownership. In the political arena thus envisioned, it is not my call to force into policy the values I am attached to, but to represent those values in the argumentative process, and in such a manner that allows me to be vulnerable to persuasion by those holding opposite values. Unless I carry myself in this way, I am not treating my fellow human beings as peers, and if I am not treating them as peers, I am not pursuing any political good, no matter how correct my values may otherwise be.

Non-manipulative politics would have the power of joining people across the political spectrum. It would not be a party, nor would it be a partisan movement. It would tend to reconcile partisan divisions, since it aims against the very thing that causes political division. The natural thing for two disagreeing peers to do is argue and seek to resolve their differences persuasively. This is not an act of partisan divisiveness, but of friendship. Division enters when one side seeks to force the other to submit by manipulative means, thus offending any ties of friendship and trust that may have been present in the relationship.

The question may well be asked whether one in our times could conduct a campaign of this style with any success. That question could be answered with another one: Why keep doing things the way we've been doing them? Perhaps the only thing keeping us doing politics in the manipulative way we have been doing is because we have become addicted to it. The reason for the addiction is rather obvious, but does not amount to utter compulsion. Manipulation is capable of yielding a short-term advantage. As long as political campaigning is defined as individuals competing for office where the only successful campaigners are those who win, we are setting ourselves up for continued addiction. The way to break the addiction is to understand that the manipulative way does not even count as a striving for the social good, but is rather a knowing sacrifice of the social good for short-term individual gain. A successful campaign ought not be measured merely in terms of individuals winning elections when they are not even striving for the social good.

The least that could be said of a movement such as this is that it is morally well motivated. If a movement such as this were to succeed, it would do so based on attracting adherents who would not measure the value of their efforts in terms of short-term individual gain, which is the only relative advantage of manipulation. Such adherents would not be discouraged by losing elections as long as they were expanding the awareness of their cause. That is what political success can be defined as: a state of affairs in which non-manipulative political action thrives. In such a state, everyone would be represented, and politics would be serving a social good.

As a final note, it is not such a difficult thing to be non-manipulative. Our social instincts point us in that direction, which is the direction of building firm and enduring relationships with others.

Manipulation is more of the intruder upon our ordinary customs. It's the way we train animals or discipline a group of unruly schoolchildren. Even in the latter case, the caveats of experts point more and more to minimization of the practice. At any rate, these two examples should not serve as analogies of the political process.

CHAPTER TWENTY-SEVEN

Is Genuine Democracy Possible?

One of the great puzzles of human history since the advent of agriculture is the interweaving of the almost relentless tendency toward economic and political oligarchy with the growing popular expectation of democracy, both economic and political. Before agriculture, contrary to a popular misconception, democracy had been the norm; this on account of the fact that non-democracy is not possible in the absence of those unguarded power advantages that spawn it in the first place. The latter, in turn, are not possible without stored wealth, which ultimately derives from stored food, which agriculture made possible.

The production of surplus food generated a pattern of ever-increasing division of labor. One type of specialization that soon becomes necessary to this process is the management of stored wealth, both in the public sector—politicians of various types—and the private sector—the entrepreneur, etc. These specializations are at once necessary to a developed agricultural society and a threat to its well-being. The threat they pose is the potential overwhelming of the ongoing human struggle to create and maintain both economic and political democracy, the birthrights of human community. Unless we can avert this threat, society is eventually doomed, since the snuffing out of democracy ushers in its opposite: alienation, the bane of organizational life and society as a whole.

Unfortunately, neither of these two threats—of economic and political despotism—can be averted once and for all, but require an ongoing social commitment to prevent the accrual of unguarded power advantages derived from privileged access to concentrated wealth. In both the public and private sectors, democratic culture will be fostered by preventing not the accrual of concentrated wealth, which is necessary to the social good, but unguarded access to it.

Historically, popular ideology has been divided into two camps on how to militate against unguarded power advantage, with one camp focusing on the public sector and the other on the private. Our inability to focus our efforts simultaneously against both has set the stage for the manipulation of the masses by those harboring anti-democratic intentions, using a strategy of divide and conquer. The fact that political parties themselves, tragically in the name of democracy, have traditionally aligned themselves on either side of this ideological fault line has only served to hasten the demise of democratic traditions in both sectors, either side playing against the other as the bad guy. The sad fact is that vigilance against unguarded power in one sector alone only serves to proliferate unguarded power in the other sector.

In the midst of this confusion, we have made the mistake of casting democracy itself to be a newly minted and experimental tradition rather than part of humankind's original patrimony. This envisionment creates in us the false impression that democracy is a precarious thing that has to be invented, as if it were a machine with precise parts needing to be fitted just so in order to produce its intended results. Or that it is something that may not be suitable for some pursuits, most commonly economic ones.

Thus, the focus on creating constitutions or formal plans based on conviction in the ideal that unguarded power advantages can be balanced once and for all by a set of rules. Moreover, even these efforts are usually restricted to one sector or the other and not both.

In fact, democracy does not need to be invented by us but only rediscovered, motivated by the recognition that we cannot and ought not trust that any invented political or economic system can produce democracy for us. Such devices should be viewed as instruments subject to constant readjustment and intended primarily to prevent or regulate pockets of unguarded power in government and the economy. Not only must we keep our eye on both, but we need to recognize our doing so as part of a game or games we need to play. As games, we must maintain vigilance over their rules, monitoring them and changing them as new developments emerge.

Every institutionalized game or sport operates in this manner: its rules are constantly in flux, with a keen eye to maintaining or improving the quality of the product by modifying the rules of the game on an ongoing basis.

One example of our reluctance to act in this manner has been the Affordable Care Act. Its opponents derided the attempt at such legislation as an impossibly complex task, while its proponents contended it was a necessary step for maintaining the quality of our society heading into the future. In fact, one might easily consider both positions to be technically correct. For, arguably, not attempting some such legislation was no longer a realistic option. On the other hand, inventing a legislative package that all at once would prudently and efficiently solve our health-care problems is easily admitted to be an impossible task. But this last assertion is, in fact, a red herring. It cannot be the point of legislation to solve problems once and for all, as if we could invent laws as perfect platonic forms that would keep our affairs in balance forever. Rather, what we ought to do is consider the ACA as but the beginning of a permanent ongoing process of cooperative ongoing adjustment to correct flaws and respond to new and arising developments.

New automobile models always turn up with design flaws that will need to be fixed on the fly. Even when this is eventually done, newly arising developments will eventually necessitate further changes, and so on. We don't take all this as a convincing reason not to introduce them at all.

As with sports, automobiles, and health care, so with democracy. All that it requires is cooperation, enough to make peace between those who worry about Big Government and those who worry about the corporate takeover of government. Unless we end this fight, we will continue slipping into alienation—economic and political—instead of rediscovering democracy, the culture of universal ownership, in all our institutions.

CHAPTER TWENTY-EIGHT

Persons and Political Participation

The United States Supreme Court's 5–4 decision in 2010 in the case known as Citizens United v. Federal Election Commission, which invalidated parts of the McCain-Feingold Bipartisan Campaign Reform Act of 2002 on the grounds that it enforced an unconstitutional ban on corporations, unions, and certain other associations from their First Amendment–derived right of using Treasury funds for direct political advocacy, has rekindled debate on what constitutes being a person. Although the issue of personhood is not explicitly cited in the principal documents of the case, the motto of those favoring the Citizens United decision has been that "corporations are persons."

The personhood question sneaks into the debate via language provided by Section 1 of the Fourteenth Amendment, ostensibly regarding another topic, according to which "no State shall ... deny to any person within its jurisdiction the equal protection of the laws."

Since it is part of the common terminology of US state laws that corporations are "legal persons" in the sense that they may be sued or sue in court, some connect this sense of the term to the term as used in the Fourteenth Amendment.

All of the above moves us to reflect on what it really means to be a person. Adequate clarity will be achieved when we arrive at a criterion that will be effective in distinguishing persons from non-persons as well as persons in a limited sense from persons in an unlimited sense. It will have to also be effective in illuminating us on which sorts of agencies have the right to unlimited political participation and which don't.

One issue not at stake is voting, since this form of political participation is by law limited to citizens; in most states to citizens not serving time for felonies, and in some states to citizens never having been convicted of a felony. Political participation, however, is more than just voting, and a healthy democracy requires all kinds of political participation. The question here is whether some kinds of associations do not have the right to unlimited political speech, or whether unlimited freedom of speech applies to all corporations, unions, and associations.

The key concept to defining personhood is moral agency. Moral agency is the attribute that makes one liable to praise or blame. Dolphins are very smart, but they are not persons. If they were, then we would be treating them very differently than we do: we should be persuading them to do tricks rather than training them; we should be subjecting felonious dolphins to various fines and punishments, etc. But it is quite clear that no matter what dolphins do, we do not hold them morally responsible, for they lack moral agency.

A moral agent is distinguished from a brute animal agent in the following manner. Whereas decisions made by the latter are always functions of their immediate survival context—which never can be extended past those desire- and fear-inducing impulses that impress themselves upon the animal at the decisive moment, causing the decision to be made—moral agents, to the contrary, have the ability to extend their deliberations to freely conjured imaginations and freely recalled memories judged to be relevant to the decision to be made, thus affecting the quality of the decision.

As clear as it is that personhood is about moral agency, personhood ought not merely be equated to it, since there are different varieties of moral agency to be considered. The two most important type distinctions of moral agency are autonomous vs. subsidiary and continuous vs. discontinuous. I argue that only continuously autonomous moral agents merit the unreserved title of "person" as cited in the Fourteenth Amendment, and only they have the right to unrestricted political participation without legislative regulation.

A subsidiary moral agent is one whose range of deliberation is limited to an invented social context, much as a game piece within a game. Within this artificial context alone does it act as a moral agent, and even there only according to the charter defining its existence. One example of a subsidiary moral agent is a corporation.

A moral agent is autonomous if it is not subsidiary.

A discontinuous moral agent is one whose deliberations, considerations, and experiences of values, etc. are not ever ongoing but are broken up into distinct, noncontiguous stretches of activity and inactivity. Imagine if, *per impossibile,* someone were to invent a computer that genuinely had moral agency. Still, it would be a discontinuous moral agency since, unplugged, it would have no moral experience whatsoever. Imagine using as your exculpating alibi for some terrible crime that you happened to have been unplugged at the time!

Of course, a moral agent is continuous if it is not discontinuous. I would argue that any invented moral agency is discontinuous, because just as we create any such agency by enactment, we can discontinue it simply by ceasing to "run" it.

We all accept that human individuals are persons. Our moral agency is autonomous, not subsidiary; we exist in the world at large, we don't just exist in artificial limited contexts. Also, we have a continuous moral agency: we can't exculpate ourselves by tuning out or going into recess. We may choose to tune out, but we will still be held responsible for doing so.

Since the only continuous and autonomous moral agents we now know of are individual human beings, it follows that these are the only persons we should consider to be entitled to unlimited political participation. And this makes good sense: first, because subsidiary moral agents are by their own constitution unable to be motivated by the big picture, since their entire existence is played out within a limited, artificial game world; and secondly, because discontinuous moral agents cannot be held continuously responsible. Like viruses—whether good or bad ones—they only exist when they act.

I should take a moment to respond to criticism that an agency such as a corporation is not any kind of moral agency at all; or that it, like a felon serving time, a discredited moral agency; or like an infant, an undeveloped moral agency; or, like a rogue country, an underdeveloped moral agency.

A corporation cannot be an amoral agency, because we rightly hold it responsible within its limited sphere of existence. Admitting it to be amoral is to take it off the hook, giving it, as it were, a "black market mandate."

A corporation *per se* ought not be considered a discredited moral agency, since to argue such implies that corporations ought not exist. It would be impossible to sustain a prosperous human existence without corporations.

A corporation cannot be considered an undeveloped moral agency either, because it is run by moral agents who have social responsibility for its moral status. People cannot be reasonably held responsible for something over which they have no control, as would be the case if a corporation were really analogous to an infant. We know, moreover, that we have reasonable expectations of members of organizations to manage the organization responsibly.

Finally, a corporation should not be likened *per se* to a rogue country which, because of its position in the world with respect to other nations, has over time situated itself into dysfunctional relationships in such a manner that its very existence has become parasitic and inimical to human peace and prosperity. We can easily see that most corporations have good reasons to exist: they exist to provide a product or service, and they are mostly successful in doing so. If all corporations were parasites, we could have never made it this far.

According to the argument presented here, it would follow that Congress does have the right to limit the political participation of corporations, unions, and other associations similar to them, in that these are not the persons referred to in the Fourteenth Amendment, but are only subsidiary moral agencies, created by us to exist in special, artificial contexts of limited moral purpose.

PART VII
PROFESSIONAL ETHICS

CHAPTER TWENTY-NINE

Pharmacological Fuzz

As a college ethics professor, my attention has long been trained to warning against the dangers of recreational intoxication, which is the deliberate impairment of one's moral judgment by means of drugs or alcohol, done for the sake of entertainment or social ease. My argument against it has been twofold: the goods thereby gained are at best dubious, while the loss is significant. The loss is of the ability to be one's own caretaker. Although we may take it for granted, we are all entrusted with the sacred duty of taking good care of ourselves. This being so, deliberate intoxication is analogous to permitting the babysitter to get drunk or stoned while caring for your children. Worse yet, this recklessness is engaged in for the sake of dubious goods: prompting oneself to do or say things one would not do or say in a sober state.

The attention properly due to the moral problem of recreational intoxication should not make us fail to see another related problem emerging in our society: loss of recognition for the value of maintaining a baseline of complete sobriety. This problem has emerged largely because of the proliferation of the use of psychoactive drugs as mood- and performance-managers. As such, it is becoming increasingly more common for people to be under the influence of these drugs all or most of the time. Although usually not bringing about a state of intoxication, they work collectively to erode away our society's baseline of sobriety. The most disturbing aspect of this phenomenon is that, for the most part, it is not even seen to be a problem at all. But it is a problem—a moral problem—and we are in trouble if we don't do something about it.

I am not here advocating against the use of psychoactive drugs when necessary for mental health. Nor am I against the occasional nonintoxicating use of drugs such as alcohol for social purposes. Rather, I am arguing for the importance of the value of establishing and routinely maintaining a baseline of complete sobriety in our lives, such that each decision we make even to go slightly under the influence of a psychoactive drug be made weighing the good to be gained against the evil of the partial loss of sobriety it entails.

If we fail to see the importance of doing this, we usher in a slippery slope whereby our recognition of the moral advantage of the sober perspective becomes less and less clear to us, until we reach the point of considering sobriety as just another mental state, not privileged among its less sober alternative states. But in fact, the sober state of mind is privileged in that it is our most alert state of moral awareness *per se*, in which we are most available to others in friendship, socialness, loving, and caring. The collective loss of sobriety entails, therefore, the erosion of all these goods.

It is important for us to see complete sobriety as a virtue, not for the sake of producing a teetotaler society, but for the sake of producing a society that makes the wisest use of its psychoactive drugs, abstaining from their continuous ongoing use unless genuinely necessary.

Unfortunately, one of the symptoms of the loss of the recognition of sobriety as a virtue is that our view of what constitutes justified use of psychoactive drugs is itself changing, erring more and more on the side of less caution. To be sure, medical judgments are involved here, but one moral issue germane to the topic is the extent to which the experience of pain and suffering (from here on, "pain" will refer to both) is normal, healthy, and even necessary to a life well lived.

We all should concede there is such a thing as dysfunctional pain, and that this is the kind of pain psychoactive drugs are intended to address. But at the same time, we should also recognize that most pain is functional. Whether physical or mental, it gives us important information about the world and ourselves that we need to be aware of and act on in order to improve our lives. We seem to have more trouble acknowledging this point with respect to mental pain than physical.

We have a pretty good idea of what debilitating dysfunctional physical pain is, and that to the extent to which it conveys no further vital information to us, it is good to medicate ourselves against it so that we may return to the activities of our lives. The drugs involved are usually not psychoactive *per se*; i.e., their effect is not achieved by causing changes in our mental state, although sometimes they may have slightly woozy side effects. In only the most extreme cases is the change in mental state significant.

The pharmacological treatment of mental pain is a different story. In these cases, the drugs do their work by altering our mental state, since it is in the mind where we are experiencing the pain. It is not rare for someone to be taking several such medications simultaneously, or that their prescription(s) cover at least the bulk of their waking hours, with other complementary medications to be taken at night. Here the mental cost of erosion of our baseline of sobriety is significant. Whether the tradeoff is worthwhile depends on the value or disvalue of the pain being suppressed.

Specifically, how important are certain kinds of mental pain to us? Let me cite a few cases of mental pain important enough to our well-being that they probably ought not be targeted by medications unless not doing so threatens sanity:

+ The pain of genuine moral guilt.
+ Sadness in response to bad news.
+ Sadness in response to broken, troubled, or failed relationships.
+ Stress and anxiety in reaction to recognition of work that needs to be done or efforts that need to be made.

These are the pains we need to guide us through the most important decisions we make in life: moral reform, repairing damaged relationships, picking up the pieces after failed relationships, attending responsibly to the troubles of our lives. If these pains are deadened, so will our resultant decision making become less responsible. It's what I call "pharmacological fuzz."

If deliberate intoxication is the "holocaust sacrifice" of sobriety—its complete, all-at-once surrender—then pharmacological fuzz is its piecemeal sacrifice: a gradual erosion of our baseline of sobriety, leading ultimately to a loss of appreciation for the value of sobriety *per se*. The gravity of the latter problem is growing as more and more people sign on to the regular use of these psychoactive drugs. We need to do a better job of counting the costs and reassessing the criteria for justified use of these drugs.

CHAPTER THIRTY

A Challenge to Capitalism
Presented by Technology

Many hail capitalism as the economic engine responsible for bringing modern society through a golden age of technological development. That notwithstanding, capitalism appears also to have set itself up as a stumbling block to attaining and maintaining the proper applications of those technologies of which it has spawned so rapid a development. Capitalism's relationship to technology is in the form of a double-edged sword. It hastens the development of new technologies, but then it directs us to an irresponsible use of them.

It looks like a case of the "invisible hand," of Adam Smith[1] dropping the ball. A *laissez faire* solution of consigning ourselves to the mechanical churnings of market forces seems only to go further toward turning certain great technological achievements into unmanageable monsters. In sight of this fact, it behooves us to reconsider the nature of our social commitment to capitalism. Does the management of new technologies require us to take a few steps away from capitalism toward a more socialist approach?

In this paper, I argue that capitalism typically fails us in the distribution of products and services that rely on new or complex technology, on the grounds of the following premises:

1. Capitalism fails us in a particular respect to the extent that the result it brings is clearly not the best we should expect.
2. Lacking reliable information about new products and services is clearly not the best we should expect.
3. Reliable information depends on its chief source's uncompromised intention to be truthful.
4. In a capitalist economy, the seller is typically the chief source of information on products dependent on new and complex technology.
5. In a capitalist economy, the seller does not have the uncompromised intention to be truthful.
6. The proper distribution of products and services that depend on new and complex technology is contingent upon the consuming public being reliably informed enough to make responsible decisions.

---

1   Helen Joyce. "Adam Smith and the Invisible Hand." http://plus.maths.org/issue14/featuresd/smith.

I will develop this argument in reference to three examples of what can be considered products or services depending on new or complex technology: steroids and supplements, nuclear power, and genetically modified organisms (GMOs).

First, I define capitalism as an economic system of an unplanned market with a minimal core of proactive regulation supplemented by a slow-to-act reactive regulatory function. The minimal core consists of bankruptcy protection laws, antitrust laws, and anti-collusion laws. These are so fundamental to capitalism that they are usually not considered as government interventions, though surely they are, since they place limits on both the natural tendencies of economic competitors and also some of the harsher consequences of that competition. The slow-to-act, reactive regulatory function is just as characteristic of a capitalistic economy. Although it implies a tacit acknowledgement that capitalism here and there might need to be tweaked, the temptation to do so is supposed to be resisted until it is clear that market forces will not solve the problem without intervention.

Conversely, I define socialism as a planned market system, in which the economy is treated in a manner analogous to a corporation, to be defined proactively by a plan. Of course, reactive amendments to that plan will, from time to time, be enacted, just as in the case of a corporation amending its business plan.

One has not really sufficiently defined capitalism until one has addressed the question of its ideological justification. Here, capitalism over the years seems to have developed quite a split personality. On the one hand is the classical approach of Adam Smith, whose justification of capitalism was perfectly utilitarian: that it produces the best results for society.[2] In fact, in Smith's time and thereafter, capitalism was promoted right alongside utilitarianism and democracy, as one big utilitarian social-agenda package.[3]

On the other hand, and quite more recently, is the Ayn Rand/social Darwinist vision of capitalism, according to which "greatest results for the greatest number" don't matter, and all that matters is that the strong are allowed to prosper while the weak are allowed to die out according to a process of natural selection that is supposed to improve society in the long run.[4] Although one could press the point by arguing that this is just another kind of longer-term utilitarianism, it is far from the classical utilitarian conception, which is not given to terms of immeasurably long length.[5]

My comments here mostly regard the classical rather than the Ayn Rand conception of capitalism.

The decision to ignore the latter is based on my judgment that it is the less defensible vision of capitalism, which neither contributed to capitalism's initial ascent in popularity as an economic theory, nor ever argumentatively overtook the classical vision. It just sort of seeped into our culture; in such a manner as many of us hope it will seep back out.

By "new and/or complex technology," I intend technical production or service abilities born from advances in scientific research, the details of which have yet to be digested or adequately grasped by the educated public. Indeed, it is not rare that even specialists within a field disagree about some of the ramifications of a technology already being pressed into service for the manufacture of some new product or service soon to be—or already—on the market.

Premise 1 would be a self-explanatory corollary of Adam Smith capitalism were it not for the fact that capitalism is taken by some to be an all-or-nothing proposition. It is rather common to hear concessions made to the faults of capitalism, with the surprising rejoinder that "it's still better than socialism," with the implication that there are only two choices.[6] But, in fact, there are more than two choices. The fact that even diehard

---

2   Ibid.

3   *Malaspina Great Books.* www.malaspina.com/site/person_841.asp.

4   Leonard Peikoff. *Objectivism: The Philosophy of Ayn Rand.* http://www.peikoff.com/opar/capitalism_moral.htm.

5   "Mill's Utilitarianism." www.msu.org/ethics/content_ethics/texts/mill_utilitarianism.html.

6   "Red Pepper." October 2004. www.redpepper.org.uk/Oct2004/ESF/x-Oct2004-pga.html.

capitalists accept the occasional tweaking of capitalism in the form of some new regulation is testimony to this. The critique of capitalism can be market by market, situation by situation. Anyone can point out situations in which capitalism seems to be working well. A decent stereo console can now be purchased for less than $200 with a much better sound than top-of-the-line systems that used to go for $1,000 a generation ago.

Similar things can be said about computer equipment. Capitalism in so many cases performs as its proponents predict it should. But it doesn't always work. That is to say, it does not always produce, as promised, the best results.

Premise 2 points to an example of one case of such failure: the lack of reliable information on products and services involving new and/or complex technology. We seem accustomed to being pressed to make important decisions on products and services that we have so much difficulty gaining reliable information on. It's a jungle out there—a jungle of half-truths, where the seller is charged with a truth-oriented task without being supplied with the motivation to be truthful. Other voices have trouble being heard besides those of the sellers; there simply isn't enough money behind their voices for them not to be drowned out. Any amount of reflection on this fact should suffice for us to conclude this is not a situation we ought to accept, and that it is sheer cynicism to assume there is no better way.

Premise 3 is the keystone of the whole argument—no informer is reliable who does not have an uncompromised commitment to be truthful. This is not an unrealistic expectation. We expect so much of teachers and researchers of any kind. Whoever among this group lacks this intention simply does not belong. Nor is it "against human nature" to want to be truthful. It is not too much of a stretch for us to see that flirting with falsehood is a dangerous thing for us, and that, no matter whatever else we'd like to accomplish, we should do so in a manner consonant with being truthful.

In the context of a competitive game such as capitalism, however, truth becomes a secondary consideration. Did I have my foot on the line when I made the shot that was credited as a three-pointer? If so, one point should be taken off the scoreboard. If I know my foot was on the line, it's not for me to tell; it's up to those officiating the game. That's the nature of competitive games. But this just begs the question of who is doing the officiating in the game of capitalism. We don't seem to have worked out that part of the game yet. And we've been playing it a long time!

It's not just a matter of regulations; it's a matter of having officials to apply the regulations. But who are the officials of capitalism? Each of us? But we're playing it too, so we'd be biased.

This is not a question without an answer. There are many ways to address the problem. It is quite simply a question about capitalism that has yet to be properly addressed. Any competitive game needs good officiating to work properly—not just rule-makers, but officials. It's not that we don't have them at all; we have them in some areas, but not in others. Or we have them for a time, then no longer.

The truth of premise 4 is seen from the fact that new technology, to be economically useful in a capitalist sense, has to be shrouded in secrecy until the product or service is brought to the market. This brings about the initial effect that most of the information available comes ultimately from the seller.

But as premise 5 suggests, the seller's purpose is to sell, not to tell the truth. If the seller tells the truth, it's because telling the truth in this instance has been deemed to be the most effective sales tactic. In fact, if anything, capitalism motivates the seller to be selective in the kind of information he releases, emphasizing the sales-favorable information while suppressing what would be unfavorable to sales.

All of which leads us to the final premise (6), which expresses the fact that it is not a sign of success of an economic system that the consuming public is prodded into making purchasing decisions on high-tech products and services in a manner that is, after all, irresponsible, in that they are made in the absence of reliable information.

Before entertaining criticism of this argument, let us in further elaboration hash over several extended examples of what I am referring to, as I promised earlier.

THE CASE OF STEROIDS

If you type the word "steroids" on any search engine, it becomes easy to see how the abuse of steroids by athletes, teenagers, and bodybuilders has come about. Even today when, at last, the scientific and medical communities have really started to get out the truth about steroids, most of the information is by far geared toward their sale. If it is that way even today, one must assume the balance of information was even more tilted toward steroid use last year, even more the year before that, and so on. The difficulty in getting accurate information compared with the ease of getting pro-steroid propaganda naturally will make it quite easy for those already tempted to do so to give in to their temptations.

It is not just that for every scientific website warning about the dangers of steroids, etc. there are five or six promoting the use of steroids.[7] It is also the tactics used, which include discrediting scientific websites for having a political axe to grind (without really saying which axe that would be[8]), and the advertisement disguised as a pros and cons fact sheet.[9]

I am not in this case arguing against personal responsibility. Any person ought to know by now that steroids are dangerous to health and are life-shortening. But as long as there are people who have a vulnerability to them, stemming either from body image problems or competitive interests, their likelihood of using steroids goes up proportionately to the pro-steroid, pro-supplement information being put out.

In a way, professional athletes are sitting ducks. They are professional competitors. It is their job to be constantly looking for a secret advantage over their competition. This is just the nature of competition. If an athlete hears about a new product just out of the labs that will give him a noticeable gain in his performance, he has to be interested. If there are no rules in his sport against the use of this product, or if there is no rigorous enforcement of rules against its use, his likelihood of using them goes way up—especially if he senses other athletes may be using the substance.

Health concerns come into play more or less, since athletes are still human. But it just happens to be an occupational hazard of professional competitors that their competitiveness makes them more likely to ignore their health for the sake of performance. The great NFL quarterback Joe Montana is hailed as a sports hero for continuing to play on and win another Super Bowl years after his physician warned him that his spine had been weakened by all the hits he'd taken over his career and that one more hit in just the right spot would mean total body paralysis.[10] Ronnie Lott, the Hall of Fame cornerback, had his finger amputated so he could keep playing football.[11] It is an occupational hazard of professional competitors that they are disposed to trade away long-term values for short-term values. What they do to gain a competitive edge, even short of taking steroids, may not be in their long-term interests. It is not unreasonable therefore to come to the conclusion that they should be protected against their own inclinations.

Even more so for teenagers, who are still minors. Yet, even websites for children run advertisements for creatine.[12] Although not a steroid, it is a bodybuilding substance currently banned by the NFL and the NCAA on mounting evidence that it overworks the kidneys and eventually leads to kidney damage.[13]

---

7   Just type the word "steroid" into a search engine and you can see for yourself.

8   Creatine Information Center. http://www.creatinemonohydrate.net.

9   Frank A. Melfa. "Steroids: Information on How Steroids Work and the Risks Involved." www.thepumpingstation.com/steroids.html.

10   Larry Schwartz. "No Ordinary Joe." http://espn.go.com/classic/s/000729montanaadd.html.

11   David Falkner. "Passion Play," football star Ronnie Lott, cover story. *The Sporting News*, October 24, 1994.

12   "Making Magic Muscles." http://www.kidzworld.com/site/p1281.htm.

13   "Creatine." www.umm.edu/altmed/ConsSupplements/creatinecs.html.

NUCLEAR POWER

We know the potential that good nuclear power represents: independence from fossil fuels and a solution to the problems of the greenhouse effect, air pollution, etc. We also are familiar with the worst-case scenarios. We have seen them played out at Three Mile Island[14] and Chernobyl.[15]

What we have a difficult time knowing is, with current technology, the real likelihood of such a catastrophic event occurring today. We need to have such information to argue about what kind of risk would be an acceptable one. We can't know whether we should be using nuclear power more or less than we are now unless we can have accurate information about the risk levels involved. But the sellers and promoters of nuclear power are not motivated to come clean on this topic. Most of us are not in a position to learn these things independently of the people in the nuclear power industry; we can only speculate.

This applies also to the problem of storing nuclear waste.[16] Do we have enough space to store the waste far into the future? Do we have low-risk ways of delivering the waste products to those sites? Do we have the logistics to keep those sites forever secure? Will those sites make us more vulnerable to attack? Will the secrecy required to secure those sites make it impossible for the public to monitor how well they are being kept secure?

The point is, we may now be ready to use nuclear power safely on a larger scale, but because of the market forces of capitalism that make the intention to be truthful secondary to the intention to sell, we can't easily rely on the information we're getting.

GENETICALLY MODIFIED ORGANISMS

We know that human beings have always been genetically modifying the plants and animals that we use, ever since we began growing them ourselves. This was done traditionally by two means: inbreeding and crossbreeding. In these methods, using the natural channels of sexual reproduction, we derived new breeds of animals and plants that had more of the desired traits we wanted. As time passed, we'd realize that often the new breeds turned out also to have undesirable traits that they didn't have before. Our breeding processes had inadvertently brought out some undesirable traits.

In more recent times, we have developed methods of gene-splicing that are more fine grained than breeding methods, in that they don't throw the entire genetic material of the organism back into play, but rather select out a segment of an organism's DNA to be spliced into the genetic material of a host organism, which does not have to be of the same species. Theoretically, this should allow for more control of the outcome, since only a small percentage of new DNA is being added without losing control of the rest of the organism's genetic content. The intended result is the highlighting, introduction, or elimination of a new, selected trait without the inadvertent introduction or loss of any other trait. This sure seems like an advance over breeding technology. But there are problems.

First, to date, most of the genetic materials to be spliced into host organisms include an indefinite amount of peripheral DNA surrounding the targeted genes.[17] Despite reports of genomes having been mapped, what we have accomplished for the most part is not the identification of the exact DNA sequence of each gene, but

---

14 "The American Experience: Meltdown at Three Mile Island." www.pbs.org/wgbh/amex/three/.

15 "Chernobyl Nuclear Disaster." www.chernobyl.co.uk.

16 "Finding a Solution for Nuclear Waste." www.ocrwm.doe.gov/youth/solution.htm.

17 "Genome Mapping: A Guide to the Genetic Highway We Call the Human Genome." http://www.ncbi.nlm.nih.gov/About/primer/mapping.html.

the rough locations of each known gene on the DNA strands.[18] What we have done is identify sites on DNA strands where this or that trait is genetically ordered. When we select that area of a DNA strand for splicing, we know the gene for the selected trait is in there somewhere. But we don't know what effects the spliced DNA segment will have besides ordering that trait.

Much of the length of a typical DNA strand of an organism is, as far as we know, inoperative as far as the ordering of traits is concerned. So the splicing technique is still pretty fine grained. The chances are high that no other major trait besides the selected one will be affected by the act of gene-splicing. But it is not as sure a bet as some make it sound.[19]

Another problem is the undetermined likelihood that a gene that orders the production of a known trait may order—or contribute to the ordering of—another unknown trait.[20] There is no hard and fast rule such as "one gene, one trait." We are still dealing in the unknown to a certain degree when we are splicing genes.

A second problem is that researchers are learning that hereditary traits are not just a simple function of nuclear DNA, but that genetic material outside the nucleus plays a role we have yet to map out.[21] This makes knowledge of the interplay between nuclear DNA and extranuclear genetic material central to the future of GMO technology. Since gene-splicing usually involves the splicing of the nuclear DNA of one organism into the host cell of another, there is considerable room for uncontrolled results, due to the unmonitored mismatching of intranuclear and extranuclear genetic material.

A third problem involves which traits the sellers are aiming for in their new GMO breeds.

Capitalist market forces dictate that sellers aim for traits that would boost profitability of their enterprises: increased durability, resistance to insects and harsh weather, increased volume.

So we can readily expect that GMO technology is making the organisms that we use bigger and stronger. But will it make them better? We need to be arguing not only about whether and to what extent we should be making use of GMO technology, but also about which traits ought to be targeted by GMO technology. Capitalism does not make this kind of dialogue likely.

My point here is that we as consumers can't afford to simply play the role of judge in a Frankenstein beauty contest. We ought to be involved in the earlier stages as well.

In all three of these cases, there is a question of research pace. Capitalist research understandably puts a premium on a speedy pace. Nonetheless, research pace ought not be determined by market forces, but by scientific principle.

Also pertinent to all these cases is the fact that processes that keep the public under-informed about new high-tech products and services also lead to the festering of unreasonable suspicions and fears. This further clouds the waters, making it yet more difficult for us to make responsible decisions in these areas.

To be sure, it can be argued that the interests of truth can be served without the chief source's uncompromised intention to be truthful, since an educated public has the wherewithal to independently evaluate the claims made by sellers. In many cases, this is clearly true. When I see an advertisement, I know what to expect. I know I can't simply accept the information given in an ad as true. Moreover, I have the ability to look things up on my own. I can find out for myself what studies are out on the active ingredient of this prescription drug or that artificial sweetener. Information such as this is out there, accessible to everyone.

---

18   Ibid.

19   Ibid.

20   "Gene Therapy." http://genome.gsc.riken.go.jp/hgmis/medicine/genetherapy.html.

21   "Behavioral Genetics: Family Matters." http://dx.doi.org/10.1038/421491a.

But what if the information isn't out there? Or what if the seller has launched a campaign to discredit disinterested sources as being politically interested? What if the seller puts out so much propaganda that it has the effect of drowning out the critical voices?

All these things happen. Producers of high-tech products and services have trade secrets containing information to which the consumer has no access. Seller-supported media sources very often do their best to discredit their critics by *ad hominem* attacks suggesting they have ulterior motives. And the seller-sponsored sources usually vastly outnumber the independent sources.[22]

Moreover, the advertisement is often disguised as scientific research, and seller-sponsored sources are often pedaled off to the consumer as scientific sites. There are all kinds of deception going on.

In short, although no one should take consumers off the hook, I don't think the blame for the abuse lies principally on their shoulders, any more than the blame for our drug problem lies principally on the shoulders of addicts.

Maybe the critic deserves one concession here: that much of the problem I am pointing to is limited to cases where the seller still has privileged access to significant product information. The less this is the case, perhaps the more we can abide by the dictum *caveat emptor*.

This might, however, have the effect of extending my case beyond the limits I'd originally imposed, which were high-tech products and services. As an example, I might also point out whether we ought not buy certain kinds of meat on the grounds that the animals are raised in a cruel manner. In fact, it's not easy for me to know how veal or turkey or chickens are raised now and whether and to what extent those animals are suffering from cruel treatment. So much of the information I would need is proprietary. Animal husbandry techniques are trade secrets.[23]

Evidence of this is that so much of the data that anti-veal groups circulate is from the seventies.

Does that make the information obsolete? I don't know how I could know. And I have tried.[24]

In short, up to this point I have tried to establish that capitalism fails us in preventing or not giving us a way to be reasonably informed about products and services dependent upon new and/or complex technology. This failure also seems to extend to any situation where information critical to making responsible consumer decisions is proprietary, privileged, or shrouded in secrecy. This is a problem we really need to solve.

Various regulatory remedies come to mind, such as laws limiting the right to corporate secrecy. In fact, laws such as this already exist, including the law requiring pharmaceutical companies to share research findings in the search for cures to serious diseases.

But regulatory changes alone won't solve the problem. A law only takes a small, if distinct, bite out of the problem, leaving people, if unchanged in their basic intentions, to find their way around those laws. What is required is a change of attitude.

In particular, what we need to do is let go of the whole capitalist ideology; i.e., the cultish devotion to the notion that the main driving engines of our economy must all be competitive ones. Competitive mechanisms are good but we need also cooperative ones. Competition is a vital economic value, but so is cooperation. An economy cannot function without a healthy balance of the two.

If competition is the value that should govern our playing of the economic game, then cooperation is the value that should govern our establishment, maintenance, and monitoring of the game. No competitive game can give a good result without rigorous officiating and constant monitoring and adjustment of the rules. It is

---

22 This paragraph refers back to notes 7, 8, and 9.

23 "Laws and Regulations." http://las.rutgers.edu/manual/ch2regs.htm.

24 "Carolyn Stull." http://ucce.ucdavis.edu/datastore/detailreport.cfm. Compare also a "pro" site: www.vealfarm.com, to an "anti" site: www.noveal.com.

this cooperative function that makes Adam Smith's vision come true. Without it, capitalism is just the black market. Just to assume that competition on its own will bring the best result for society is rash.

A first step in the direction of letting go of the capitalist ideology is to recognize that we are not as capitalist as we think we are. We already have many socialist mechanisms built into our economy: the graduated income tax,[25] Social Security,[26] welfare,[27] public postal service,[28] public works,[29] and public schooling,[30] to name a few.

More telling perhaps than any of these is the fact that our local economies are often more socialist than they are capitalist, because of two mechanisms: zoning laws and town planning boards. Because of these two downright socialist mechanisms, we manage to protect the local environs of our more well-to-do communities from the scarring effects of unmitigated capitalist growth and decay. In these communities, which are typically the ones in which our most prominent capitalist tycoons choose to live, the local economies are planned. Predictably, there will be no body-piercing salon on Connecticut's Greenwich Avenue, and you won't find a McDonald's in Darien—except for the one on the interstate. Predictably, there will probably be no body-piercing salon or McDonald's on the main streets of our wealthiest municipalities; just as predictably, the adult bookstores and discount liquor stores will be conveniently located just across their borders with less affluent communities.

I am not suggesting it is wrong for communities to plan their local economies. I'm just calling for a general acknowledgement that this is what we are doing, and that it is socialist, and therefore we are not as capitalist as we think we are. Once we recognize this, perhaps we can be free to consider the possibility that here and there it may be necessary to introduce other socialist mechanisms into our economy to remedy problems.

Economic organizations don't live in a vacuum; they live in the community. As such, they have to be attentive to their relationship to the community. If the community has a clear expectation of them, organizations are usually compelled to respond. They know their lifeblood depends on good community relations. That is why public relations are a basic component of corporate infrastructure.

Corporations have the ability to scale back their competitiveness for the purpose of joining in a cooperative effort, if they have assurances their competitors will not be taking advantage of them for it. Sure, there is fierce competition in the economy, but the competition typically takes place within the prescribed parameters of the game. If we change the rules of the game to require more interorganizational and more public-private cooperation in the development of new technologies for the purposes of keeping the public responsibly informed (and extend this change, perhaps, to other cases where the public has a vital interest in evaluating the private workings of an industry, such as many believe to be the case with respect to the veal industry), we have reason to expect cooperation would occur. But the public has to be behind it.

---

25   Both sides agree: www.wjmiller.ne; www.sochealth.co.uk.

26   Here, too: www.ncpa.org; www.socialistappeal.org.

27   Robert A. Sirico. "The U.S. After the Welfare State," *American Civilization*, v. 1, Issue 4, March 1995.

28   Sheldon Richman. "Separating School and State: How to Liberate American Families." www.sntp.net/education/school_state_main.htm.

29   "Social Democracy: New Deal Liberalism for Today's America." www.geocities.com/fineyoungsocialist/newdeal.html.

30   "The Socialist" (January 2005). www.socialistparty.net/pub/pages/socialist002jan05/6.htm; Jacob G. Hornberger. "The Conservative Commitment to Educational Socialism." www.fff.org/freedom/0998a.asp.

CHAPTER THIRTY-ONE

Does Bilingual Education Work?

Many seem to have been persuaded that bilingual education should be abolished on the grounds that it "does not work." This is often supported by anecdotal reference to immigrant children succeeding in school without it. Such anecdotes typically begin with a small child arriving on our shores speaking her native tongue and "not a word of English," and end with that child having become "fluent" in English, speaking "with no accent" and speaking "nothing but English." This kind of story speaks to a surprisingly large group of people in our country, who seem to have been sour on the idea of bilingual education from the start.

A small but dedicated group of anti-bilingual education researchers gives an air of respectability to what might otherwise be more clearly seen as a movement guided by a fear that any kind of public embracing of first languages other than English is a threat to national unity. These researchers rarely state this to be their concern. But the name of at least one of their websites tells another story: www.onenation.org.

As Jeff MacSwan of Arizona State University points out, those who oppose bilingual education have public sentiment in their favor, and know it ("Facts Elude Politicians's Perspective," *East Valley Tribune* [Arizona], Nov. 13, 2000). They are embraced by the mainstream virtually without even having to make a case for their position. "There's just so much overt and covert racism in our society to fuel [opposition to bilingual education] and so much suspicion that large groups of immigrants are opposed to assimilation. Many people are just looking for an excuse to vote against bilingual education." The convenience of this marriage with public sentiment affords them the luxury of spending nearly all their energy in discrediting bilingual education without having to be concerned with the quality of their arguments. It is a strategy of attrition, of jumping on bandwagons and riding them full tilt, in which all that really counts—or is counted—is the headline.

Prefatory Note: This essay was written in 2001, before Bilingual Education as we then knew it became illegal in Massachusetts, my state of residence. In 2002, Massachusetts joined California and Arizona in banning Bilingual Education in most of its forms. While the movement to make Bilingual Education illegal in states has since stalled, it is holding its ground in the states where it succeeded.

New batches of such anecdotal reporting typically follow on the heels of media articles hinting at the ineffectiveness or at least non-necessity of bilingual education—such as Louis Sahagun's famous January 13, 1999, *Los Angeles Times* front-page article—or of mere editorial mention of it months, or even years, later. Sahagun's article was a progress report on the performance of language-minority students in the Los Angeles area roughly a year after the California legislature, with the passing of Proposition 227, had officially abolished bilingual education throughout the state's public school system. The article noted some scattered but noteworthy short-term improvement in standardized test scores among these students since 227 had been put into effect, and hinted that perhaps these students were better off without bilingual educational services.

It is important to note, as does Stephen Krashen ("Why Bilingual Education?" in *ERIC Clearinghouse on Rural Education and Small Schools.*[1] See also, by the same author, *Condemned Without a Trial: Bogus Arguments Against Bilingual Education.* Heinemann, 1999) that the article in its entirety is no glowing appraisal of Proposition 227, but only a tentative, qualified appraisal of it. It is equally important to note that the evidence on which this modestly positive appraisal is based had already been anticipated by comprehensive studies whose conclusions favor bilingual education, as we shall review below.

The paucity of proof in favor of what bilingual education opponents propose is indicated by how far afield they go looking for it. One startling example is a 1996 research review (Christine Rossell and Keith Baker. 1996. "The Effectiveness of Bilingual Education." In *Research in the Teaching of English*, 30, 7–74) that seeks support for their theory of "structured immersion" as preferable to native language instruction by citing a South African study from 1946. (E. G. Malherbe. *The Bilingual School: A Study of Bilingualism in South Africa*). This was long before bilingual educational theory as we know it existed. (There are serious questions whether this study is even about structured immersion at all. See Stephen Krashen's "Why Malherbe is NOT Evidence Against Bilingual Education."[2])

But the problem in this debate is not just ignored or overemphasized evidence. There is also a philosophical problem, regarding what is meant by the question: Does bilingual education work? Obfuscation on the meaning of this question leads to fallaciously drawn conclusions no less than does the unbalanced marshaling of evidence. These are the two issues addressed in this essay, in which I hope to establish on grounds both philosophical and empirical that bilingual education not only is indispensable but also clearly does work.

First, let us settle the matter about what it means to ask whether bilingual education works. The case that it does not work usually goes like this:

> Our main language minority group in public school systems across this country—non-English-speaking Hispanics—are typically grouped in bilingual education programs. But Hispanics as a whole have the worst educational problems, as indicated by dropout rates and performance on standardized tests. Therefore, bilingual education must not be working.

By this way of reasoning, bilingual education is deemed to be guilty by association, with the implication being that if bilingual education worked, Hispanics wouldn't have worse educational problems that their non-Hispanic peers. It is apparently not imagined by those who argue this that the causes of these educational problems may be other than bilingual education, and that bilingual education may even be taking a significant bite out of these problems. A further insult to sound reasoning is the frustrating fact that the evidence regarding the educational problems of Hispanics is most often unanalyzed ethnically grouped data that fudges together the

---

1   http://ericae.net/ericdb/ED403101.htm
2   http://www.languagepolicy.net/archives/Krashen4.htm

statistics of all Hispanic students, whether they are in bilingual education programs or not, with no allowance made for new arrivals, etc. The troubling evidence might actually favor bilingual education if the problems are shown to be caused by not enough bilingual educational services being provided.

When I speak of the prejudice against bilingual education, I am not suggesting that those who oppose it are necessarily prejudiced, nor that they are the originators of it through their research. Prejudice, by definition, is established before research. It comes from gut feelings that we are tempted to trust because they fit into our worldview so well. Everyone wants to feel comfortable at home, and we feel less comfortable when we encounter foreign or alien elements on what we consider our "home" turf. Of course, as rational beings, we are called not to fall victim to our prejudices.

It seems clear, though, that opponents of bilingual education have given themselves over to a politicized approach. Their argument strategy is not to themselves provide proof for their theories, but to force a stalemate, one they believe would favor an end to bilingual education, which by their description is a very expensive program. Of course, expensive programs that can't be proven effective should be terminated. It all seems so logical.

But there is a problem. They are playing one of the oldest argumentative tricks in the book: instead of trying to prove something yourself, demand comprehensive proof from your opponent. Then chalk up your opponent's failure to produce one as conclusive evidence of the stalemate you were angling for. This way of arguing is a trick because no one can ever provide comprehensive proof. One can always take issue with something, whether regarding the claims of the research (which it hardly ever is for critics of bilingual education) or the methodology (which it usually is).

Besides the fact that their overall argumentative strategy is based on what is essentially a logical fallacy, they are still mistaken in their claim that bilingual education research is stalemated. A genuine stalemate in research is arrived at only when research cannot advance or bring progress to a field of study. In this respect, bilingual education research is clearly not stalemated. I can cite several examples of universally accepted results of bilingual educational research that no one, not even its opponents, contends with.

1. Despite the disfiguring caricatures, bilingual education, led by uncontested research, has been moving away from "pull-out" programs that segregate English-language learners from mainstream students, and have been finding increasingly more ways to integrate. The best example of this movement is the dual language approach, in which native speakers are grouped with language learners so that the English learners can learn a second language while the English learners learn English.

2. Again, cued by uncontested research, bilingual education has been moving decisively toward a two-language model, whereby English learners work on their literacy skills in both languages simultaneously.

3. Following decisive research findings, bilingual education has in recent years stressed the intimate connection between its two key components: native-language instruction and second-language instruction (ESL), and geared the latter more toward subject-area instruction supplemented by a variety of types of non-verbal "comprehensive input."

These changes have kept bilingual education on the cutting edge. With that in mind, it is difficult to see how someone could consider the research that led to these changes stalemated. Moreover, any attack on bilingual education that ignores the existence of these now central features of it ought to be considered obsolete.

But let's be fair. The question might be asked: Who's politicizing? This is a charge that can be thrown cheaply either way. Therefore, I propose the following definitions to be the basis for deciding if a perspective is politicized.

A perspective is politicized if it shows persistent lack of regard for the common-ground details of a subject matter in a way that aligns itself with superficial public sentiment on an issue.

Moreover, let us attend to a distinction between considered public opinion, on the one hand, and superficial public sentiment on the other. Considered public opinion is the prevailing view of the public on a matter about which it is sufficiently well informed, whereas mere public sentiment is the prevailing view of the public on a matter without regard to how well informed it is.

As suggested in Hakuta and August (see citation below, page 8, paragraph 2), much bilingual education research is politicized to the point where it is of dubious scientific value. To be fair, they were pointing an accusatory finger in both directions. But I think the case against the opponents of bilingual education is far more serious, since they are clearly putting up a unified front aimed not at gaining more insight into an educational program, but at discrediting the program wholesale. This strategy goes directly against the recommendations of Hakuta and August, which opponents so often cite.

I identify eight features of the case fashioned against bilingual education that indicate quite clearly that it is a politicized rather than scientific perspective:

1. They accept public sentiment against bilingual education as an objective indictment of it, even though, as all would have to agree, prejudice against bilingual education is widespread.

2. Bilingual education is characterized monolithically as a method that segregates English-language learners from their native-speaking peers, despite the common awareness that updated methods of bilingual education do not have this feature. (Jim Cummins. *The Ethics of Doublethink: Language Rights and the Bilingual Education Debate.* University of Toronto[3])

3. Bilingual education is described as if it consists almost entirely of native-language instruction, even though they are well aware that the preferred methods are intended to include an equal component of English-language instruction (ESL or ELL).

4. They fail to challenge the notorious myths of second-language-learning that their less knowledgeable but more famous allies trumpet as cornerstones of their case against bilingual education.

5. They engage in wild mischaracterization of research in an attempt to show how neutral parties and even bilingual education supporters acknowledge the failure of bilingual education, or that their "structured immersion" method somehow has an established track record that it really doesn't have.

6. They have clearly adopted a cynical stalemate strategy that could only be successful in tandem with the support of biased public sentiment.

7. They implicitly support divestiture in English-language learning even while claiming to be advocates of English-language learners.

8. They exploit the gap that always exists between theory and execution, fallaciously considering bad execution as proof of bad theory.

As reported in an interview (*The Valley Advocate*, April 11–17, 2002), Dr. Rosalie Porter was by her own description surprised by the fact that Spanish-speaking parents "did not demand native-language instruction. They asked only that their children learn English ..." She apparently considers this as evidence against bilingual education.

Dr. Christine Rossell also considers this a major point against bilingual education ("Statement of Christine H. Rossell." 105th Congress House of Representatives. *Hearing on Reforming Bilingual Education.* April 30, 1998).

---

3   http://iteachilearn.org/cummins/researchbildebate.html

In fact, I am rather startled that researchers should base their conclusions on the quality of a controversial program in significant part on unqualified public sentiment. If you ask people their opinion on matters in which they are not well-informed, or feel social pressures, the views they express cannot be regarded as reliable indicators of their considered opinion expressed after having been sufficiently well informed and inoculated against the social pressures of perceived prejudice in the mainstream.

One can easily imagine what Hispanic or Vietnamese or Russian or just about any immigrant parents would say to their children's teachers: "We want our children to learn English as well and as quickly as possible. We don't want our children to be taught in their native language if that would be an impediment and not a help to their becoming fluent and literate users of English." If you then plant the notion that the antecedent is in fact true, then naturally they will accede to the consequent.

Everyone knows this is what parents want. What we disagree on is what is the best way to do this. Opponents of bilingual education ride the wave of prejudice against bilingual education that inclines one to believe the best and quickest way to learn English is by being immersed in it without the support of native-language instruction.

Monolithic depiction of bilingual education is unprofessional, regardless of one's eventual judgment about it. Characterization comes before judgment; the reverse is a fallacy. Porter monolithically depicts it as a program that segregates English-language learners from their native-speaking peers. In the Introduction to her 1990 work, *Forked Tongue—The Politics of Bilingual Education* (Basic Books, 1990), she calls bilingual education "essentially segregative."

Porter and Rossell continue their monolithic sketch by depicting bilingual education as almost all native-language instruction. In her article, "The Federal Bilingual Education Program" (*Brookings Papers on Education Policy 2000* (2000), 215–243)[4], Rossell defines bilingual education as "native tongue instruction, characterized by learning to read and write in the native tongue and learning subject matter in the native tongue and eventually transitioning to English." Porter largely follows suit. In the above-cited interview in *The Valley Advocate*, it is clear she is using "bilingual education" as a synonym for "native-language instruction," as she does in most of her writings. All this, despite the fact she occasionally makes mention of other more current models that do not fit this description, such as two-way and integrated models.

In fact, the transitional bilingual education model—the model prevalent in the United States—requires, on the whole, equal components of instruction in native language and English as a Second Language (English only), tapering off more and more to favor the latter as the student progresses in the second language.

Prejudice against bilingual education is supported by different myths. (Krashen, "Bilingual Education Works"[5]; Barry Mclaughlin, "Myths and Misconceptions of Second-Language Learning"[6]) One myth in particular stands out most egregiously, namely that children learn second languages quickly and easily. Ronald Unz says this flat out in a post-Proposition 227 interview with Ben Wattenberg. As Krashen remarked at the time, he should know better. So should Porter and Rossell—and, of course, they do; yet they are quite silent on this point. One should distance oneself from faulty support of one's convictions. Intellectual alliances ought not be based on common conclusions alone, but also on common grounds. This kind of catering to prejudice is demagoguery.

The fact is, children in an integrated environment usually learn to assimilate street talk or playground talk rather quickly, including very often dropping their native accent; but this is no indication they are on the road to academic proficiency. Oral proficiency and literacy are two very different things. Success in one is not

---

4   http://www.jstor.org/discover/10.2307/20067223?uid=2&uid=4&sid=21104208791123

5   http://www.rethinkingschools.org/special_reports/bilingual/Bi152.shtml

6   http://www.cal.org/resources/digest/myths.html

a reliable indicator of success in the other. A child in need of bilingual education, left to her own devices, will typically develop language acquisition disorders (LAD). These are survival adjustment language learners that become serious obstacles to full, literate fluency in the second language—and even in the first language! People with LADs typically have parceled out language skills alternately to their two (or more) languages, so that they end up without a complete set of fluency and literacy skills in any one language. Proceeding in this manner usually blocks full literacy in any language, locking the affected person into a semi-literate trap that is very difficult to exit later on, and that can carry severe social consequences.

If we pay attention to the details of language learning and get past the myths, we see that it takes years to become literate in a second language, and the process is more complicated when one lacks literacy in the first language. This is the indisputable grounds for concluding that English-learning students should have the benefit of native-language support time blocks as long as they need them, and always interspersed, as bilingual education theory has long insisted, with English-immersion blocks, or ESL. The exact combination of the two should be determined and adjusted according to a balanced consideration of the values of subject area learning, literacy skills, and level of English language proficiency.

Porter demonstrates the propensity to widely miss the mark in interpreting the literature in her article, "The Benefits of English Immersion":

> Most disturbing of all, the high school dropout rates for Hispanic students (Spanish speakers) has not improved in the past quarter century. Two-thirds of the limited-English children in U.S. public schools are Spanish speakers, the group most heavily involved in native language instruction programs.
> (US Department of Education. February 1998. Executive summary. *No more excuses: The final report of the Hispanic dropout project.* Washington, DC.)

Porter's parenthetical comment, significantly, is incorrect, and in fact notoriously caters to the prejudiced conception that whatever is wrong with Hispanic students is the fault of bilingual education. Most Hispanic students in this country, by far, are never in bilingual programs (nor are they all, by far, Spanish speakers). In contrast, a much higher percentage of them, for example, live in poverty or are from broken families. The report covers all Hispanics, and states that all Hispanics enrolled at one time in US schools have a 20% dropout rate.

That most bilingual students in this country are Hispanic is not significant to linking bilingual education to the high dropout rate among Hispanics. The significant statistic is what percentage of Hispanics are in bilingual education.

At any rate, Porter surprisingly misreads even the intent of the US Department of Education publication that she cites. Here's another quote taken from the same page she cited from:

> Gaps in school completion rates between Hispanic and non-Hispanic students remain even after controlling for the social class background of students, for their *language proficiency*, and for their immigrant status [italics mine].

The clear inference to make from this study, then, is that the cause for the gap is, quite to the contrary of what Porter infers, something other than lack of language proficiency. So clearly, her attempt to pin the high Hispanic dropout rate on bilingual education is not supported by the very study she chose to cite.

---

7   http://www.ascd.org/publications/educational-leadership/dec99/vol57/num04/The-Benefits-of-English-Immersion.aspx

Porter revealed more of the same line of thought in her interview with *The Valley Advocate*, in which she says her turn against bilingual education—she was once, as she puts it, a "believer"—is moved mainly by a 1997 federal study conducted by the National Research Council of the National Academy of Sciences:

> The study looked at 30 years of bilingual research and came up with two stunning conclusions: the first is that there is no evidence that a program of native-language instruction has any greater benefits than any other kind of program. And the second was that teaching children to read in English first, instead of in their native language, does not have negative consequences.

The study Porter referred to is titled *Improving Schooling for Language-Minority Children—A Research Agenda* (Diane August and Kenji Hakuta, eds. National Academy Press. 1997). But she is incorrect in her assessment of the study's conclusions. The thirty-year research review contained in this study did cover another study, published in 1978 (American Institutes for Research Study. Dannoff, MN.), that came to the conclusions she stated. But this study was not endorsed by August and Hakuta. Maybe this was the source of Porter's confusion.

The real gist of the study is this, in the words of August and Hakuta themselves:

> It is difficult to synthesize the program evaluations of bilingual education because of the extreme politicization of the process. ... [M]ost consumers of this research are not researchers who want to know the truth, but advocates who are convinced of the absolute correctness of their positions. (August and Hakuta, p. 148.)

In short, the reason the committee headed by Hakuta and August were not able to say anything more definitive was because they were stymied by the politicization of the topic.

In his above-cited article "Doublethink," Jim Cummins also notes that Porter is sometimes criticized by her own allies on this point, as when Keith Baker in two articles—one a critical review of Porter's book *Forked Tongue* (Baker, 1992), and the other from the journal *Phi Delta Kappan* (Baker, 1998)—criticizes Porter for misreading the gist of two reports. In Baker's words:

> She summarizes a report from El Paso (1987) as finding that an all-English immersion program was superior to bilingual education programs. The El Paso report has no such finding. What Porter describes as an all-English immersion program in El Paso is, in fact, a Spanish-English dual immersion program. The El Paso study supports the claims of bilingual education advocates that most bilingual education programs do not use enough of the native language. It does not support Porter's claims that they should use less.

and:

> " ... Like El Paso, San Diego has an extensive two-language program. Like El Paso, there is evidence that the extensive bilingual education program worked better than the typical bilingual education program. ... Like El Paso, the results of the San Diego study argue for more bilingual education programs, not fewer as Porter maintains" (p. 6).

Rossell herself seems to be way off in her assessment of the Malherbe study (1946, cited above) as supportive of what she and her associates call "structured immersion." Still in "Doublethink," Jim Cummins, himself Canadian, is astonished at how widely Rossell misses the mark in her interpretation of Canadian language studies:

Her arguments for structured English immersion programs are based overwhelmingly on the documented success of bilingual and trilingual programs. Rossell and Baker ["The effectiveness of bilingual education." *Research in the Teaching of English, 30, 7–74.*] reviewed a large number of program evaluations and cite ten research studies which they claim show structured immersion to be superior to transitional bilingual education (TBE). Specifically, they claim that in comparisons of reading performance in TBE versus Structured Immersion, no difference was found in 17 percent and structured immersion was significantly superior to TBE in 83 percent of studies. These statistics sound impressive but they obscure the fact that nine out of ten of the so-called "structured immersion" programs were actually bilingual or trilingual programs.

It is remarkable that none of this sloppiness has hurt the popularity of their cause. It is equally stunning that their failure to cite evidence of the effectiveness of the program they propose to replace bilingual education has not noticeably slowed their movement either. By the almost impossibly rigid standards they set for what would constitute good proof that bilingual education works, I don't think their method would stand a chance.

But none of this really matters, for they have the trump card in their hands, and one has to believe that they know it. That trump card is the prejudice of the masses. The vast majority of those who support the cause against bilingual education do not do so on account of Rosalie Porter's works or Christine Rossell's research reviews. Their minds were already made up.

The way that Porter and Rossell argue their cause doesn't make sense except on the assumption they understand and intend to exploit the fact that public prejudice is on their side. Rather than try to argue that bilingual education doesn't work, they claim that research roughly indicates a stalemate. This appearance of stalemate is created by the especially rigid criteria they use to weed out the most favorable studies as not constituting evidence at all, coupled with their characterization of their own research reviews as part of the research base itself. More surprising is that they go from the seemingly passive position of stalemate to infer audaciously that a stalemate in the research is reason enough to drop bilingual education and try something else. Something else cheaper.

The American prejudice against bilingual education has two components. First, Americans fear that people coming to our shores lately don't want to assimilate. We fear that people's desire to retain their native languages, a privilege many of us sourly recall was not enjoyed by their own ancestors, is an indication that they intend to resist learning English. They tend to see bilingual education as a political entitlement extracted by immigrants, mostly Hispanic, during the civil rights movement as a means of resisting their assimilation into the mainstream.

The second component of our prejudice is a notion that no researcher on either side would accept: that second-language learning for children is automatic, requiring only intense exposure to it without "interference" from the native tongue. So the blame goes on continued use of the native tongue, and the prescription is to abandon the native tongue. Going not so far back into the past, this was the explicit recommendation made to immigrant parents: speak to your children in English only if you want your children to succeed. I dare say, this is still the way most Americans think, though even Porter and Rossell would have to admit it to be quite wrongheaded. Nevertheless, it is from people who think just this way that their movement draws the bulk of its support.

To be sure, Porter makes it clear she does not want to see a return to the way things were before bilingual education (*The Valley Advocate*). But banning the use of the native language is what she recommends, and that is the essential ingredient of the way things were.

In short, their stalemate strategy gives them the luxurious illusion of being in the catbird seat. This allows them to continue presenting to the public cases of bad execution as indictments of the theory itself. Just as tellingly, they continue ignoring how the actual positive results of the research have transformed the methodology beyond the reach of their criticism seen even in the best light. They can do all this because public sentiment is little concerned about how effective their "structured immersion" method will be. No one will ever call them on the carpet for the eventual failure of this method, because its failure will never be noted. Instead, it will be attributed to other kinds of failure within the immigrant community itself. This is the advantage of playing on the side of prejudiced public sentiment. Prejudice always excuses itself.

To get to higher ground, I propose that we accept the meaning of the question whether bilingual education works as the following:

> Are language minority students limited in English proficiency better off with bilingual education than without it?

If the answer to this question is affirmative, then bilingual education works.

We are being biased if we consider scattered anecdotes as making, even collectively, a serious case for the abolition of bilingual education. For anyone who cares to look, there is, in fact, good evidence that bilingual education works. There is evidence in the form of long-term studies, not mere anecdotal evidence or one-year snapshots. This includes studies funded by those who had set out originally to discredit bilingual education; e.g., the Reagan administration in 1983 (see J. David Ramirez, *et al.* 1991. *Final Report. Longitudinal Study of an English Immersion Strategy and an Early-Exit Transitional Bilingual Education Program for Language-Minority Children.* San Mateo CA: Aguirre International; and Julie A. Miller. "Native Language Instruction Found to Aid L.E.P.'s" in *Education Week*, v. 6, #9, Oct. 31, 1990, p. 1) along with other respected scholars such as Wayne Thomas and Virginia Collier (1997. *School Effectiveness for Language Minority Students.* Washington, DC: National Clearinghouse for Bilingual Education). McQuillan and Tse (1996) report that between 1984 to 1994, 87 percent of academic studies on bilingual education were favorable ("Does Research Really Matter?" in *Bilingual Research Journal*, 20 (1): 1–17).

The long-term studies conducted by Virginia Collier reveal something a bit surprising at first, but which would account for our propensity for coming up with short-term anecdotal indictments of bilingual education: doing without bilingual education *does* give a short-term boost to test scores; however, that is paid for dearly later on, in the form of a definitive fizzling out of academic and cognitive performance.

We need to see that the education of a child is a long-term project, and ought to be judged in the long term. If I want to build a tall tower but lack patience, I might neglect to first build a wide, sturdy foundation in order instead to attain a measurable height more quickly. After a short time, I might be praised for the height of my tower, while my more patient neighbor, who took the time to build a proper foundation, gets criticized for not having attained a certain height. As the years go on, however, it will appear evident who has followed the wiser policy. My neighbor, building on a wide, sturdy foundation, will eventually be able to reach heights that would cause my tower, on its narrow, flimsy foundations, to crumble.

The issue is not how quickly these children learn to speak English, but how well they can acquire literacy skills in English. A young immigrant child can learn to speak street English without an accent in a year, but that is no measure of her progress toward literacy or academic success.

Nor is the issue—surely we know better—whether or how quickly a child loses the use of her own native tongue. I can't imagine why educators should consider this a good sign.

Some of us, apparently, have difficulty conceding the simple fact that learning a second language requires the supportive use of one's native idiom, especially at the rudimentary stages. If a child succeeds in learning a second language from scratch without native-language support in the schools, you better believe she's been receiving it elsewhere. This kind of extracurricular support typically occurs with middle-class immigrants or immigrants with well-organized community support systems. But not all of our young immigrant students have either of these luxuries. It would be a grave violation of our duties to wash our hands of providing these services to those in need of them.

One way or the other, our immigrants do learn English. But all too often, as anyone close to them can see, they develop language acquisition disorders, which stand as serious obstacles to their ever really becoming literate—in any language. It is a typical scourge of children left to their own devices. Just as children who learn to swim without formal instruction usually end up with defective strokes, non-native speakers of English who lack good bilingual educational services usually develop language acquisition disorders. Non-native speakers, especially in the early stages, have different educational needs than native speakers. If these needs aren't addressed, they won't turn out well educated. Addressing these needs is what bilingual education is all about.

Some of us are rankled by the fact that instruction is being given in languages other than English. They don't see how this could be helping a child learn English. But it is really not hard to understand the connection. Most of the people who begin receiving bilingual educational services are children who have not acquired literacy in their native tongues. Literacy in a second language comes much more easily if it has the support of first-language literacy. The "immersion" strategy only works with handpicked groups of students who are already literate in their native idioms.

The preliterate, non-English-speaking child clearly has more work to do to become literate in English than do preliterate English-speaking children. Why so many of us expect them somehow not to require more time for the task is a mystery to me. While we're on the subject, another mystery that baffles me is why we think taking away the use of a child's most significant learning instrument—her native tongue—will expedite the process of her becoming literate in English. To the contrary, it should be recognized that acquiring literacy in one's native tongue should be the best means to expedite the process of acquiring literacy in English.

An irony of the attack on bilingual education is that a major component of English as a Second Language (ESL) involves teaching the English language *using* English, which is just what the abolitionists seem to be calling for. I should think they would want to emphasize this component, and favor whatever is required to strengthen its effectiveness. This is where they would be most surprised to learn what ESL teachers consider as indispensable to their own success: the support of native-language instruction.

In *Roads to Freedom* (Routledge, 1970), British philosopher Bertrand Russell noted:

> If a man is offered a fact which goes against his instincts, he will scrutinize it closely, and unless the evidence is overwhelming, he will refuse to believe it. If, on the other hand, he is offered something which affords a reason for acting in accordance to his instincts, he will accept it even on the slightest evidence.

I think this characterizes our national attitude toward bilingual education: we oppose it because it goes against our culturally bred "instincts," not because the evidence warrants opposition to it. The proof of this is in how we pounce on and magnify the least alleged shred of anecdotal evidence against bilingual education, while ignoring the great balance of well-researched evidence in its favor.

Out of our frustration at seeing the disproportionately poor academic performance rates of Hispanic students, coupled with their disproportionately high dropout rate, we have hastily come to the conclusion that bilingual education has failed and should be abolished. This is no more justified than coming to the same conclusion about mathematics, given the dismal performance rates of students nationally. The correct conclusion is that, without pointing fingers, we need to do what we can to improve and perfect bilingual education.

Pointing fingers is inappropriate, since the main causes for student failure in this country have overwhelmingly more to do with what is or is not going on at home than at school.

Bilingual education works in the sense that, in the long run, we would be much worse off without it than with it. Let's focus our efforts not on abolishing it, but on making it work better.

CHAPTER THIRTY-TWO

Academic Narcissism

In the struggle for economic stability and success, higher educational institutions compete against one another on a variety of playing fields: diversity, affordability to students, compensation of faculty, the fine-tuning of admissions standards, physical plant, breadth of curriculum, and landscaping are among some more easily noticeable ones. But there is one area of competition, one particular, highly coveted quality, which, in spite of its abstractness, stands out to academic marketers as a definitive selling point, a defining quality of academic hegemony: prestige.

In pursuit of this elusive quality, institutions of higher learning may to some extent try to create it themselves, perhaps, for example, by tightening admissions standards—if they can afford to. But by and large, prestige is a quality that cannot be generated or grown on the spot in a short term. As a result, it needs to be imported in the form of bringing in professors who have attained this precious, if subtle, commodity within their disciplines. Therefore, the gain and retention of prestigious professors, or those at least on the verge of prestige, is pursued as a principle way of increasing and maintaining institutional prestige itself.

This shifts the question to how professors acquire prestige in the first place. We should not fail to acknowledge that some professors may gain prestige without directly seeking it, simply based on the public notice of the excellence of their work. Yet although we may wish or pretend that all individual academic prestige is acquired in this manner, we would be dishonest not to acknowledge that many academics pursue prestige directly as a central focus of their professional ambition. They may do this either because they were drawn to this career in the first place for the sake of prestige, or probably much more commonly, they feel pressured to do so by the knowledge that the extent of their attainment of prestige is the main criterion upon which they ultimately will be judged in their fields and by their employing institutions. In either case, it is this academic demand for prestige which is the spur for both the accretion and development of academic narcissism in higher education.

Note to reader: This was written as part of an extended reflection on the recent experiences of a former student who is now a graduate student at another institution. I omit mention of details not only for the sake of confidentiality, but also for prudential reasons, as the case is ongoing. This paper was inspired by recognition of the fact that this student's situation is not unique, but is related to troubles common to academia.

To be sure, there is nothing wrong with prestige, per se. But arguably, it is not a quality that should be pursued directly, on the grounds that for individuals to do so corrupts the mind and promotes narcissism, a quality detrimental to academic institutions in several keys ways discussed below. In fact, perhaps we can agree that not genuine but only ostensible" prestige can be acquired by direct pursuit as a fulfillment of one's ambition; this since genuine prestige is in turn dominated by the quality of moral integrity, which shuns self-aggrandizement for the sake of pursuing collegiality.

Dr. Sam Vaknin, author of Malicious Self-Love: Narcissism Revisited (2001), defines narcissism as a disordered self-love which brings about "infatuation and obsession with one's self to the exclusion of others" combined with "the ruthless pursuit of one's gratification, dominance, and ambition." Clearly, it is not the mere love of self that concerns us presently, for self-love is an essential feature of healthy and happy human life. Narcissism is a peculiar disorder afflicting self-love with harmful and antisocial features.

The reason the academic profession is prone to a higher incidence of those afflicted with this disorder is that academic culture craves prestige, and the obsessive quest for prestige has the unfortunate effect of attracting and cultivating narcissists.

We could just write off academic narcissism as a minor personality flaw that comes with the trade, and no doubt many cases of it are perhaps minor enough to be treated in this manner. But narcissism in academia all too often rises to proportions so harmful as to be, at least in the longer run, socially and institutionally detrimental and dysfunctional. In what follows I discuss the following harmful effects academic narcissism leads to in far too many cases:

1. The mistreatment or alienation of students, or negligence toward them
2. The bullying of colleagues
3. The prevention or stultifying of progress in the disciplines
4. The sensationalism of academia
5. The alienation of academia from society and social utility
6. The politicization of academia
7. The intractability of academic narcissism itself

Narcissistic professors are not all bad. Often, their narcissistic goals may happen to dovetail nicely with good and healthy professorial behavior. What we are concerned with here is when they don't; that is when harmful consequences develop and all too often cause significant harm. Keep in mind that, as a psychological disorder, narcissism may grow more acute over time, turning what may have started out as a professional peccadillo into something quite more horrendous as time goes on, even to the point of insanity.

Perhaps the greatest sin of academic narcissism is how students may be hurt by it. It is often the cause of their being ignored or underappreciated by professors too distracted by their own ambitious professional development to give due attention to their teaching vocation. Perhaps such professors will cherry-pick a few among their students and dote upon them to the exclusion of their other classmates. It is easy to see how harmful this can be to student morale, leading perhaps to an alienated disaffection for the subject matter of that discipline, if not for academia generally. There are credible stories about how professors vying for tenure are advised not to concern themselves with teaching —let the teaching take care of itself—while they tend to grooming their portfolio and professional image to impress those who would grant them tenure.

Professors who are adherents of competing schools of thought within their discipline are supposed, none-theless, to get along, to be friendly and collegial with one another, to not take their professional differences personally, and to not seek one another's harm. A narcissistic academic may have trouble toeing this line, since he sees the threat of his position in the field being diminished or lost. Like a planet, he would control the area of his orbital sweep, pushing out or keeping the area clean of whatever is incompatible to his career work while absorbing into his own sphere and as much as possible to his own credit the work of scholars around him that jibes with his own. In the process, some of these co-orbiting bodies—research colleagues, graduate students, etc.—may have had their work distorted in the process of either fitting into or fitting out of the academic narcissist's sphere of influence to the point where their own academic integrity has been marred.

This, in turn, leads to the stultification of progress with the disciplines, since the work of some has been unduly discredited or rejected, while the work of others gets accepted only in distorted form and the credit of still others is usurped by the narcissist, hampering their ability to function autonomously within the field. In all three cases, the will of those victimized by this kind of academic violence is likely to have been weakened, not rarely causing a loss of talent from the field.

Since narcissists crave attention, their academic interests are likely to gravitate not toward the vital questions of the field as much as toward those around which they can build their personality cult. Thus, the lean toward the more sensational, including at times extremism over moderation, or conceptually peripheral over central topics. But academic progress cannot be built on our jumping from one sensational item to the next; it clearly requires the discipline of avoiding the temptations of sensationalism.

Higher educational institutions exist ultimately to serve the community. To accomplish this goal requires a keen vocational focus on service. Higher educational institutions affected by narcissistic decision making are thereby affected with a blurred focus that will eventually alienate them more and more from the public, making it more difficult for them to be genuinely useful to society. Relationships with the community cannot be strong when those at the helm are not community-oriented to begin with; narcissists cannot be genuinely community-oriented, since they are obsessed with the cultivation of their own prestige. Whether or not people notice their narcissism, it will have a negative impact on their ability to form strong ties with the community, boding ill for higher education.

When narcissists are entrenched within institutions, they become an obstacle to its ordinary healthy functioning so that detours commonly have to be made to appease their need for attention and accolades in order to prevent their interference with even routine matters. They interfere even in these mundane matters because of their need to be accommodated, and maintain their dominion over what they consider to be their identity-defining territory. Thus is academia politicized by narcissism, in the sense that ordinary academic or intellectual matters now become delicate personal matters in which diplomacy looms larger than truth. Along the way, the intellectual substance of hard academic labor gets corrupted, and innocent academic zeal gets frustrated and befuddled, if not altogether killed.

It would be bad enough if academic narcissism could fester in this manner for a time, only to be periodically uprooted when it goes too far. But in fact, narcissism in higher education does not seem to be something easily uprooted; It is more likely shifted from position to position within an institution, or transplanted from one institution to another, than stamped out, because the academic narcissist holds in his hand the valuable playing card of carefully cultivated ostensible prestige, which always looks good to those craving it, enough even to tempt hiring institutions to ignore the troubling backstories that tend to follow these people wherever they go. The rumblings may matter, but they don't have much of a chance of dimming the brilliance of the meticulously crafted images presented in their resumes and bios. The ostensible prestige they have accrued cannot easily be stripped from them, and unless it is, institutions will be craving it. Short of being convicted of heinous crimes, it is difficult to imagine what it would take for an academic narcissist to lose the advantage of this carefully honed weapon.

Besides their craving for prestige, what else makes academic institutions particularly vulnerable to narcissism is the common policy of posting positions internationally. Although this stems from the innocent motivation of fair hiring practices, it insures that, given the glut of academics produced by our overabundant supply of graduate schools, only applicants who look best on paper will get on short lists. In contrast, local academics who are better known by the hiring institutions and whose maintenance of employment at this level is based more on the quality of their service than on how they look on paper will not be likely to compete.

Of course we cannot recommend a departure from fair hiring practices. But perhaps we can look into doing a better job of acknowledging the merit of good service, even weighed against the more traditional resume virtues of publishing, research, and outside speaking engagements. This might tip the scale more in favor of the cultivation of the academic profession as a vocation and less in favor of its cultivation as a personal ambition.

PART VIII
SEXUALITY

CHAPTER THIRTY-THREE

Asexuality

In the seventies going into the eighties on college campuses across the country, the expected mantra to be pronounced at parties and scribbled on bathroom walls was "Sex, Drugs, and Rock & Roll." The peer pressure to conform to this ideology, at least in appearance, was rather strong. In short, you were expected to be a partier and a "player."

It's not that there was some kind of thought police force out to check on everyone's beliefs about such things; it was more that one felt rather alone if one had more conservative attitudes that discouraged intoxication and non-committal use of sex. There were no easily visible support groups for such people, except for sectarian ones, which usually required a significant and specific religious commitment.

During my grade school years I felt the pull of the SDRR ideology quite strongly. It was an ideology that went largely unchallenged in my friendship circles, while very little mention of it was made by adult authority figures in my life. I was never quite able to conform to the ideology, but yet could not pull away from it either. A deeper sense of intimacy within me caused me either to balk or not pick up the subtle cues that people "on the make" typically send one another to promote "hookups."

By the time I got to college, I had a firm conviction against intoxication, regardless of the substance. I had also grown to awareness that my sexuality was a precious thing that should not be misused. I wasn't quite sure where exactly to draw the line between proper use and misuse, but I was appreciative of the importance and goodness of sexual abstinence. Permanent abstinence struck me as an acceptable option, but only in the abstract, since I was preoccupied by thoughts of eventual marriage.

Today, although we still have a culture that pushes sex, there is more support for those people, especially young people, who favor a lifestyle of abstinence—either temporary or permanent. Among these, there is a burgeoning movement of those who identify as "asexual." They differ from mere abstainers in that they claim simply to lack sexual desire.

The reaction to the asexuality movement falls into two groups, not necessarily mutually exclusive: those who consider some or all asexuality to be a disorder, and those who consider some or all asexuality to be an ordinary sexual orientation or choice. The consideration of either position carries the possibility of both physiological and psychological ramifications. Finally we might want to reflect on the extent to which even permanent lifestyles of abstention or asexuality may be healthy to us.

First off is the question whether asexuality can be a physiological trait, whether ordinary or abnormal. Physiologists have been aware of it mostly as a disorder. And there is no doubt that unhealth of the body may bring about privation of sexual desire. Such cases would objectively be considered as disorders, even though the person experiencing such a thing may conceivably welcome the condition.

Physiologists and psychologists are likewise aware that sex drive varies considerably among humans and even from time to time in the same person. This variation is generically considered to be ordinary *per se*. A matter to speculate is whether this ordinary variation in human sex drive may include at one extreme the complete and permanent lack of sex drive. Evolutionary biologists might insist an affirmative answer be contingent upon identifying what sort of selective benefit this might confer to the human species, that some of us have a complete privation of sex drive. My response to such a demand would be it is not inconceivable that social species gain a selective advantage from the trait of either indefinite or permanent asexuality being expressed in some of its members, thus making them more available as direct or indirect caretakers of the offspring of others. Bees, wasps, and ants do it; even crows do it, although the likelihood of permanence in their case is low. Why not humans?

Even if permanent asexuality exists as an objective physiological disorder, this does not compel the one experiencing it to view it as a curse, as something for which she ought to seek a cure. In this case, we could say it is a medical but not a moral disorder. For it may be that sex is not an individual need required for physical or mental health. It is a species need for obvious reasons, but for this need to be met does not require everyone to have or try to have sex. More on this below.

It may also be that any particular case of asexuality is a mentally conferred trait, not having to do with the body. In this case, whether or not to view it as a disorder is more controversial. While some report never having had an interest in sex, asexuality may also result from the loss of interest due to previous misuse of sex, sexual abuse, or unpleasant sexual experiences.

Here, too, we are most likely to view asexuality as a disorder only if it is unwanted by the person experiencing it. Still, we would want a criterion to justify its treatment as a disorder in the case of those who want the treatment. For example, what if I have some sex drive, but I want more? Do I deserve treatment to strengthen my sex drive just because I want it, or should my sex drive have to be found to be below a certain threshold?

The more pressing question is whether asexuality, whatever its cause, can be a good thing for us, a suitable and viable path to human happiness for some.

Plato noted that when we ask what good something is, we are asking a *teleological* question: what purpose it serves. One possible answer would be the one speculated on above, that selective asexuality among social species increases the pool of caretakers of the progeny of that species. In the case of the human species, we might want to broaden the notion of caretaking to include activities that might only be counted as indirect caretaking, such as increased devotion to a profession vital to the community. Although presented above as a mere speculation in the context of evolutionary science, it is a thought deserving of ethical attention as well: Should all of us be having or trying to have sex? Should all of us have or try to have babies? Or would it be better in both cases for some of us not to?

One stumbling block for some of us is the stubborn impression—in large part bolstered by the media—that sex is not just a species need, but also an individual need, essential for our overall health and happiness. If this is true, then of course asexuality is not only a medical but also a moral disorder.

But for sex to be an individual need implies that its absence will cause either physical or mental atrophy, or both. Now there are many cases in human culture of permanent asexuality, whether by choice or constitution.

Among these, we certainly do not see any pattern of physical harm. If there is some pattern of diagnosable mental harm, it has thus far escaped our notice.

The more frightening aspect of this question is to reflect seriously on the implications of agreeing that sex is an individual need. In such a case, would it be incumbent on the pregnant wife who has lost all sexual desire for the duration of her pregnancy, such that sex would be unpleasant for her, either to accede to her husband's advances anyway, or to arrange for his sexual relief in some other manner? In fact, it is not too difficult to see how her doing either might be in the long run ruinous to their future sex life, romance, and marriage as a whole.

Or worse, when pubescent children having trouble in school are sent to their guidance counselor, along with the routine questions about physical health regarding diet and sleep, ought the counselor be concerned whether the student is getting his or her sexual needs met?

Once we clear our minds of the notion that sex is a need, the controversy surrounding asexual or chaste lifestyles fades. After all, sex is trouble; it is at the root of much if not most of the trouble of human life. Perhaps for some it is reasonable to conclude that, desired or not, it is more trouble than it is worth.

CHAPTER THIRTY-FOUR

Sexual Orientation

The human species differs from other known sexually reproducing animals in that it lacks any noticeable set of biological cues that determines the object of our sexual pursuit. That notwithstanding, much attention has been devoted to searching for genotypes corresponding to our several sexual-preferential "phenotypes": homosexual, heterosexual, etc. In contrast, comparatively less and less serious attention now gets paid to the search for environmental factors that might explain human sexual preference, this despite the fact there is much evidence germane to the topic already possessed in our common social experience awaiting our due reflection.

It is not that our search for sexual-preferential genotypes is ill-conceived *per se*, although our execution of it thus far has been shoddy, to say the least. But what is lamentable about the enterprise is, first, that it is largely grounded on a fallacious motivation; second, that it ignores the proper empirical protocol that environmental causes first be ruled out; third, that it is not based on any serious attempt to connect the explanandum—the phenotypes—to the effects of the ordering of protein production in cells (which, after all, is what genes do to produce phenotypes); and lastly, that little effort is made throughout these efforts to reasonably unpack just what it is to have a sexual orientation in the first place.

Let us begin with the last point cited, since its clarification is required for us to go any further. What does it mean to claim that a certain person, say, John, is homosexual? It could conceivably mean any or all of the following things:

1. That the objects of John's sexual desires are commonly members of his own gender.
2. That the objects of John's sexual desires are mainly or exclusively members of his own gender.
3. That John is virtually incapable of having or cultivating significant sexual desire for the opposite sex.
4. That John has chosen a lifestyle of same-gender sexual intercourse.

For us to evaluate whether sexual orientation is inborn, we should first decide which of these four conditions would require any special causal explanation at all, let alone count as the genetically ordered phenomenon.

We should exclude 4 outright, unless we want to ignore free will as a human trait. After all, we do routinely choose to pursue certain desires and not others. Our lives would be miserable and short if we lacked this ability. It is ludicrous to think that human happiness requires us to pursue all our desires, or even all our strong ones, or that it is somehow dishonest to choose not to pursue a certain desire. I have a strong desire to sleep in every morning, but quite fortunately to my pursuit of happiness, I routinely and categorically choose not to pursue that desire.

We must be careful to note the distinction between harboring desires and choosing to pursue those desires. In fact, we should attend to four stages of desire:

Stage 1: Desires that just pop into one's mind, whether or not one chooses to cultivate them.
Stage 2: Desires one chooses to harbor or cultivate, whether or not one chooses to pursue them.
Stage 3: Desires one makes as conditional decisions to pursue, whether or not those conditions ever arise to trigger their pursuit.
Stage 4: Desires one actually pursues.

It is clearly the case that each of us has Stage 1 desires that don't make it to Stage 2, Stage 2 desires that never get to Stage 3, and Stage 4 desires that never get to Stage 4. It is equally clear that to have a Stage 4 desire for something requires first having a Stage 3 desire for it, which in turn requires first having a Stage 2 desire for it, etc. Moreover, it seems absurd to deny that the transition from a lower stage to a higher stage of desire is mediated by deliberate rational choice. Therefore, what we should be looking for is what makes desire for things pop into our heads in the first place.

This leaves us to look for a genetic cause for 1, 2, or 3. But as researchers have long agreed, 1 needs no special cause, since all human beings are capable of having homosexual desires. How commonly John actually harbors them may vary simply according to how far John's imagination takes him, which no doubt is a function of John's lived experience. For example, if John's imagination is tightly controlled by social taboos against homosexuality, all else being equal, he is probably less likely to acknowledge or harbor them willingly. On the other hand, if John has no taboo barrier and instead lives in a social milieu suggestive of same-gender sexual scenarios, he is on that account more probable to harbor such thoughts. There are, in fact, societies in which very little if any full-fledged homosexual activity is noted. But there are no societies that altogether lack inchoative homosexual behaviors, especially at the onset of adolescence. Typically, adolescence is a time in which two things occur in tandem: children become more rigidly segregated by gender, and children begin to experience sexual feelings. Intuitively, at least in the absence of taboos, this combination seems quite likely to produce homosexual desires and imaginations.

If we exclude both 1 and 4, as not requiring any special causal explanation, that leaves 2 and 3 as our remaining options. But in light of our explication of 1, it now becomes evident that 2 as a phenomenon could in part depend on 3. For how many homosexual desires one might have does not by itself preclude the possibility of having heterosexual desires as well. Therefore, the special cause we should be looking for is not why people might have homosexual desires, but why they might lack heterosexual desires.

Of course, there is a further possibility, namely that one might lack both heterosexual and homosexual desires. Apart from the possibility that this could be for absence of sexual desire at all, there might also be a special cause why one might lack homosexual desire as well. We have already spoken of social taboos, which, when effectively in force, discourage individuals from harboring certain thoughts. It is reasonable to think that such a factor may be the main reason why many imaginative humans report lacking any homosexual desires or thoughts. But clearly, we would have to look for another cause for the absence of heterosexual desire.

Our reflection to this point has allowed us to pinpoint the special cause behind homosexuality that we should be seeking. But we should note that as a matter of proper rational protocol, we ought first exclude the reasonable possibility of environmental factors before we go looking for a genetic cause. This is because genetic causes of specific cognitions are highly unlikely unless there is a clear physical trail to them, such as in the case of animal sexual attraction ordered by pheromones, which produce fixed, dependable results. To the contrary, the way human beings fix their sexual desires on objects of pursuit is a complex matter not leaving any obvious physical tracks.

In fact, genetic causal studies are and will remain ephemeral until some likely scenario emerges for connecting the trait to be explained with the production of proteins in cells. We are not close to being at this point regarding our understanding of human sexuality. And it is likely we never will, since there very well may be environmental causes staring us in the face that will give us all the explanation we need.

But before we get to the discussion of the latter, something should be said about the misguidedness in of thinking that discovery of a genetic cause to homosexuality in humans is relevant to the moral evaluation of it. As we all know, some genetic traits are desirable, and some are undesirable; some are functional, and some are dysfunctional. It is therefore silly for us to think the moral controversy could be settled in such a manner. We will return below to a more nuanced discussion of whether there is a reasonable controversy concerning homosexuality and, if so, then what should that discussion be limited to.

It appears evident that some people who have sexual desire lack the disposition to have significant sexual desire for the opposite sex. This may be either for certain periods of their lives or for their entire lives. That many of these people opt for homosexual lifestyles because of this fact is quite understandable. Their only choice in this case appears to be whether to choose a sexual lifestyle or not; however, the choice of a chaste lifestyle, though not unreasonable, is relatively rare. It is no doubt more rare in a society that makes room for the homosexual lifestyle.

We are well aware that homosexual behavior typically becomes prevalent in situations involving a long-term lack of physical access to the opposite sex. The most famous examples of this are prisons, but similar results occur in any single-gender institutional setting, whether military, educational, etc. We tend to write such cases of homosexuality off as artificial, if not simply ignoring them altogether. But I think they give us the key to our answer. Now, a lack of access to the opposite sex is the predominant factor leading to the choice of a homosexual lifestyle. Also, a lack of access to the opposite sex can be physical or psychological. To be sure, there is something "artificial" about the prevalent homosexuality in prisons, etc., in that the lack of access causing the prevalence is physical; once most of these men and women regain physical access to the opposite sex, their heterosexual behavior is likely to return, prescinding from the likelihood of lingering sexual associations from previously gender-sequestered lives.

What we have failed to consider is that lack of access to the opposite sex can be deeper than lack of physical access: it can be lack of *psychological* access. In such a case, degree of physical access is irrelevant. For the barrier in this case is psychological.

As to the cause of this lack of psychological access, one may speak of two causes: subjective and objective. An objective cause would be the perception of an alienating trait in the opposite sex generally; a subjective cause would be the perception of an alienating trait in one's own sex generally.

A key example of an objective cause would be fear of the opposite sex. Most of us can recall the fears of the opposite sex we had to deal with in adolescence. Some of us may no longer have these fears, while some of us may have never quite shrugged them off. To many of us, these fears have not proven prohibitive; however, it is more than reasonable to think that for some of us, they have. We all know how daunting fear of the opposite sex can be. Moreover, there are different kinds of fear of the opposite sex: fear of the unknown, fear of being harmed, fear of losing one's identity in the clutches of the other gender, fear of incompatibility, and performance anxieties. There is no guarantee that our fears will not overwhelm us in any particular instance, and there is no guarantee people will respond to their fears in the same way as others.

A key example of a subjective cause alienating me from my own sex would be what might be called the "stereotype straitjacket." To gain access to the opposite sex as a potential suitor, I have to occupy a social niche. These niches are subject to cultural elaboration and may become quite cumbersome and even socially dysfunctional. They might require us, for example, to suppress some key aspects of our own self-conception in order to occupy the niche. To be sure, there may be no fixed set of niches, and it may be possible with greater effort to more or less carve out one's own niche, but these are difficult things to do, especially during childhood, when we are expected to accomplish them. There is no set age at which we first take on such tasks, but we gradually back into them as we become socially aware.

One common deal breaker in this regard, especially for men, is the desire for same-gender intimacy. While some may equate this already with homosexuality, the desire for same-gender intimacy, however great it may be, is not a sexual orientation. Nonetheless, many of us consider it at odds with heterosexual life, such that there is a pressure to suppress this desire. Those who find this to be an unconscionable exclusion may thus be in a bind.

In short, I may lose access to the opposite sex because I could not identify with any of the social niches through which such access could have been gained. My failure to accomplish this task may not be my "fault" or even indicate any mental defect, since I may have reasonably judged the options to be tantamount to various forms of self-immolation, in which my occupation of any such niche would entail divorcing myself from some key aspect of my personality. Mind you, this may have nothing to do with sex *per se*, although the result is loss of access to the opposite sex.

Thus far our reflection has been limited to what may be called non-incidental homosexuality, or homosexuality caused by lack of psychological access to the opposite sex. But there are also several forms of incidental homosexuality we should take note of to avoid confusion. These are forms not based on lack of access to the opposite sex.

One form of incidental homosexuality is monogamy-induced. A person who has sexual desire for both sexes at some point may choose to commit to a monogamous relationship. To the degree the monogamy is permanent, that person will be seen as homosexual and probably will begin to identify more and more with homosexuality.

Another form of homosexuality is habitual. As stated earlier, with puberty typically comes separation from the opposite sex. Just at the time we are beginning to have explicit, adult-grade sexual desires, we tend to find ourselves in a variety of private situations with members of our own sex, such as camping trips, pajama parties, sleepovers, etc. In the absence of effective social taboos, it seems unlikely there would not be some kind of at least inchoative sexual experimentation in such situations. Given that sexual desire is a great reinforcer of behavior, it is possible that these experimentations might spawn sexual habits that persist into adulthood.

A third type of homosexuality is by convenience. Although it has often been said that the choice to be homosexual in our society is inconvenient, there is a certain convenience to it that cannot be overlooked. Members of the same sex are more likely to have matching libido, arousal patterns, sensitivities, etc. A same-gender partner is likely to be more readily aware of her mate's body and psychology; moreover, the considerable burden of maintaining good gender relations—one of the great challenges of human socialness—is lacking.

I cite these three types of incidental homosexuality just to acknowledge their occurrence is not covered by the principal explanation given in this paper—absence of psychological access to the opposite sex—that pertains only to non-incidental homosexuality.

A critic might contend we have no right to exclude humans from the sexual determinism we see evident in the rest of nature. In fact, so many other sexual species have elaborate sexual behaviors involving complex animal decisions, yet it is all determined by biological cues. Why should we think we are any different? Perhaps there are biological mechanisms at work that are just too elaborate for contemporary science now to analyze. But the least we can do is search for statistical evidence even if we cannot identify any "physical trail" from DNA through proteins to behavior.

I answer this criticism by pointing out that in the higher animals, at least, there is a certain amount of *residual* sexual desire, undetermined by biological cues, which the animal is left to imaginatively project on any convenient object in its environment. Male moose during mating season are notorious for mounting and attempting to mate with all kinds of large, inanimate objects, provided they seem to have four legs. Dogs, both male and female, adopt the embarrassing habit of humping a human leg every so often. Are we to conclude then that certain dogs are human-leg-sexual by nature? Of course not! It is simply the case that they experience some sexual desire that occurs to them in the first instance disassociated with any object, and it is left up to them to project that desire onto some convenient object in their environment.

As with moose and dogs, so with humans. Except, whereas these other animals still have the object of most of their sexual desire predetermined by biological cues, there is no evidence that any of our sexual desire is preordered to set objects in that manner. Thus, all of our sexual desire is "residual"; we are born neither homosexual nor heterosexual; just sexual. It is up to us individually and collectively to decide the objects of our sexual desires.

As to whether there should be any moral controversy to our choice of sexual orientation, this hinges upon our knowledge of the purposes of human sexuality, a subject about which we have been quite bashful to entertain in a productive dialogue. At any rate, there is certainly no cause for discrimination or social shunning of any kind. The sexual choices we make are an intimate and private part of our pursuit of happiness, to which we all have the same sacred right, limited only by our commitment not to interfere with that same right possessed by others.

CHAPTER THIRTY-FIVE

The Purpose of Sex

There is long-standing controversy over what constitutes a healthy use of human sexual intercourse. Non-consensual uses are universally condemned. Most societies have strict rules against certain kinds of sexual unions, such as incest, adult-minor, etc. There are other commonly accepted restrictions of sex in the workplace and among coworkers even off-duty, while psychologists and others warn of the dangers of premature sexuality. The moral status of same-gender sexual intercourse has been a hotly debated topic; moreover, modern values lean heavily toward permanent monogamous commitment as an important condition of good sex.

We will not be able to engage fruitfully in a dialogue over these prescriptive matters until we have a descriptive discussion on the purpose of sex, which is the aim of what follows. By "prescriptive discussion" is meant discussion of judgments of what is better or worse; by "descriptive discussion" is meant ascertainment of the features of a thing relevant to making prescriptive judgments about it.

Often we run into difficulty at the outset when trying to describe the purpose of a human activity. This owes to the fact that the thing typically motivating an individual to enter the activity is other than the purpose of the activity as a whole. Although basketball players play the game to win, winning is not the purpose of the activity of basketball. Similarly, although individual investors typically invest their money into stocks to make money, individual investors making money is not the purpose of stock investment. The purpose of basketball is the aesthetic beauty of excellent human performance; the purpose of investment is to share along a wider base the risk of failure of large, growing companies to promote stable growth of the economy. In both cases, the individual's incentive to participate is but the carrot in front of them to encourage the activity. Without such incentive, the purpose of the activity itself could not be met for lack of adequately motivated participants.

Similarly, the purpose of eating is not the enjoyment of food consumption, but the nourishment of the body and the provision of food for organismic activity. Although lack of appetite in an animal is a serious problem often foretelling death, nonetheless, humans do well to remind ourselves that the purpose of eating is not to obtain pleasure, but to nourish ourselves to maintain our health and vital functions.

Likewise with sex; humans would do well to remind ourselves that similar to eating, its purpose is not to obtain pleasure, although the pleasure is of course quite welcome. But here is where the waters get a bit murky for us, since it is hard to say exactly what the purpose of sex is for humans. Or perhaps I should say: purposes.

To be sure, one of the purposes of sex for us, as for other animals, is reproduction. But unlike most other animals, whose sexual activity seems more strictly ordered to that purpose, human sexuality has specialized into a more pervasive activity which, far from being directed by natural cues to occur only when conception is most likely, persists even after menopause into old age, and often throughout the female's reproductive cycle, including even pregnancy. For humans, sexual activity is not primarily cued by reproductive readiness in the female, as it is in other animals. All this suggests that our species has developed other important purposes for sex than merely reproduction. Not that we have moved on from the latter purpose, but that other purposes have been added.

When speaking about the extension of human sexuality beyond reproduction, we are speaking specifically about changes to the female. For in all species, the male is ready when the female is ready—at least biologically. So the question is, of what purpose is the extension of human female sexual interest beyond the times of reproductive readiness?

There are also signs in the male that human sexuality has taken on new purposes other than reproduction: human sperm is notoriously weak in proportion to that of other closely related species. Moreover, our overall infertility rate is high in comparison with other animals, high enough to suggest there may be other important purposes for sex in human life.

It is now widely accepted that of the extant hominine species, we are most closely related to chimpanzees and their close cousins, the bonobos. These two members of the genus *Pan* have evolved quite distinct sexual behaviors. Although both species are pervasively both polygynous and polyandrous, the chimpanzee female is sexual only during her time of reproductive readiness, and only then is she attractive to the male. In contrast, female bonobos have extended sexual readiness approaching that of humans. The purpose that extended sexual interest seems to play in bonobo society is increased socialization of the male. Compared with his chimpanzee counterpart, the male bonobo is pacific and cooperative, not engaging in the typical violent practices of male chimps such as infanticide, killing rival chimps, physical abuse of females, and forced sexual intercourse. It is reasonable to suppose that the extension of sexual interest in female humans has the same purpose: to increase overall human socialness by socializing the male.

But this is at best a partial explanation, since humans are quite unlike their chimp and bonobo cousins in that we develop socially over the history of our species, and as our socialness increases, we gravitate more and more toward monogamy. Whereas we were never a polyandrous species, polygyny in earlier times was often considered preferable for men who could support multiple wives. (The importance of lifelong parent-child relationships is a cornerstone of human socialness, and is probably the reason why our species has largely steered away from polyandry, since it makes it difficult to know who the father is.)

The increasing human preference for monogamy over human social development coincides roughly with our transition to the agricultural mode of survival. In earlier times, polygyny may have been preferable to those who could afford it as a form of social security in old age, or as a hedge against population shortages, or shortages of men. In hunter-gatherer times and even during the long transitional stages leading to the agricultural lifestyle, including horticulturalism in some places and pastoralism in others, there were more ways for young men to die than young women, including hand-to-hand combat and—at least among horticulturalists—hunting expeditions for large animals. In those times available fertile women were assets human society may have felt it could not afford to delay utilizing, and a prosperous man already married may have often been considered a more secure match than a young unmarried one. Security came with attachment to larger families.

As the human race settled into the agricultural mode of existence definitively and human social groupings became increasingly larger, the older concerns favoring multiple wives faded, and the disadvantages of polygamy became more felt. Polygamy reduces or nullifies the romantic bond between man and wife, and this separation in turn negatively affects father-child bonds, thus reducing human socialness. Conversely, monogamy increases human socialness by increasing the bond between man and wife.

Monogamy in nature is closely connected to biparentalism. In such a setting, the male's genetic survival is maximized by his own co-parenting, since the offspring are with rare exception sired by him. For various reasons, the survival plan of some species requires more intensive parenting, either because of a dangerous predatory environment, as in the case of many species of cichlid fish, or in the case of humans, because our adaptation of higher intelligence brings with it the tradeoff of a longer period of maturation, including an extended period of infantile helplessness. Monogamy is a common response in nature to the need for more intense parenting.

The evolved relative weakness of human sperm reflects not only an ancient move in the human line away from females having multiple partners, thus curtailing the need for sperm competition, but probably also a move toward more extended use of sexual intercourse in pursuit of increased socialness. Unlike the bonobo, whose extended utilization of sex beyond the purposes of procreation is primarily inchoative, not resulting in insemination, the human extension of the use of sex typically does involve ejaculation. If this extension were for the sake of increasing reproduction, we may not have expected such a weakening of the human sperm as we have seen. Therefore, it is likely we evolved this way in pursuit of social rather than increased reproductive purposes.

Reflecting on the fact that the human species is a historically developing species capable of improving itself, passing on those improvements from generation to generation, we ought also consider that a more specific purpose of extended sexual activity in humans may be the improvement of gender relations, or gender communion. In many animal species and especially in most of the higher ones, males and females typically don't get along, and it is typically the testosterone that gets in the way. The males are not only less social than females, even among themselves, but they are particularly antisocial with the females, killing their offspring and even sometimes interfering with pregnancies to hasten their own sexual access to the female, and in the case of chimpanzees brutalizing females to keep them submissive.

Humans, in fact, do have and have always had a gender relations problem, but it has been less severe than in other species. Moreover, our historical social development has coincided with and arguably has been contingent upon improved gender relations. As human society becomes more complex, we perhaps can no longer afford the social inefficiencies that come with bad gender relations, including especially the underinvestment in girls and women concomitant with less intimate, nonmonogamous uses of sex.

In short, the purpose of sex in humans beyond mere reproduction seems to be our increased social bonding accomplished by the increased socialization of the male and, in particular, increased gender communion. Good monogamous sexual relationships can produce this not just for the participants, but for society as a whole. If my socialness is increased, I can then pass it on to my children and, to some extent, even to my friends, in my ordinary interactions with them. Moreover, when a man and a woman establish a firm and abiding bond, this bonds them more to each other's gender cohorts as well; it counteracts gender alienation.

The psychology of human sexuality backs this point. Sex is a celebration of sorts—a celebration of gender. In this celebration, each participant offers his own gender to the other in return for the reception of the gender of the other into his own self. It is an intimate mutual appreciation of, and identification with, each other's gender.

It is important to be mindful of these purposes of sex, especially given that in our commercially hyper-sexualized culture, we are often led to use sex in ways not conducive to these ends or even contrary to them, thus leading to the contrary effects of decreased socialness and gender alienation.

How the purposes of gender communion and increased overall socialness are supposed to fit with the purpose of reproduction is an interesting question. But we will not be able to answer it unless we first come to grips with what cognitive role the reproductive purpose of sex should play in humans. For no one considers it a misuse *per se* for infertile couples or elderly couples to have sex. The fact is that by far most individual human uses of sex are infertile. Is it yet incumbent on us to be in some way mindful of the reproductive purpose, so as not to contradict it? What would count as a contradiction of it? To merely ignore the reproductive purpose altogether would be tantamount to a vain fantasy of pretending that we weren't animals. Perhaps it is simply that we ought to be mindful of the reproductive potential as an integral part of the meaning of sex. After all, we are not just rational beings, but rational animals.

There may be some resistance to this line of thinking among those who suspect it of being intrusive on personal privacy. But what is true about the human species, even what is true about what is helpful and harmful to humans, is not a private matter; on the other hand, the choices humans make in pursuit of happiness are indeed a private matter. Neither this discussion nor the one it hopes to enable is geared toward infringing on such privacy. My friends reminding me that I should take it easy with the sweets does not infringe on my rights to choose my own food. I wouldn't consider them friends if they thought they should not remind me of such things if they believed I might need being reminded. This counts also for points of disagreement. My vegan friend might think it her duty to remind me to cut down on my meat intake because she is worried for my health. Although I may disagree with her on the facts, I should still appreciate her act of friendship and not consider it an infringement of my pursuit of happiness, unless she were taking measures to manipulate me into compliance with her wishes. In short, there is plenty room for friendly dialogue on these points.

Another objection might come from someone committed to the notion that, despite the fact we are a species, we, unlike the other animals, can dictate to and for ourselves our own actual purposes, and that such purposes are true independently of any facts, such as those considered above, related to our common species belonging. Accordingly, some might argue that for one person, the ultimate purpose of sex may be, say, mere pleasure without any romantic commitment, and that this may be so just by that person's own fiat. To this objection I answer that it is dishonest for us to ignore the fact that we are animals, and it is errant for us to ignore the truth about what is helpful to us and harmful to us as animals; or that there are common species facts about what is helpful and harmful to us.

Finally, someone may be suspicious of the recommendation of monogamy because of its association with modern Western matrimony, which has been criticized as sexist. This line of thought began with Friedrich Engels' critique of marriage in modern capitalist society in his work, *The Origin of Family, Private Property, and the State (Der Ursprung der Familie, des Privateigenthums und des Staats, 1884)*. It is important to note that Engels was never a critic of monogamy itself, nor of matrimony generally, but just matrimony in a capitalist or *bourgeoisie* setting. In fact, he held monogamy itself in high regard, so much so that his critique of *bourgeoisie* matrimony was on behalf of true monogamy.

At any rate, we should take care not to confuse marriage as a particular institution with monogamy generically. I would argue, alongside Engels himself, that monogamy is intrinsically an egalitarian relationship, in contrast with polygamy, which is not.

If these are the purposes of sex for humans, the next step would be to discuss how good sex, or sex that is good enough not to be considered a misuse, relates to them. Although we may surmise that humans are better off the better we achieve our purposes, including sexual purposes, certain questions remain. Can sex be good without meeting all of its purposes? Are we to judge act by act, or relationship by relationship? Are some of the purposes of sex more vital than others? Are some or all of the purposes met by imperfect compliance; i.e., by many or most cases of sex meeting it? Do any of its purposes stand alone as necessary conditions to good sex? I hope this essay has brought us closer to a meaningful discussion of these questions.

PART IX

FAITH AND THE SUPERNATURAL

CHAPTER THIRTY-SIX

Relating to the Supernatural

Is it rational to seek out a relationship with the supernatural? One approach to this question is to answer in the negative on the grounds there is no supernatural. We will return to this later. Otherwise, we are left in a perplexing spot, expressed by the question: Is the supernatural itself familiar to us, or unfamiliar? In other words, are we to define the supernatural as that which is beyond our experience? If so, then how could we ever relate to it, even if we wanted to? In the end, this may be the principle motivation for denying the existence of the supernatural: that it has been defined as that which is beyond our experience. After all, our experience, taken in the widest plausible sense, is our evidence base, the basis of all our judgments.

In light of this, I would offer the following conditional answer to the question posed at the beginning of this essay: If the supernatural is not in our experience (in the widest plausible sense), then it is irrational to seek out a relationship with it, since it is irrational to judge without evidence that something exists or might exist.

Whether this conditional answer turns out to be a moot point hinges on whether we can recognize the supernatural in our experience. If we can, this will open a pathway to an affirmative answer to the same question.

Either the supernatural is in our experience or it is not. If it is, then it is already familiar to us, whether or not we are acknowledging it for what it really is. In light of this essential logical truth, we ought to avoid the pitfall of prejudicing the question by defining the supernatural as something outside of our experience. Taking this step requires us to accept as a preliminary possibility that our experience in the widest plausible sense may be a mixed bag of natural and supernatural elements. Failure to take this step, or even to see the necessity of doing so, is exactly where many people get lost on the question.

Of course, the prospects for an affirmative answer to our question hinge also on a "yes" answer to the more fundamental question: Is it rational to seek out a supernatural explanation? If the answer to this question is "no," then we ought to acquiesce entirely in natural explanation, since by our admission just made, there would be no good reason to believe there is any other explanation to be had beyond it. For supernatural explanation would be just that: explanation beyond natural explanation.

The conversation to this point prompts the following two queries:

1. What is natural explanation?
2. Is natural explanation limited?

If natural explanation, whatever it is, is limited, this would open the door to the rationality of seeking supernatural explanation based on the following argument:

1. It is rational to seek sufficient explanation for things.
2. Limited explanation is insufficient.
3. Natural explanation is limited.
4. It is rational to seek supernatural explanation.

I take premise 1 to be self-evident, since unless we are to deny its face value entirely—in which case we have no business discussing the matter at hand—sufficient reason is the obvious purpose of rationality.

I take premise 2 to be uncontroversially true by definition. So the point will be proved if premise 3 is shown to be true.

WHAT IS NATURAL EXPLANATION?

Rationality is occupied with seeking answers to two kinds of questions: closed questions and open questions. Closed questions are "closed to argument" in the sense they are answered or to be answered by observation, calculation, or some combination of the two: How many people are in the room? What is the cause of smallpox? Who shot the bullet that killed JFK?

Open questions, on the other hand, are simply questions that are not closed. That is to say, not being answerable by observation or calculation, they are thus "open to argument" in that they can only be answered by some argumentive process, some kind of weighing of pros and cons: Is the man who shot the bullet that killed JFK guilty of murder? Do humans have souls? What is the purpose of human suffering?

In short, closed questions are the questions of empirical science, mathematics, and the like. All these fields are limited endeavors in that they have no prospects of ever answering open questions. Open questions, in turn, are the questions of philosophy and the like: questions about morality, the supernatural, and other non-empirical and incalculable matters.

Our rational life, then, is taken up by two types of endeavors: closed question and open question. It is logically impossible for one type of endeavor to encroach upon, subsume, or replace the other. Both types are vital, meaningful, and even necessary to our quests for truth and happiness.

Natural explanation is typically by its own admission identified with closed-question endeavors. It's not typically considered to be up to natural explanation whether we have souls and, if so, whether they are immortal, whether God exists, etc. The fact that this identification of natural explanation with closed-question endeavors is not more clear is that our intuitive recognition of the distinction tends to be corrupted by a magical view of science: that if we wait long enough, it will explain all things. I call this view "magical" because it being accepted, even as plausible, rests on imagining that one day open questions will be perfectly translated—*salva significatione*—into closed questions, which in turn will then be answered by science. But in fact, closed questions and open questions are irreducible to one another. To see this, consider the case of death.

Loosely speaking, we know what death is. But we don't know exactly what death is and therefore cannot say exactly when it occurs. Death *per se* is not empirical; the question "What is death?" is, therefore, an open question. Nonetheless, for practical reasons, we need a closed-question, empirical analog-concept of death.

So we develop clinical definitions of death, which consist in series of observations of the body and behavior of the subject resulting in a judgment of death—"legal" death—if all observations turn up negative: no pulse for ni minutes; no heartbeat for nj minutes; no detectable brain activity for nk minutes; etc. These definitions inescapably have arbitrary elements such that the same subject may be legally dead in one jurisdiction and still alive in another!

We all know that being legally dead is not the same as being really dead. Even as we work to synchronize our legal definitions internationally and improve them to approach more closely the ideal of being coextensive with real death, the categorical gap in meaning will always be there. Real death will never be, even in part, defined by the subject's heart stopping for a certain number of minutes.

In short, natural explanation will always and forever fall short of telling us exactly what death is. Hence, natural explanation is limited. If so, then it is rational for us to seek explanation beyond it: by definition, supernatural explanation.

Moreover, if natural explanation is limited—i.e., insufficient—then it is irrational for us to summarily deny the supernatural, the only reasonable grounds for which had been that natural explanation was sufficient.

The questions that need to be answered, which natural explanation cannot answer, are open questions. They are open because science, mathematics, and the like cannot answer them. They are questions among which are those regarding the most vital and intimate aspects of our existence.

To be sure, open questions and closed questions may be related in important ways. Answers to closed questions may inform open-question endeavors in important ways, just as open-question endeavors may inspire or lead the way to closed-question endeavors. What is being denied here is only the reducibility of one to the other, not the dialog between them.

Even if we accept the rationality of seeking supernatural explanation, the question remains: how to relate to the supernatural. (Keep in mind, we have not here proved the existence of any particular supernatural being, nor even that we can find solid answers; we have only proved the rationality of sometimes seeking supernatural explanation.) There are two possibilities to consider: that the source of supernatural explanation is personal or impersonal. In the latter case, then some sort of manipulative approach would be called for, according to which those forces might be channeled and guided according to our own best judgment.

If, on the other hand, the ultimate source of supernatural explanation is personal, then a manipulative approach would be just as inappropriate as it is in our own ordinary personal relationships, in whose image we would then be advised to govern our relationship with the supernatural.

One question looms large in deciding whether the supernatural is personal or impersonal. We know that we ourselves exist as personal beings. Personhood is a remarkable and mysterious anomaly in the world. Is it possible that our own personhood has an impersonal cause, that personhood in fact reduces entirely to impersonal elements? Perhaps some attempt could be made through complexity theory to depict personhood as an emergent feature, something similar to how harmony can emerge from the playing of several notes but is yet distinct from those notes, or how the appearance of a rainbow emerges via light rays from the sun passing through a mist of falling water droplets at a certain angle. This kind of explanation may yield an explanation of the emergent features as appearances. But is personhood just an appearance ultimately set off wondrously by the dancing of so many elementary particles? This question strikes me as an opaque or impenetrable mystery. For in the case of harmony begotten by notes played and rainbows begotten by sunlight and water droplets, the things begotten, in the end, have no greater reality than what begets them and possibility even less; whereas personhood seems far greater than dancing particles, etc.

If, on the other hand, our own personhood has a personal cause, I would consider this a penetrable mystery—and although not fully comprehensible, I can understand the explanatory principles in play: of like begetting like, that causes are proportionate to their effects, etc.

We all should agree that unnecessary appeals to mystery ought to be avoided. But sometimes all we have is a choice between mysteries. Given a choice between an opaque, impenetrable mystery and a penetrable one, I think reason favors the latter.

CHAPTER THIRTY-SEVEN

Faith and Reason

There has been an odd conspiracy in effect for centuries between many religions and many who oppose or are alienated by religion—a strange sort of common ground that has served to establish an unreasoned separatism that has done its best to sequester religious thought from rigorous rational scrutiny and vice versa. This conspiracy takes the form of the accepted premise that faith is opposed to reason. This, in turn, has become the grounds for two contrary positions: fideism and rationalism (in which context we are to ignore other senses of this latter term), as described in the following couplet: faith is opposed to reason, so much the worse for reason (fideism); faith is opposed to reason, so much the worse for faith (rationalism).

I say "for centuries," but perhaps in a sense this is also a timeless conspiracy. Tertullian's dictum *credo quia absurdum* probably should count as fideist; as possibly even Martin Luther's description of reason as a "whore." Nonetheless, in recent times it has taken on a more distinct and perduring form, to the extent that it is prevalent (and perhaps even more so!) even among intellectuals on both sides.

The effects of this movement have been to cripple so much religious thought by exempting it from rigorous rational scrutiny, while stultifying so much otherwise rigorous rational scrutiny by the unquestioned acceptance of the postulate that anything related to faith discourse is irrational. On the one hand, the social effects have been to promote unscrutinized acceptance of religious dogma as an entry fee into religious cultures, while on the other expecting alienation from religion to be a key marker of rational acuity. The costs of these effects are hard to measure, but one might well suspect them to figure largely in the sociopolitical divisiveness of our era.

As any conspiracy, it is a pact of sorts. But unlike most pacts, which are agreements to cooperate in some ongoing way, this is largely a pact of non-cooperation, in which the only thing shared is one common foe: those who would have collaboration between faith and reason. In this sense, it is more of an anti-pact than a pact, since its intent is purely destructive (of dialogue).

This fight between fideists and rationalists is interrupted only by their one collaboration: to oppose the reconciliation of faith and reason. Since both sides have staked their identities in the mutual antagonism of faith and reason, it is in their common interest to ignore the possibility of reconciliation. The signs of this are clearly visible in our culture, which in key instances pits science against religion as if their reconciliation is out of the question.

What brought this feud to the forefront in modern times was the creeping ideology of empirical skepticism. Known also in more focused contexts as scientism or positivism, it is the denial that we can have knowledge of claims that cannot be answered by observation or calculation. If this were true, it would mean that any claims to knowledge besides those within science, mathematics, and the like would be unreasonable and spurious. This would put the entire discourses of faith and religion, including all the claims made in them and through them, in crisis. Either these would be nullified by rigorous skeptical scrutiny, or they would have to be protected from it by some ideological rationale. The first pathway leads to rationalism, while the second leads to fideism. In fact, this dilemma only rears its head thanks to an uncritical acceptance of empirical skepticism. There is something odd about an unquestioning concession to a position which itself stems from a tradition of rigorous ongoing scrutiny.

At issue is not so much whether empirical skepticism is true, but whether, and on what grounds, it should merit such deferential acceptance. Skeptical theories are fair game, but the great divide between science and religion is not caused by a mere preponderance of skepticism in our culture; rather, it is born from an uncritical deference to it, for which there is no justification.

I suspect humans have always had a tendency to flirt with skepticism, that we sway back and forth during the course of our lives in our degree of adherence to such theories. But as long as we recognize there is no good reason to exalt any form of skepticism above the fray of the rigorous scrutiny upon which skepticism itself is based, we could still have a good basis for dialogue between religion and reason. The hampering of this dialogue can only be based on acceptance of empirical skepticism not as a theory of knowledge, but as an ideology. In consequence, we must recognize both fideism and rationalism as ideologies themselves: systems of thought whose premises are programmatically protected from serious critical evaluation.

Let us go so far even to suppose for the sake of argument that empirical skepticism is true. Still, we could not know it is true, since knowledge of its truth would be of a nonempirical claim, which by the theory's own lights would be impossible. So even in this best-case scenario for empirical skeptics, there would be no grounds for its uncritical acceptance. If this is the case, then neither should it be justified to dismiss offhand the possibility of nonempirical knowledge.

A point we have ignored up to now is the credible prospects for nonempirical knowledge that we, in fact, do have. If an empirical question is one that can only be answered by observation or calculation and, hence, is "closed to argument," then nonempirical questions must be those that are "open to argument" or answerable only by means of an argumentative process. Now, we know the conclusion of any argument is true if the argument is valid and the premises are true. Such an argument is said to be sound. So nonempirical knowledge would amount to establishing that an argument is sound. It seems rather odd to insist we can never do this. For the determination of validity is merely a matter of calculation, so all that is left to determining soundness is the evaluation of premises; how can it be that we are unable to ever judge whether premises are true in argument contexts? This is tantamount to conceding that despite the fact we are rational animals, reason itself cannot play the role of arbiter of truth. No reasonable person has ever claimed that reason performs such a function infallibly, but it seems equally ludicrous to suggest it cannot perform the function at all. All it comes down to is a sort of weighing of the pros and cons regarding a matter; something a rational being should be fit to do.

It may be we are worn down by the fact that genuine controversies are characteristically perennial and, hence, do not seem to be solved the way empirical problems often can be solved. But this appearance of non-resolution may be only a mirage. Individuals and groups do, in fact, resolve controversies. True, this does not imply universal consensus in the public forum. But the absence of universal consensus is not proof of non-resolution; whether we can have argumentative moral or religious knowledge is only answered by a process of ongoing dialogue, not by observation of universal consensus. Not only may a universal consensus on a matter be wrong, but it is not required for something to be considered known. In fact, even empirical knowledge sometimes fails the test of universal consensus. We don't consider science stymied by the fact that some otherwise educated people think the world is less than seven thousand years old. So why should the fact that many people doubt God's existence be considered as proof we can't have knowledge of the matter? The proof, if there is one, is in the quality of the ongoing argumentative dialogue.

Nor should we consider it a mark against nonempirical knowledge that its proof is not all at once, but ongoing; for so too is scientific knowledge. There is never a point at which we are permitted to close the books and decree any theory of science to be true. By their own nature, these theories must continue to be put to the test forever, leading either ultimately to refutation or to ever-increasing corroboration. So why should we expect more of nonempirical knowledge than we expect of science?

At any rate, whether justifiably or not, this is how things have gone, and as a result philosophy in the eyes of many was thus demoted from its role of general arbiter. This, in turn, led to predictable results: the falling into disuse of philosophy from the role of providing what Thomas Aquinas called the "preamble to faith" and the loss of respect for any but scientific authority. The latter, in turn, led both to the general acceptance of religious revelation as either unreasonable (rationalism) or utterly beyond reason (fideism), as well as to an ongoing array of misguided attempts either to "prove" or "refute" religion by scientific methods. All of these effects are doors slammed in the face of sound rational principles.

In the first place, the notion of a philosophical preamble to faith is an acknowledgment that religious dialogue requires a pre-established philosophical context. We don't go to religion to learn whether God exists, whether we have souls, or whether souls are immortal. These are questions whose primary treatment is philosophical. It is only having given them their due philosophical treatment that we can approach religion with mature motivation. If we are discouraged from doing this, then ultimately the quality of our religious dialogue will suffer. Religious dialogue presupposes previous philosophical treatment of its fundamental concepts and claims.

The loss of a healthy sense of authority on nonempirical matters has put us in a position in which our social dialogue has become stunted. Acceptance on authority is nothing other than trust of our fellow humans' experience and accrued wisdom, individually and collectively. Without any acceptance of authority, we would have no reason to read books or go to school. In fact, the progress of human knowledge is based largely, and in so many ways, on acceptance of authority. But this all hinges on a sense of trust that progress can and is being made. If this sense is lost, then the motivation for acceptance of authority is lost.

To be sure, a healthy acceptance of authority is not blind; rational beings are still called upon continually to verify one another's trustworthiness. But this scrutiny cannot be administered unless trust is given in the first place. I liken the situation to a married couple. Marriage is ruined both by lack of trust and by blind trust. Lack of trust prevents the marriage from being a real marriage, while blind trust enables one spouse to exploit the other and ruin the marriage that way. What is called for is trust with ongoing verification. If I am expected home at seven and don't get home until midnight, I owe my wife an explanation; if I don't give her one, then she ought to investigate the matter.

To apply this to the question of religious authority, let us consider Genesis, Chapter 3: the Fall of Man. In a mature first reading of this chapter, an honest reader unencumbered by any disabling ideology should be able to discern and accept that the author(s) had a serious moral purpose. This is not just any meandering myth. Moreover, the reader should easily discern the story is not really about this one man Adam and this one woman Eve, but about all of us. It should be seen that the author is attempting to convey a dramatic universal truth about the human condition. Although it may be challenging for us to pinpoint the precise nature of this truth, a process that will no doubt involve hashing over various theories, this bodes well for the progress of religious thought, as long as the preliminary steps described above have been taken: steps for acceptance of authority that if not taken will force us simply to dismiss the matter as an old fable, curtailing the possibility of any progressive discussion.

This dismissiveness of authority on nonempirical matters puts us in a quandary when it comes to the next step of exegesis of the scripture in question, which is the determination of whether it is by divine revelation. For if we have any knowledge that this or that is by divine revelation, it can only be either by our own direct intuition, which is rare, or by the authority passed down from others. If we deny nonempirical authority, the only pathway we have left for judging divine revelation is our own individual experience, which we then shall not be able to pass to anyone else. This not only turns religion into a non-communal self-service institution—if it could be called an institution at all—but cuts off the possibility of social scrutiny of the revelatory claim. For if divine revelation, if it comes at all, comes only by direct individual intuition and is not transmittable by authority to others, then there is no way for the intuiting individual to receive any help from others in ascertaining the veracity of his religious experience.

This seems so odd and so unhuman. In fact, we are so overwhelmingly a social creature that it ought to be said that all human knowledge—even human intelligence—is social. If we tried to portion out human knowledge into individual contributions, we would end up with nothing. Every single thought in my mind, even if it is genuinely of my authorship, has roots in the thoughts of others. So the notion of acceptance of authority, far from being a dictatorial intrusion on human free thought, is an ordinary and routine part of it. In fact, it is the reasonable acceptance of authority that puts us in the position to properly scrutinize authority in the first place. All human ongoing endeavors are social, and all social endeavors require trust. This necessity of trust as an enabler of dialogue is the basis for the reasonable acceptance of authority in every human endeavor.

This reasonable acceptance of authority might extend not only to original authors, but to those who have cultivated and transmitted traditions to us. The authority we accept might come at least in the form of the conviction that there must be some important truth to be discovered here, even if we can't exactly agree on what that truth is.

Since the question of the reasonability of claims of divine revelation is tied to the question of the reasonability of the acceptance of human authority on nonempirical matters, the rejection of the latter gives us no option but a fideism based on solitary religious experience for accepting the former. But solitary religious experience being by definition impervious to social scrutiny, any acceptance of claims of divine revelation would have to be judged unreasonable.

The denial of nonempirical authority would effectively leave science as the only remaining pathway for criticizing religious claims—something we have been awkwardly attempting to accomplish, even though it involves a category confusion. It is not that science has no legitimate interface with nonempirical endeavors, but it cannot replace the function of sound critical scrutiny in its own right. In illustration, let us discuss two examples: archeological searches for religious objects and setting conditions of falsification for faith claims.

There is, of course, nothing wrong *per se* with searching for ancient objects of religious interest. But it is probably a poor use of archeological resources, which are more adapted to learning about cultures through the patterns of artifacts they leave. To funnel those resources into searches for singular objects of real or legendary history is therefore very unlikely to give a good return for one's investment. Ironically, this seems to be one of the more clever ways for archeologists to attract funding. There is considerable religious interest in using science to verify religion in this misguided way, so anyone doing archeology on biblical times and in biblical places will be tempted to characterize their study as a search for some singular religious object, such as anything belonging to John the Baptist, for example. Just as the hundreds of churches in the world that claim to possess the remains of the head of John the Baptist (maybe they all have a piece of it!) are bound to receive more visitors because of the mere claim, even though the supposed remains are almost never on display, so too do archeologists, who, although in their hearts may have more seriously scientific motivations for their study, feel almost compelled to cater to this interest.

The chief criticism of this archeological sensationalism is that it lends the false impression that the credibility of religious doctrine is somehow on the line one way or the other. So much scientific energy has gone into determining the age and provenance of the Shroud of Turin, it is somewhat like watching a very slow tennis match. When results come back matching the intentions of the faithful, they feel their faith to have somehow been vindicated. Then when the tide turns and results seem to conflict, the other side rallies and the faithful only then seem to be concerned with the inherent tentativeness of science. In fact, the shroud itself, regardless of its real age or provenance, neither proves nor disproves faith. If there happens to have been some miracle involved in its manufacture, the exact nature of the miracle may be quite different than what one might suspect. If, on the other hand, it is really datable to the time of Christ, then it might still be the burial shroud of one of the many other poor souls of that time who were crucified. The point is, the credibility of faith and religion ought to be recognized as standing or falling on their own merits, not somehow on the merits of scientific authority.

All this is not to suggest that physical relics may not be of religious value. We cherish the physical signs of those we love whether they are alive or dead. If the Shroud of Turin happens to be Jesus's own burial cloth, that of course would give it added intimacy, as does even the likelihood that it may be such. Science may be consulted to rule out fraud and forgery, and to specify time periods and provenances. But none of this alone is what confers religious value to the object. At best, science plays a subsidiary role, not a definitive one.

One rationalist criticism against faith and religion is that the faithful do not subject their own faith claims to the test in the way scientific claims are typically put to the test. The challenge is that faith claims should be conceived against a background of the conditions of their own falsification. So, for example, my commitment on faith to the proposition that God always will deliver me ought to be interpreted in such a manner so it can be publically verified whether God in fact always delivers me. To accomplish this, I should have to commit myself to a certain "clinical" definition of what it means for God to deliver me, and then keep close tabs on whether those conditions are met. This would at least give faith claims a chance to earn their credibility in the manner empirical claims do in science.

The problem with this is that it requires a translation of nonempirical claims into empirical constructs that no longer mean what they mean. To believe that God always delivers does not imply that he will do so in a manner preconceived by me, or in any particular set time frame. It means only that God will always take care of my best interests in one way or another, over the time frame of my entire existence. Thus, any partial observation of my life might not perfectly show the deliverance; nor would any period of observation framed additionally by an empirical facsimile of my nonempirical conviction.

It is simply not for science to criticize faith convictions in this manner; rather faith convictions are to be criticized on their own merits, by means of rational scrutiny with the aid of reasonable acceptance of nonempirical authority.

CHAPTER THIRTY-EIGHT

The Idea of the Unlimited Being

In everything we seek to explain theoretically, we are seeking to get to the bottom of a matter. To get to the bottom of a matter is to settle it entirely and comprehensively. We know what it is to do that, but alas, as finite knowers, we can't do it. Our knowing tasks are in fact infinite, and our capacity to tackle them is finite. As a result, we cannot have a comprehensive grasp of anything, for, as Leibniz famously noted, to know any one thing fully is to know everything.

Nonetheless, it is the mandate of rational awareness that we seek to get to the bottom of things: unconditioned knowledge, comprehension. This determines the direction of all inquiry. For though we cannot achieve this kind of comprehension, we can get closer and closer to it, as we go along, individually and socially. It makes no sense to deny the sensibility of the unconditioned merely on the grounds that it is something we cannot definitely and fully possess, for to do so would impugn by implication all theoretical inquiry. For in order for any inquiry to be sensible, it must be going in the right direction; i.e., a productive direction, a direction that allows us to approach unconditioned comprehension ad infinitum.

So although we cannot, given our finite knowledge capacities, reach full comprehension of the unconditioned, or the ultimate explanation of all things, we are in position at least to imagine what it must be, if it existed: unconditioned or unlimited being. For otherwise, it would just be yet another intermediate explanatory plateau.

Such an imaginative reflection does not, of course, constitute a proof of its existence, but at best a proof of its possibility, setting the stage for attempts to prove or disprove its existence.

But what, if anything, can we say about unlimited being? First off, it would have to have all and only qualities which do not imply limitation. It would have to have them all, otherwise it would be limited. It would have to have only such qualities, otherwise, possessing limiting qualities, it would, once again, be limited. Secondly, it would have to be the unlimited being; for supposing there were two such things, the one would be the limit of the other, which would be a contradiction.

Moreover, to be the ultimate explanation, it would have to possess qualities proportionate to all that required explanation, and not accidentally, but essentially. For accidental explanation is by that very fact conditioned by fortuitous circumstance, which in turn would require further explanation. All this would require the unlimited being to have the power to do or make all that could possibly be done or made. This is the quality of omnipotence.

If the unlimited being were omnipotent, it would also be omniscient, since indeed, knowledge is power, and lack of knowledge implies limitation of power. Furthermore, if the unlimited being were omniscient, it would have to be omnibenevolent as well. To be omnibenevolent is to always choose best. Now there are two ways not to choose best: by innocent error or by self-deception. But an omniscient being as such is incapable of both. Innocent error depends on lack of knowledge, whereas an omniscient being can have no such lack. Such a being could not be self-deceived, either, for all deception is based on the exploitation of blind spots in the awareness of the deceived, whereas the omniscient being could have no blind spots to exploit.

The unlimited being would have to exist necessarily, for otherwise, not existing in some possible scenario, it would be powerless there as well, which would contradict its omnipotence.

Finally, it would have to be accountable for all that requires explanation; otherwise it would be unrelated to those things independent of it and hence limited from and by them.

In short, the unlimited being, if it exists, would be unique, omnipotent, omniscient, omnibenevolent, necessarily existent, and accountable for all things.

Before we can conclude that the unlimited being is possible, we have to rule out internal contradiction, incoherence, category confusion, and meaninglessness of its conception. For something is possible if its conception is meaningful, coherent, noncontradictory, and not exhibiting category confusion.

The idea of God can only be contradictory if there is a contradiction between being and unlimitedness. But there is not. To be is to exist, and to exist is to act. Acting is the instantiation of more or less power. Our imagination easily teaches us that if someone runs fast, it is possible at least in principle to run faster; if someone is smart, it is possible to be smarter. In other words, if someone's existence falls within the bounds of certain limits, it is conceivable that those limits be expanded. Some qualities do not have fixed maxima to them and therefore are conceivably expandable ad infinitum. If this is the case, then there is no contradiction between being and unlimitedness.

Even if not contradictory, an idea would yet be incoherent if it has unexplainable conceptual gaps. For instance, what would you say about the claim that I saw a generic mammal in my front yard the other day. That is an incoherent claim, not because there is any contradiction to being a mammal, but because being just a mammal and nothing more specific is a notion with an unacceptable gap in it. There is an incoherent lack of detail that makes it an absurdity. The idea of God would, then, be incoherent and thus absurd if there were something absurdly missing from it. But what could be missing from the idea of the unlimited being? Nothing is absent from the notion except for limits. But there is nothing absurd about the imagination of unlimitedness. We imagine and strive for perfect knowledge even though we know only an unlimited being could have it. This very striving for unlimited ideals which we cannot attain is what makes us what we are as rational beings. The fact that we can even pose these infinite ideals to ourselves, the striving for which is what gives our lives transcendent meaning, proves that their notion is not absurd, and that therefore neither could unlimitedness of being be an incoherent notion.

Nor do we have cause to conclude that the notion of the unlimited being is a category confusion. For we readily recognize the appropriateness of applying the attribute of limitedness to being: I am limited by my height, weight, age, gender, etc. If the application in the affirmative of limitedness to being is not a category confusion, then neither can be its application in the negative. If it is not a category confusion to say swans may be white, then neither is it a category confusion to say they may be nonwhite. On the other hand, just as it is a category confusion to claim swans are prime (numbers), so is it equally a category confusion to call them nonprime.

Finally, it is wrong to claim the idea of God is meaningless, for we know very well that of which we are speaking: a personal being who knows, loves, and creates in a perfect and unlimited fashion. In fact, no concept can be meaningless which is neither contradictory, incoherent, or a case of category confusion unless we are speaking of artificial notions outside of the context for which they were created, such as imaginary numbers, or chess pieces. The square root of negative one is the founding concept of imaginary numbers, which are vital to mathematics. One might argue that it is not a logical contradiction in terms, and it is arguably not a category confusion, since roots, generally, do apply to numbers. Its meaning is not properly incoherent, since whatever trouble we may have with it is not a matter of something being missing. Yet outside special mathematical context, it would have to be described as a meaningless notion, just as is the chess rook outside the game of chess.

We could only consider the idea of God as meaningless in this sense if it were an invention meant for a special context with no natural meaning of its own. That this is not the case is evidenced by its universal accessibility to the human mind, the idea behind our awareness of the possibility of providence, the cornerstone of all religious sentiment, which in turn is evident in all human culture.

By this line of reasoning, then, we conclude that the idea of God as the unlimited being, with all the traits here ascribed and deduced, is possible.

CHAPTER THIRTY-NINE

Can God's Existence Be Proved?

The possibility of the idea of God as unlimited being opens prospects for proving God's actual existence ontologically, causally, and teleologically. Along the way we shall have to contend with the atheist Problem of Evil counterargument and handle the Kantian objection that all efforts to prove God's existence fail by stalemate, or paradoxes of antinomy, which, far from being a peripheral matter, go to the core of much doubting about God's existence, whether or not the doubters themselves have ever studied Kant.

This essay presupposes its companion essay, "The Unlimited Being", which argues that the idea of God as the Unlimited Being is indeed possible. Of course, I will leave it up to readers, in each case, to decide, by their own processes of critical discernment, whether any or all of the arguments presented here are sound.

When we speak of ways of proving whether God exists, we are not so much speaking of any single actual wording of each of those ways as much as we are speaking of argument archetypes. In this sense, since an argument has many possible versions, the job of an evaluator is to address the argument in its most charitable form. That is what I intend to do with all arguments discussed here. As such, the proceeding discussion will not include a historical survey of past formulations.

The categorization of proofs for God's existence referred to above—ontological, causal, and teleological—stems from the treatment of this topic by Immanuel Kant, with the exception of my use of the term 'causal' for Kant's 'cosmological', in accordance with a common contemporary custom. An ontological argument for God's existence is one which attempts to prove that God exists from the very definition of God itself. A causal argument is one whose attempt is based on the existence of the world quantitatively as something which could neither have caused itself nor exist causelessly, and therefore could only have been caused by God. Finally, a teleological argument is one whose attempt is based on the existence of detail so qualitatively intricate that it could not be explained by coincidence, and thus could only be explained by the existence of a designer apt to creating it, namely, God.

The potential ambiguity between causal and teleological proofs is inevitable, since it is impossible to separate altogether quantitative from qualitative evidence. Let it suffice for our purposes that causal arguments have a quantitative focus: the mere existence of the world, whatever it is; while teleological arguments have a qualitative one: the high, perhaps infinite, degree of intricacy of existing things.

Kant intended this tripartite categorization to be a catchall for perennial philosophical argumentation about God, and I accept it as such. Of Thomas Aquinas's Five Ways, for example, the first three are causal arguments, and the last two I take to be teleological: the fifth way more straightforwardly; the fourth way focusing on the design of rational awareness as we experience it, the cornerstone of which is our ready, immediate awareness of infinite standards far beyond our ability to live up to or even to have fashioned in advance.

These three ways of proving, which can be attempted interiorly as well as exteriorly, in essence are the ways of attempting to prove God's existence philosophically: that is, in the open public forum, without reference to privileged or private evidence, such as any purportedly revealed or inspired theological tradition or private experience.

THE CAUSAL PROOF

Perhaps the most compelling strategy for the causal proof is that represented in the contingency argument, which can be expressed as follows.

1. The world exists.
2. The world is the set of all existing contingent things.
3. Any existing contingent thing requires a cause existing outside of itself.
4. Any set of contingent things is a contingent thing.
5. The only possible non-contingent existing thing is God, the unlimited being.
C. God exists.

First, we must establish that the above argument is valid. An argument is valid if and only if its premises jointly force or entail the conclusion, i.e., if and only if the conclusion cannot be false where the premises are all true. To be sure, a valid argument may have a false conclusion, but only if at least one of its premises is false.

In this case, validity is established by the fact that premises 1, 2 and 4 entail that the world itself is an existing contingent thing. This combined with premise 3 entails that the world requires a cause existing outside of itself. But by premise 5, that cause can only be God. This forces the conclusion that God exists.

A contingent thing is something which does not exist necessarily; it does not contain fully within itself the reason or cause of its own existence.

That the world exists we may defend intuitively, without having to argue beyond the given what the world is like. It may be all thought, all matter, or some combination of the two. It may be just as it seems or quite different from how it seems. In any case, it is something existent.

That the world is the set of all contingent things we may defend by appeal to science itself, which recognizes that everything in the world is contingent in the sense that the cause of any existing thing in the world is to be found in other things. Intuitively, the term 'world' refers collectively to all such things.

That any existing contingent thing requires a cause existing outside of itself can be defended as true by the definition given above of contingency.

That any set of contingent things is itself a contingent thing is defensible by noting that a set of things per se is no more than a mere aggregate of those things, conferring then no emergent feature that would transcend the collective attributes of its parts. Noncontingency cannot be arrived at simply by the mere aggregation of contingent things, no matter how large the aggregate. This point applies temporally as well as spatially. Even a beginningless temporal aggregate of contingent things, perhaps one following another in an infinite series, is no less an aggregate than a spatial one, and therefore just as defined by the contingency of its constituents.

Premise 5 may be defended by reference to the argument made for the possibility of the unlimited being made in my essay, "The Unlimited Being". The unlimited being is the only notion of God accessible to reason alone, and thus serves as grounds for all philosophical discussion of God, per se. By this idea, God is certainly noncontingent and therefore existing, if at all, outside the world. Premise 5 is true, then, assuming that the unlimited being is possible.

If all five premises of this argument are true, then since the argument is valid, God exists. To criticize the argument, therefore, requires us to challenge a premise, presumably the premise that counts as the weakest link. Now, in theory, given the limitlessness of the human imagination, any premise of any argument may be criticized. But criticism without discipline gets us nowhere. Therefore, we are well advised to pick our fights well and criticize only premises which are genuinely controversial. After all, it is inevitable that any argument with a controversial conclusion will have at least one controversial premise.

To challenge premise 5 would be a moot point, since it is based on work done elsewhere, and as such, the challenge to premise 5 should consist in the criticism of my argument in "The Unlimited Being".

It might be considered a stretch to deny premise 1, that the world exists, especially as defined in premise two, as a mere aggregate. Premise 2, by the way, is beyond criticism as a stipulative premise, i.e., a premise giving a definition for the sake of argument. However, we may want to return to ask the question, as the British mathematician and philosopher Bertrand Russell once did, whether something like "the set of all contingent things" can really be considered as a thing at all.

Premise 4 seems hard to challenge, simply because 'world' here is defined merely as an unsystematized aggregate. It is hard to imagine how such a thing, in the absence of any internal organizations, could take on transcendent emergent features.

Further, premise 3 seemingly stands as a noncontroversial common definition of a term. If a thing contains its own full cause within itself, it is then not a contingent thing. However, we might have to look into the possible angle that perhaps some things, particularly large aggregates of things, have no cause at all.

So, we have two angles of criticism to explore: that the world may not really be a thing at all, and therefore cannot be said to exist; and that perhaps some things, particularly large aggregates, do not have causes.

The case for the first was made logico-mathematically by Bertrand Russell in what is now known as Russell's Paradox. Developed in 1901, it still is widely accepted as proof that there can be no universal set in logic. Russell related the gist of this paradox to that of the work of logician and mathematician Kurt Gödel, and controversially applied it as well to criticize the causal argument for God's existence, likening the philosophical idea of the world to the universal set.

The paradox, briefly, is that the universal set would have to be the union of any well-formed (i.e., logically specifiable) set with its complement. In order for this to be possible, it would have to be the case that the complement of any well-formed set is also a well-formed set. He proved this to be false by the example of the complement of the set of all sets that contain themselves: i.e., the set of all sets which do not contain themselves. This set is not well-formed, i.e., is logically paradoxical, since to be a member of it requires not being a member of it, and vice versa.

The only thing controversial about Russell's Paradox is his application of it to the causal proof, to the effect that we cannot say the world exists, because the notion of the world is illogical, since it would be a case of the universal set. But we could answer to this that the world is not equatable to the universal set as Russell claimed. It may be considered the set of all existing contingent things, of all contingent things that ever exist; whereas the universal set would pretend to be much larger than that: something like all possibilia. Not all possibilia are existing things. In fact, the world in our context cannot be the universal set, since by definition it would have to exclude all noncontingent things.

The second criticism is that perhaps some things, particularly large aggregates, may not have a cause, on the grounds that some aggregates are just arbitrary collections created or invented by our own imaginative whim and, though not illogical entities, lack any proper metaphysical status.

In fact, we see that science has trouble applying causal explanation to particularly large things, as is evident in the question: What made the Big Bang happen exactly when and how it did? Incidentally, science also has difficulty applying causal explanation to particularly small things, such as elementary particles. But there is no clear sense that this difficulty comes from any defect in the notion of causation per se. The difficulty in science seems to stem rather from puzzles regarding the limits to what we can observe, and perhaps even to puzzles about observation. I would agree that there is something kooky about composing an arbitrary collection of unrelated things and then asking for what caused that set of things. But, in the first place, kooky is not necessarily non-sensical. The question "what caused this here pepper shaker and me to exist" has an answer, which we can pursue by breaking down the question into separate inquiries. In the second place, there is nothing kooky about the notion of the world. It is just the collectivity of all the stuff that ever exists. To say that such a thing does not require a cause undercuts all of the proximate causal explanations of things in the world.

This reasoning applies, as hinted at briefly above, to the case of a beginningless world. Suppose the physical world does not have an actual beginning in time. This could be the case, or instance, if the Big Bang were preceded by a previous Big Crunch, or implosion of a previously existing configuration of things, which, in turn, had been preceded by a previous Big Bang, and so on, beginninglessly into the past. Some assume that such always having existed removes the need for causal explanation of the entire series. But in fact, I surely could not, since causal explanation is not merely an inquiry into how things started, but, as Leibniz aptly put it, "why things are just as they are and not otherwise." A beginningless sequence of contingent existence gives us, if anything, more to explain than less to explain.

In short, there does not appear to be good reason to deny that the world has a cause, either because it is not a thing at all, or because it is too large or amorphous a thing.

THE TELEOLOGICAL PROOF

For such a proof to have the required reach to even have a chance of success requires appeal to the witness of a level of intricacy in things that is infinite. So the argument should be formulated in a manner such as the following:

1. (At least some) things existing in the world have infinitely intricate detail.
2. Intricacy of detail is either by coincidence or design.
3. The greater the intricacy of detail, the less likely it is by coincidence.
4. If 3 then 4a it is infinitely unlikely—that is negligibly probable—that infinitely intricate detail is by coincidence.
5. If 2 and 4a, then 5a existing infinitely intricate detail of things in the world is by design.
The only thing that could design this existing infinitely intricate detail is the unlimited being, God.
6. If 5a and 6, then God exists.
C. God exists.

The validity of this argument should be evident to the reader. If intricate detail is by coincidence or design, and it is not by coincidence, then it is by design. Existing design requires an existing designer capable of producing it. If the only possible such existent is God, then God exists.

Again, a valid argument does not constitute a proof, but requires that we go on to establish the truth of the premises.

Before reviewing the premises, we should establish what is meant in this argument by infinite design. When we speak infinite design, we are not speaking of finitely ordered infinite design. This kind of design is finitely comprehensible, so would not count as infinite design for the purposes of this argument. Here, infinite design is design we can progressively understand more and more, but never comprehend.

Premise 2 can be argued true without controversy based on the meanings of the terms. Coincidence in the sense we are using it simply means not by design.

Premise 3 can be seen as true based on probability theory. A greater coincidence is composed of a larger number of parameters constituting simple probabilities less than one multiplied against one another. The more such parameters multiplied against one another, the smaller the product, or resulting compound probability.

Premise 6 can be argued true based on proportionate causation: that a cause has to be proportionate to its effect. Existing infinite design can only be produced by a designer with unlimited designing abilities. This quality in turn implies omniscience, which in turn implies unlimitedness, which can only be possessed by the unlimited being.

Premises 4, 5, and 7 are defensible as statements of noncontroversial deductive inferences from previous premises based on the meanings of the terms involved.

Finally, premise 1 is defensible based on our experience knowing, interacting with, and investigating the things of the world—especially natural kinds. Natural kinds are the things in the world we discover and don't invent. We find such things—arguably all of them—infinitely beyond our ability to comprehend them. To be sure, we can understand them more and more, but the prospect of completely understanding them in any finite time frame is intuitively off the table, to the point where it is absurd to suggest that one day we will have finished physics, or chemistry, or biology, etc. These, clearly, are infinite tasks, as is the task of knowing oneself or one another. What we find in the study of such things is an uncountable infinity of interrelated and continuous detail, both extensively and intensively. Simply put, in studying these things, though we understand them better and better, we never get to the bottom of them; to the contrary, the more we understand, the more we recognize there is to know about them. This is a clear sign of infinitely intricate detail.

Despite what has just been said in defense of premise 1, it stands as the only genuinely controversial premise of the argument. So in criticizing we are compelled to try to make a case against it.

The case against premise 1 will have to be that, in spite of the fact that the details of natural kinds appears to us ever so rich, even bottomlessly so, we have no good reason to conclude that it is in fact infinitely intricate. However daunting the detail may be for us, it may yet be finite in magnitude. Perhaps we get confused between the infinite and the very large finite.

After all, even a philosopher as great as Aristotle argued against the existence of actual infinity, making the case that infinity is a possibility we perceive and project on things, which themselves are finite. His reasoning, roughly, was that infinite means never ending. For Aristotle, to exist is to exist in time and/or space, then nothing temporally unending, or infinite, exists, for to exist it would have to exist at a certain time. Analogously, unending spatial existence cannot be executed, since to exist it would have to have spatial definition, which implies completion, which implies being finite.

Despite the fact that Aristotle himself tacitly accepted actual infinity in at least one form, that is, of a beginningless universe, his above described criticism of actual infinity cannot be dismissed on that account.

Quite clearly, Aristotle was hobbled by an implicit assumption that all that exists is either temporal or spatial or both; nothing can exist outside of time and space. He also seems to have failed to countenance the possibility of intensive rather than extensive infinity.

We can grant to Aristotle that there can be no such thing as an infinitely large object, since to be such requires having spatial definition, which requires being finite. We can also grant him that there can exist no infinite temporal process, since by 'exist' in this sense we mean at a time, whereas any supposedly temporally infinite process would at any one time be finite. (The exception to this would be a beginningless process, which we have agreed for the sake of argument not to challenge.) None of this rules out the case of intensively infinite detail. In fact, we recognize continuity of detail in natural kinds. Although a physical thing at any one time is made up of a finite number of elementary particles, the detail we notice in things does not reduce simply to those particles. We notice continuity of detail, and such notice is notice of actual infinity, or infinitely intricate detail. We notice this intricacy not only as continuous, but bottomless and ever expanding in richness of detail ad infinitum.

To the contention that this notice we have of the continuous, bottomless, and ever-expanding intricacy of detail of natural kinds is confused or projected, i.e., that we are mistaking very large finite magnitudes for infinite ones, it should be noted that the infinite is quite easy for us to grasp, conceive of, and process, and our routinely doing so right from infancy is what gives us the ability to create, acquire, and use human language.

That this is so is evident in our ready acquisition and use of common terms, that is, of terms which can only accurately be described as referring to infinite sets of things. This fundamental feature of human language can only be based on our immediate, intuitive awareness of the infinite even from infancy; not as logical constructs from the finite, which would be excessively tedious at best, but from the fact that we have immediate notice of infinity, either in the form of perceptively discerning continuous detail as distinct from discrete detail or in our ready ability to parse infinite from finite endeavors. Our awareness of such things is not born from calculation.

In stark contrast, very large finite magnitudes are exceedingly difficult to grasp. We have little chance of appreciating the magnitude of googol, which is ten to the hundredth power; certainly we have no chance with googolplex, which is ten to the googolth power. The claim that we confuse very large finite magnitude for infinite magnitude relies on the assumption that the two are easy to confuse; but they are not, since once is easy to grasp, and the other exceedingly difficult.

Here the critic might retort that the very difficulty of handling large finitudes motivates us to convert them imaginatively into infinites, permitting a neater treatment of them. But our own scientific investigations in the end break the bank on this hypothesis. For if all our scrutiny of actual existence were merely finite, then our scientific analyses would gradually be leading us—step-by-step and level-by-level—to simplicity. Accordingly, it should then be clear to us all, for example, that a single human cell is a less complex entity than a human being; or that the molecules forming it are less detailed than the cell itself; or that the atoms comprising those molecules are per se easier to understand than the molecules; all the way down to the elementary particles—electrons, quarks, etc.—whose essences should be simple in nature.

But this is surely not the case, and there seems to be no serious attempt by scientists anywhere even to suggest such a thing. In fact, the electron itself is just as mysterious to us in its own right as human life itself—or any other life, for that matter. This is not to say that our analyses are untrue, but that the intricacy of detail we are analyzing is infinite. For necessarily the analysis of any finite intricacy goes gradually from complexity to simplicity.

THE ONTOLOGICAL PROOF

Both Leibniz and Kant made the point that the soundness of the causal argument depends on the existence of an effective ontological proof; Leibniz admitted this of the design argument as well. For Kant, this was a death sentence, since he—along with Thomas Aquinas, among others—considered the ontological argument to be suspect. This was not the case for Leibniz, whose acceptance of the ontological argument was based on what he saw as straightforward modal-logical reasoning, which I will employ here.

I would argue, along with Leibniz, for granting the point of dependency of both arguments just discussed on the ontological argument. But we should press even further and recognize that the ontological argument itself depends on the proposition that the idea of the unlimited being is possible, the thesis argued in my earlier essay, which is a companion to this one. The argument can be stated in the following manner:

1. The unlimited being is possible; that is, possibly, the unlimited being exists.
2. If 1, then 2a possibly the necessarily existent being exists.
3. All things that are possible are either contingent or necessarily existent.
4. If 2a and 3, then 4a the necessarily existent being is either contingent or exists necessarily.
5. But that the necessarily existent being is contingent is a contradiction.
6. If 4a. and 5., then 6a., the necessarily existent being exists necessarily.
7. The necessarily existent being is God.
8. If 6a and 7, then God exists.
C. God exists.

For the purposes of this argument, something contingent is something which possibly exists but does not necessarily exist.

The argument is valid in the following manner: 1 through 3 imply 4a; 4a and 5 imply 6a; 6a and 7 imply C.

We defend premise 1 by reference to the case made for it in the companion essay, "The Unlimited Being" (UB).

Premise 2 is true by definition if premise 1 is true. To review, being unlimited implies existing necessarily, since possibly not existing implies a limitation.

Premise 3 is uncontroversially true by the generally accepted definitions of the terms, including the definition given above just after the premises.

Premise 5 is true by logical necessity. For that which exists necessarily cannot also not exist necessarily.

Premise 7 is true by definition, if premise 1 is true.

Premises 4, 6, and 8 are defensible as statements of noncontroversial deductive inferences from previous premises based on the meanings of the terms involved.

The remarkable thing about this argument, whose conception I credit to Leibniz, is that all its premises except one are true by logical or by accepted definition. The only premise left available to criticism in fact, is premise 1, which has already been argued in UB. On its own, premise 1 seems humble and unassuming, hardly something capable of stirring controversy. But in fact, it turns out that the whole case for proving the existence of God depends on it.

The upshot of this is that it puts us in a position such that the only rational way to deny God's existence is to deny the possibility of God's existence, i.e., the very sensibility of the idea itself of God, the unlimited being. Which is quite a difficult task, if we are to be fair, since the standard for justification of a possibility per se is far lower than the standard for proving existence. Once again, I refer the reader back to the discussion of all this in my previous essay.

THE PROBLEM OF EVIL ARGUMENT

Making a case for the possibility of the idea of God as unlimited does have one significant wrinkle to disturb theists in that it subjects us to a strong challenge against God's existence as well, in the form of the Problem of Evil argument, which can be stated thus:

1. If God exists, then the actual world is the best possible world.
2. The best possible world does not contain superfluous evil in it.
3. But the actual world, in fact, does have superfluous evil in it.
C. God does not exist.

For the purposes of this argument, we define God as the being who is all powerful, all-knowing, and all good, responsible therefore for all that exists.

A possible world is a maximal compossible option for existence, such that if God creates, God can only create one world. It comprises all created things that ever would exist—past, present, and future—according to that option.

The validity of this argument is clear enough: it is a double application of modus tollens:

If p, then q; if q, then r; not-r; therefore not p.

Premise 1 is defended as being implied by the conception of God as the unlimited being. See discussion of that topic in UB.

Premise 3 is intuitively defensible on the grounds that we see evil in this world regarding which it is unconscionable to suggest contributes in its own right to the greater good. Evil is superfluous if it is unnecessary in this way. (One can speak also of permissible evils if there are several options of this sort of prudent or preventive evil to choose from).

The logic behind premise 2 is that any possible world, no matter how good, can be surpassed in net goodness by the mere removal of some superfluous evil in it. It makes sense in a finite arithmetic way. We can even go further and say that if we accept the limitation that possible worlds can only be finitely good, then premise 2 is true.

Some philosophers have criticized premise 3 on the grounds that the actual world is mysterious to us; that we cannot appreciate the big picture; that perhaps only God Himself is in a position to see the big picture. Leibniz, in fact, argued in such a manner, but only because he felt constrained, for some less than obvious reason, to accept the limitation that a possible world can only be finitely good. Under this constraint, then the only option left for the critic is to deny premise 3. (That Leibniz argued this way is particularly puzzling, since he was a philosopher who, unlike Aristotle and many other philosophers of note, accepted actual infinity in the world.)

I take the position that the criticism of premise 3 is unreasonable on the grounds that in order to accept it, we have to impugn our moral sensibilities altogether. For what is at stake is not subtlety: all the rape, murder, and genocide that occur now have to be considered as necessary or permissible evil on the grounds that it somehow contributes to the overall goodness of the world. If we are to accept that, then what are we to reject? Why even have moral deliberations at all? It pulls the rug out from under any further moral discussion.

Since we cannot reasonably write off our own consciences in such a manner, I thus conclude that we cannot accept the big picture criticism of the Problem of Evil argument.

The best option for criticism, I think, is premise 2. By challenging the tacit assumption that possible worlds can only be finitely good, we can skirt the decisive inference that the net value of a possible world is increased by subtraction of superfluous evil from it. Supposing the best possible world is infinitely good, then it would not be made better by the finite subtraction of evil from it.

And why should we not suppose that the best possible world is infinitely good? If God exists—and we are permitted for the sake of argument by this argument to make this assumption until and unless we arrive at a contradiction—then it should be reasonably within his creative powers to create an infinitely good world. To be sure, we cannot expect God to create God, since God is no creature. But being infinitely good is not tantamount to being unlimitedly good, for there are limited infinities. A possible world might be infinitely good in any or all mutually compossible respects compatible with being created.

That there are limited infinities is easy to see by the mathematical example of infinite quantities: a line is a one-dimensional infinity, a plane a two-dimensional infinity, etc. The same may apply to a variety of infinite qualities, such as priceless values, etc.

At any rate, the very notion of a finitely good best possible world is arguably nonsensical in the same way as is the notion of a greatest possible natural number. All natural numbers are finite, and for any such finite magnitude, a greater magnitude is conceivable. So arguably, the very notion of a greatest possible finite magnitude is nonsensical.

This criticism does not allay the fact that the superfluous evil we encounter in the world is mournful in its own right. We are justly disturbed by it, so much so that we may still have reservations about a world containing such evil. We might, for example, ask why God would permit such evil ever to exist in the world. Here we might make appeal to the notion of an evil which is not prudently preventable by God. Unlike the big picture argument, this is not justification of the evil; it is based, rather, on the claim that perhaps there are some evils God permits because to prevent them he would have to annihilate or never create some other good which is necessary for the world to be the best possible world. The case I am referring to is the existence of free-willed creatures in the actual world. We can argue that all the superfluous evil in the actual world, however mournful it is on its own account, is not prudently preventable by God on the grounds that to do so would require the annihilation or noncreation of free willed creatures, who are presumably indispensable to the actual world being the best possible world.

So now we must question this presumption: What is so good about the existence of free willed creatures in the world that their inclusion in the world is worth all the superfluous evil that enters the world as a result? We know that free willed beings are the only ones endowed with moral agency, such that they are held as praiseworthy or blameworthy according to the quality of their deliberate choices. Could it be that it is this feature that makes us priceless, this feature that is the basis of our ability to form intimate, disinterested love relationships—even with God, presuming, as we are entitled to do here, that God exists? Poets sing the virtues of love, but is love really worth all that trouble? I suppose it is, if our loving nature, given enough time to develop in history, is reliably destined to prevail over evil. But can we count on good prevailing in the long run over evil?

I think we can! For good will is based on sound and well-ordered judgment, which once it takes root is easy to sustain. On the other hand, bad will is based on unsound and disordered judgment, which like a lie becomes ever more burdensome and harder to sustain over time; bad will, rather, goes from one biased rationalization to another, like an addict wasting one vein after another with his sorrowful addiction. It is reliable, I think, that good ultimately prevails over evil in the indefinite long run; but at any one time, there is the possibility of a disturbing setback in the opposite direction, requiring us to rely on providence to provide the most favorable conditions for preventing this and allowing good will to thrive. If God exists, I think we can rely on him to come through in this regard, since as the unlimited being, God is willing, able and knowledgeable enough to deliver providence to us.

DO WE HAVE A STALEMATE?

Apart from how each of us may judge the success of the above arguments, many of us doubt there can be a knowledgeable outcome to this kind of argumentation, based on the notion that compelling arguments can always be given in support of opposite conclusions. There is no closure to such an argument process, so the door is always open to a further round of dialog. Some interpret the infinite nature of this process to imply a stalemate, such that no reliable progress toward the truth of the matter is possible. They look at human axiomatic science such as math and logic and see finite, definitive demonstration that we can build on and advance to other, more advanced topics. Then they see philosophical argument, always going back to the same perennial point of controversy, and despair on account of this that any progress has been made.

This is echoed in Kant's notion of an antinomy, in particular his antinomy of the necessarily existent being, or what we here are calling the unlimited being. Kant despaired not that reasonable argument could be made for such a being, but that there is both reasonable denial and reasonable affirmation of it, leaving us in a position of stalemate as far as concerns getting to the bottom of the matter.

Must we despair of approaching knowledge on this matter simply because the argument process itself is infinite? Cannot an infinite process yet lead us reliably toward the truth, even if it doesn't deliver us truth once and for all? To be sure, we must concede that we are not ourselves omniscient and therefore are unable to complete or comprehend an infinite endeavor. But surely, we can approach truth infinitely as an asymptotic limit. At any one time we have to admit a deficit; but as a running judgment over time, we may justifiably conclude whether we are on the right track or not, and adjust accordingly.

To the oft repeated question: "Who is to say?", I answer we all are—all of us and each of us. As to what we should do if there is still disagreement, I answer: argue some more. But argue cooperatively in friendship, as partners in the pursuit of truth.

CHAPTER FORTY

Non-Fideist Religion

Throughout the centuries until recent times, humans have more or less passed down religious traditions received from their forebears in a manner similar to language, almost imperceptibly adding something, subtracting something, or tweaking it as they passed it along. Most of this transmission has been as uncontroversial as the transmission of language.

In recent times, given the vast confluence of heterogeneous cultures, the transmission of religion has become problematic to the point that in many cases it has all but stopped. What was once a seemingly automatic process has become stunted by lack of confidence in the content transmitted and has led to the widespread if uneasy practice of critical comparison of religious traditions—with one another as well as with the various possibilities of what might substitute for religion.

Many questions arise from this critical process which require our steadfast attention if we are to find a way to settle our troubles on this matter. And indeed we are troubled, individually and collectively, whether or not we adhere to any particular religious tradition. To continue the analogy between religion and language, it is for each of us as if the use of our native tongue, or even human language generally, has suddenly become called into question as morally suspect, so that we might now be called onto the carpet for using it at all. Of course, we might respond by choosing not to speak, or by only speaking secretly. Or we might try to dodge the critics by insisting that we are not speaking to them, thereby blunting the point of their critique. But these responses are not healthy, since it is the nature of human language to be public and interactive, not private. Moreover, it is a primary expression of our humanness, such that to suppress or discourage it is a suppression or discouragement of being human.

Similarly, religion taken collectively is a longstanding tradition of connecting with, reaching out to, and interacting with one another and the supernatural in so many vital ways, or at least ways once considered vital. How can we now suddenly be off the critic's hook by insisting religion is and ought to be kept private?

For most of the existence of our species, religion was not even a count noun, but a generic institution, existing in some similar form in every human culture. Except for those reports with obviously ulterior political or economic motives or abject bias, there were none we could still take seriously today in the light of more developed social science of traditional societies with no religion at all. Religion was found to be everywhere, and it was because of this confrontation of heterogeneous cultures at various times and places in human history that religion gradually became a count noun.

Now, two different religious traditions contradict neither necessarily nor, if they do at all, in their entirety, but only in particular respects. An early and still ongoing common response to religious diversity has been to reconcile them to one another in some way, either by syncretism, reduction of one to another, or blended co-existence. But with regard to religious contradiction specifically, a more aggressive response has been the attempt to impose a religious standard by either informal or formal political action. This response muddies the waters horribly, since its typical result is forced or hustled conversions, which most often remain in some significant recalcitrant manner as false fronts concealing underlying resistance and leading to the degradation of religious integrity—all regardless of the intrinsic quality of the religious judgments behind the political action.

In the age of the widespread advocacy of religious liberty, we find ourselves now still having trouble coping with religious diversity, to the point where this trouble may make us wonder whether religion as we have known it is any longer a good thing at all, if it ever had been.

Can religion be a good thing, important and vital? We now no longer have the luxury—and perhaps, in the long run, it is a benefit to have lost this luxury—of easily acquiescing in a monolithic religious tradition that embraces all aspects of our lives without requiring from us any sustained action of rigorous critical scrutiny. The only chance we have of regaining the pristine confidence of our perhaps now remote ancestors in choosing whether or how to be religious is by envisioning the possibility of critical religion. Only if we do this can we have a chance to decide whether it is sensible for us to embrace such a thing.

Religion is or strives to be providential community. The recognition of the possibility of providence is what grounds the motivation to be religious in the first place, and has ever been a notion fundamental to human awareness. Providence is the entrustment of ourselves and our lives to a cooperative force apt to guide us in all that we do and think. If there is providence, it must be in the form on an unlimited being, for no lesser being would be capable of delivering on such a promise.

Providence would entail intimate collaboration between divinity and humankind, a collaboration ever rich in singular, personal, intimate contact constituting an ongoing relationship in time. The substance of the history of this relationship is the deposit of faith.

Philosophers in recent times who have advanced the notion of a natural religion, natural in the sense of being completely derived from reason, have done so eschewing the notion of a deposit of faith as something not only irrational, but dangerously divisive, on the grounds that the claim that God has spoken to me, or to us, in some singular way, giving us his singular message, implies that God has not in this same sense spoken to anyone else. In fact, this might indeed be divisive, unless the deposit of faith thus allegedly delivered were a source of providence for all, not just for the sacramental community first receiving the deposit, or even, if extended to others, extended just to those explicitly converted to the sacramental community, such that only the members of this community confessing full adherence as believers were the saved and all the rest were lost. Requiring confession of belief as a starting point for community is divisive because it ignores the psychological and epistemic complexities of belief which block the way for many. In the first place, belief is not merely a matter of good will; nor is it possible to believe just by choosing to out of the blue; nor would that be a good thing to do even if we could do it! Moreover, if it is all true that a) religion is salvific, b) belief in the deposit of faith is required to access its saving graces, c) access to the deposit of faith is gained primarily by acceptance into the community of faith, and d) access to the evidence capable of producing such belief comes primarily from access to the deposit of faith, then what can religious divisiveness—the exclusion of unbelievers—do but remove them from the opportunity to benefit from whatever good the religion offers?

This kind of self-defeating corporate logic makes it clear that the question of how one becomes a religious believer needs to be settled.. If such belief is but a supernatural gift requiring no natural deliberative process on the part of the one coming to believe, then religion itself is utterly beyond reason and fideist. But if religion is fideist, then no description of sane human psychology could accommodate it, much less account for it. This indeed would be the height of divisiveness.

If, on the other hand, religious belief is not genuinely acquired in this fideistic manner, it would then have to be based on some intimate collaboration between faith and reason and thus take the form of an ongoing dialog between the two, faith in this sense referring to the communal participation in the deposit of faith and the evidence gleaned from such experience.

Yet one might wonder how even such a dialog as this could be genuinely inclusive rather than divisive. For dialog proceeds from controversy to reconciliation. But if religion itself is based on common acceptance of a deposit of faith, then it seems in the first place that there can be no dialog until some faith agreement is established, after which, to the extent this has already been accomplished, reconciliation has already been achieved, so there is no longer a need for dialog. This is the dilemma that stands in the way of our seeing the possibility of genuine religious dialog, or to be more clear, of seeing religion as dialog. What will its starting point be, other than orthodoxy? And if that is to be its starting point, then where does it have to go from there?

In fact, no dialog is genuine unless it departs from the shared common grounds of its participants, whomever those happen to be. If this point is accepted, then the first horn of our dilemma is solved. But a problem still remains as to the second horn, what the aim of the dialog is to be. Since genuine dialog is a collaborative venture, how can we insist, as religion seemingly must, that the endpoint of this dialog still be fixed at orthodoxy?

Clarity might be gained in answering this question by our identification of who the parties to this religious dialog are to be. We know one party will be the sacramental community, or those having received and now transmitting the religious tradition. But what about the other party or parties? The only serviceable answer to this question is any party, any party at all. For if we give any limitation to who may be party to religious dialog, we fall back once again into divisiveness.

On the other hand, if religion is to be genuine dialog, how will this not threaten to contradict the deposit of faith on which the religion is based? For if being, say, Catholic means nothing more than being party to the Catholic dialog in the more open sense just suggested, then this seems to permit even atheist Catholicism.

In the first place, this concern is overwrought, since it would not apply to religious belief in the sense pertaining to the sacramental community. Even so, believing Catholics really should not be disturbed by such a thought. For regardless of official affiliation, people's actual beliefs are all over the religious map, and most of us aren't quite sure what exactly to believe. There is a significant discrepancy between de dicto belief—what we confess, and de re belief—what we are really persuaded to be the case. The fastidious tailoring of de dicto belief is suitable if we are concerned merely with the maintenance of appearances. But that it is not what religion should be about if it is to be a worthwhile institution.

To be sure, it is reasonable to expect of religious dialog that it remain true to the deposit of faith which defines it. We can see how this might be accomplished if we note a distinction between two kinds of dialog: focused and open. An open dialog has no fixed endpoint to arrive at, while a focused dialog does.

Focused dialogs can still be genuine as long as no finite time limits are imposed on the discussion, such as would render them artificial. (It is well worth noting that this point applies to open dialog as well!)

That said, we may now conceive of non-fideist religion as a focused dialog aimed at the explication of the deposit of faith and departing from grounds held commonly between the sacramental community who have received the tradition and would transmit it, and what we might call the adventive community, i.e., those who are approaching the faith. The concern that this arrangement may result in a sort of condescending patronism should be allayed by the recognition that no party to the religious dialog ever achieves comprehension of the faith, whose content is infinite while our capacity to come to a developed awareness of it is finite. Now in matters of infinite dimension, every perspective is vital. This assures, therefore, that all parties benefit and thrive from one another's perspective, and that therefore no one is in a position to be patronizing.

Lest it yet be thought that such an inclusive approach will surely dilute religious content or destroy the integrity of the religion, it should be kept in mind that a religious community is assumed to be graced by the guidance of the divinity, who is the great reconciler. If we want to be reconciled, we must be willing to put ourselves in a position to receive such a blessing. We cannot reasonably hope to have reconciliation unless we invite everyone to the table.

The only discipline we need to impose on the dialog of religion is mutual good will, especially not taking mere difference of opinion even on important matters as evidence of evil or dishonest intent, retaining instead an openness to mutual persuasion within the accepted bounds of discussion. For religion is no place for polemics, which, after all, is not oriented to the truth, but to the defeat of one's opponent. At best, polemicists are motivated by the uncritical presumption that the truth is entirely on their side. But even in such case, polemics are nonetheless inimical to truth by being formally indifferent to it, dedicated instead to achieving selfish victory. Truth is not well served by methods of deception such as polemics.

All parties to religious dialog must consider it their sacred duty not to fall to the temptation to reduce their apprehension of the content of faith to an overwrought or narrowly conceived finitude, thereby making of the deposit of faith itself an idol of their own invention, no longer suitable for representing the divinity, but rather serving only their own social convenience.

Although in religion we seek to behold the unlimited being, we have to accept that our apprehension of it will always be a bit blurry. So the worry that all-inclusive dialog might blur religious content is just something we need to learn to cope with; otherwise it will lead us not only away from reconciliation but toward idolatry, in the form of our seeking contrived, finite clarity at the expense of infinite, all-inclusive truth.

Finally, this dialog need not be conceived by all its parties to be within the same official institution, such that, e.g., Jews would have to leave their institutions and traditions to dialog with Muslims or Christians and vice versa; to the contrary, they may take place in situ, both distributively and collectively. Moreover, our considering ourselves as belonging prospectively to one faith community should not be considered per se as contradicting our membership in another community.

PART X

AESTHETICS

CHAPTER FORTY-ONE

Variable Interpretation: Cooking, Music, Divinity, and Idols

When an old friend asked me for my gnocchi recipe, I sent him what amounted to an essay on gnocchi. I was unable to live up to the classical recipe format, because it would not have captured how I make gnocchi. It's not only that I don't use exact measurements of ingredients. It has more to do with the process: it is not entirely scripted, but varied. In short, it is a process with key decisions to be made at various junctures, with each decision depending, in part, on how the previous decision was made. And I can't really say how many decisions there are to be made; it depends on how finely grained I set the information threshold. The more I think about it, the more information I could give. Of course, too much information will ruin a recipe, just as will too little. But even how much information is optimal varies according to many factors, including the person sending the recipe as well as the person receiving it.

This is not a problem unique to gnocchi, but relates potentially to all things. Think of having to teach any skill that is typically done as second nature to someone who lacks that skill, such as getting in and out of a car, swinging a golf club, or pitching a baseball. The instructions involved are potentially infinite, yet we never have an infinite amount of time to instruct. Moreover, an excess of information overburdens the instruction process.

Therefore, in most such cases we prefer to instruct by direct demonstration, or by apprenticeship. Somehow, seeing how something is done oneself, having it modeled, gives so much more comprehensible input than by instruction through language or symbols. But direct demonstration is not always plausible. Sometimes the need is to convey a skill or the ability to perform an operation to an audience or group of performers inaccessible to direct demonstration. In such cases, we are forced to face the above-described information paradox.

This paradox regards not so much the avoidance of the opposite pitfalls of both too little and too much information; this alone would not be a paradox, but a delicate balancing act. The real paradox is how to convey an infinite amount of detail in a finite amount of time, and in a finite number of words or symbols. Reality as we perceive it is continuously detailed; continuity of detail implies infinity of detail. We can grasp such infinity all at once, synthetically, but we can only describe or analyze it finitely. That's why I have trouble writing gnocchi recipes.

This paradox applies even more to cases in which one must instruct others to perform an operation that one cannot do oneself, or at least wants to be done by others. At least the gnocchi cook gets to experiment in his own kitchen, cooking gnocchi over and over until he gets it right. But imagine having to conceive and send out a gnocchi recipe without ever getting to experiment in the kitchen. This is the lot of composers of ensemble music. In most cases, these composers do not play all the instruments for which they are writing, and even if they do, it is unlikely they play them with the proficiency they would hope for in the performance of their compositions. But even if there were such a composer, he or she still would not be able to play all the parts simultaneously. And yet, the composer must conceive the piece, and give adequately descriptive instructions for its performance, as an ensemble piece.

To be sure, we now have the ability to record parts separately and then mix them in the studio, with often pleasing results. Sometimes a piece may even be conceived to be performed in such a manner. Some of Stevie Wonder's compositions were done just that way, with him playing all or most of the parts. More often, however, this is a concession to the lack of opportunity to prepare and assemble the required musicians at the same time and in the same place to perform the work. Moreover, the ensemble sound never gets to be heard until the studio mix is completed.

In fact, it is typical that composers of assemble pieces employing a wider variety of voices or instruments will be hoping to get the best performers for each part, those who specialize in singing at just that vocal range, or playing just that instrument. This presumably will maximize the probability that the compositions will be performed closest to the composer's intentions.

But here comes another snag: assuming the best musicians would be brought together for the performance of a certain composition, how is the composer to prepare each of them to play his or her part? Typically, the composer instructs each musician individually with written symbols and technical terminology, then gives an additional set of written instructions to the conductor. All of these sets of instructions are intended to jibe in a Leibnizean fashion, with each performer, including the conductor, being conceived as a separate "monad," while the composer alone has the divine task of making sure all these monads fit together; that the results of everyone executing his own instructions are the experience of an ensemble performance.

Extending this analogy, if the composer is a "good god," then the only way the experience can be a failure is if one or more of the performers fails to execute the instructions given. If all the musicians perform impeccably and the ensemble experience still fails, then the composer would be a "bad god."

A performer can fail in two ways: first, by failing to execute well-understood instructions, and secondly, by failing to understand the composer's instructions. The first kind of failure is minor in the case of competent musicians, who, though they do make mistakes, are adept at minimizing the deleterious effect of these on the performance as a whole. But the second type of failure brings us back to the paradox described above, since the odds of misunderstanding between composer and performer are multiplied by the number of performers involved. To be sure, the conductor is the one who is charged with the task of mediating such gaps in understanding, or interpretation. But it is really a monumental task, since the overall sound of an ensemble piece can be considered not merely as the sum of the individual parts performed, but also of all the interactions between the parts played: two-way, three-way, etc.

To make this point clearer, imagine a photographer at a gathering of twenty who wants to take a picture of every possible combination of his guests, including solo shots. The result would be more than a million photographs (1,048, 575, to be exact: $2^{20}-1$).

Now, this might all be seen as making a mountain out of a mole hill. After all, ensemble compositions are written and performed all the time. Audiences dress up, sit in theaters, listen, clap, and go home; composers take their bows; musicians take their bows; critics write their reviews—some bad, some good. So what's missing from this picture?

What's missing, for all we know and for all even the composer himself knows, is the extent to which the piece performed was actually the piece conceived by the composer. Let's ignore the fact of errors made in the execution of a piece and focus solely on the communication between composer and performer. One could argue that the odds of successful conveyance of an ensemble composer's intentions to each performer, especially according to the Leibnizean conception, are negligible, on the grounds the composer's envisioned conception of the piece is essentially something infinite, but can only be conveyed by finite means. As a result, what inevitably gets performed is not actually the composer's conception, but merely a surrogate of it, made up of a finite facsimile of the composer's intentions and filled in and made whole by the musical intentions of the performer, who "micro-composes" his performance to fill in for the deficit between the infinity—i.e., continuity—of the composer's intentions and the inevitably finite description of it that the composer is able to give.

It's much the same as when we read a novel. The author imagines a continuous scenario but can only convey it finitely. It is left to the reader to fill in the gaps and thus derive for himself—and for himself only—a continuous vision of the story told. Each reader of a novel is therefore a "micro-author" of it.

Those authors or composers who out of an obsessive desire to more perfectly inform their audience or their performers of their vision may attempt to convey their instructions and descriptions in a more and more fine-grained manner, but the gap between infinite and finite can never be bridged that way; just as an infinite quantity is not increased by adding finitely to it, so, too, a finite quantity cannot become infinite by adding finitely to it. Furthermore, the more information one gives, the greater the odds of that information being misunderstood. Therefore, it is dubitable whether composers would communicate more effectively with a more fine-grained system of notations than they have now.

If we cannot solve or avoid this paradox, the next question is how best to cope with it. Composer James Nicholson has what I consider to be an enlightened response to this question: let composers embrace performers as co-composers, and conceive and write their compositions accordingly. In this way of composing, which he calls "variable interpretation," the music that is eventually performed is not stultified by the inevitable communication gaps that result when performers conceive themselves as mere executors of someone else's intentions. Since performers inevitably must micro-compose, why not acknowledge and embrace that fact, and compose in such a manner that encourages such co-composing?

Humans have always struggled to bridge the gap between the finite and the infinite. We sense the presence of the infinite, the sacred, the divine, then in response we sculpt finite "idols" as surrogates of them. To be sure, some may take these idols to be mere symbols of an infinite reality beyond them. Nonetheless, the idol *per se* tends to become more of an obstacle to our encounter with the infinite than a conduit to it. But idols may be hewn out of things other than stone. We have idols of thought as well, and of sound. If our ultimate fulfillment is in the appreciation of the infinite, then we have got to find a way to get past the idols blocking our way. Variable interpretation is a way of attempting to do that in music.

CPSIA information can be obtained
at www.ICGtesting.com
Printed in the USA
LVHW060421290820
664475LV00003B/37